Cambridge
Advanced English

Leo Jones

CAMBRIDGE
UNIVERSITY PRESS

Published by the Press Syndicate of the University of Cambridge
The Pitt Building, Trumpington Street, Cambridge CB2 1RP
40 West 20th Street, New York, NY 10011–4211, USA
10 Stamford Road, Oakleigh, Victoria 3166, Australia

© Cambridge University Press 1991

First published 1991
Third printing 1992

Printed in Great Britain at
the University Press, Cambridge

ISBN 0 521 33697 X   Student's Book
ISBN 0 521 33698 8   Teacher's Book
ISBN 0 521 33517 5   Set of 3 cassettes

VN

Contents

EDUCATION WEAVER

Thanks

First of all, I'd like to say how grateful I am to:

Jeanne McCarten for her inexhaustible patience, support and
  encouragement throughout my work on this book,
Alison Silver and Lindsay White for their friendly editorial expertise,
Peter Ducker for the design of the book, and
Peter Taylor and Studio AVP for producing the recordings.

Thanks very much also to the following teachers who used the pilot edition
with their classes and contributed detailed comments on it and who
evaluated and reported on subsequent revised units. Without their help, this
book could not have been written:

Pat Biagi, Christ Church College ELTU, Canterbury
Jenny Bradshaw, Christ Church College, Department of Language Studies,
  Canterbury
Sylvie Dawid, Beverly Langsch and Monty Sufrin, Berne
George Drivas, Moraitis School, Athens
Tim Eyres, Godmer House, Oxford
David Gray
Amanda Hammersley, British School of Monza
Chris Higgins and staff, Teach In Language and Training Workshop,
  Rome
Tom Hinton
Roger Hunt, International House, Madrid
Ruth Jimack
Christine Margittai
Laura Matthews, Newnham Language Centre, Cambridge
Joy Morris and staff, British Institute, Barcelona
Jill Mountain and staff, British Institute, Rome
Julia Napier
Patricia Pringle, Université II, Lyons
Lesley Porte and Diann Gruber, ESIEE, Paris
Rachelle Porteous, London School of English
Tom Sagar and colleagues, Collège Rousseau, Geneva
Katy Shaw and colleagues, Eurocentre, Lee Green
Elizabeth Sim and staff, Eurocentre, Cambridge
Lynda Taylor
Kit Woods

Finally, thanks to Sue, Zoë and Thomas for everything.

Welcome!

Each of the 24 units in *Cambridge Advanced English* is based on a different topic and is designed to help you to develop all your skills in English. You'll find exercises and activities in each unit that concentrate on different skills, helping you to revise and consolidate what you already know and to develop and extend your knowledge further.

The odd-numbered units are 'Theme units' and they contain:
- informative Reading texts from a variety of authentic sources, with tasks, exercises and activities to improve your reading skills. You can prepare many of these in advance at home
- Listening exercises with tasks and activities to help you improve your listening skills
- Effective Writing exercises to help you develop useful techniques you can use in your writing
- realistic Creative Writing tasks to give you an opportunity to express yourself in writing

The even-numbered units are 'Language units' and they contain:
- shorter Reading texts or Listening exercises
- work on Grammar revision: the 'problem areas' of English grammar are dealt with in a thought-provoking and interesting way
- Word-study exercises to help you to develop your vocabulary skills
- Functions sections to help you to practise the functional language needed in different situations OR work on Pronunciation

Every unit contains:
- exercises on vocabulary connected with the topic of the unit
- opportunities for discussion
- work on idiomatic expressions and phrasal verbs
- integrated activities where, for example, a listening task leads on to discussion, which in turn leads on to a reading task, which may then lead on to a writing task

Activities shown with this symbol ▣ are Communication activities, where you and your partner(s) are given different information that you have to communicate to each other. These are printed at the end of the book but in random order so that you can't see each other's information.

▭ indicates that there is recorded material on the cassettes.

▣ indicates that you should use a fluorescent highlighter to highlight useful words or expressions you come across in a text or exercise.

Enjoy using *Cambridge Advanced English*!

1 Desert islands

1.1   A year on a desert island

> ● **UNINHABITED TROPICAL ISLAND ADVENTURE.** Writer wants "wife" for one year. 01-935 8384

A   The advertisement above appeared in *Time Out*, a London weekly magazine. Work in pairs or small groups and discuss:
– what kind of person would place such an advertisement
– what kind of person would reply to it
– why the word "wife" is in inverted commas

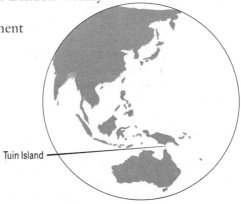

Tuin Island

B   You'll hear part of a broadcast about Lucy Irvine and Gerald Kingsland who spent a year together on Tuin Island in the Pacific Ocean. It was Gerald Kingsland who placed the advertisement in *Time Out*.

Before you listen to the recording, look at the questions and see which answers you can GUESS without hearing the broadcast.

Listen to the recording and note down your answers.

Was it Lucy (L) or Gerald (G) or both of them (L + G) who . . .

wrote *Castaway* **L**	wrote *The Islander* **G**
had lived on another tropical island	had worked in a tax office ....
was 24 years old	was 51 years old ....
caught fish	tried to grow vegetables ....
did the cooking	was going to write a novel ....
was bad-tempered	went off for long walks alone ....
fell in love with the island	wrote a diary ....
was bitten by insects	couldn't walk ....
lost a lot of weight	had an irritating voice ....
lost touch with reality	drank salty water ....
did repairs for local islanders	went to Badu for Christmas ....
wanted to stay longer on the islands	wrote a best-selling book ....

C Good listeners are often able to ANTICIPATE what a speaker is going to say. It's often possible to guess what is about to be said from the context and from your knowledge of the subject matter.

Work in pairs. Look at this transcript of the last part of the conversation and write down the missing words. The first is done as an example.

1 Then the rainy season came: enormous storms and very _rough seas._
2 So they left the island to visit Badu for Christmas. They had to stay till the sea was .... for them to return.
3 Gerald told Lucy she should be the one who would write ....
4 So both of them happily spent the last months of their time on ....
5 When the time came to leave, he wanted her to ....
6 The idea would be, you know, he'd repair engines to make ....
7 But she didn't want to. She felt that she was too ....
8 And she wasn't in ....
9 So she left to go home and write the account of their ....
10 And her book was a best-seller, called ....

📼 Listen to the recording and check if your guesses were right. If you didn't get the exact words, did you at least get the gist of what was said?

D Work in small groups. Discuss with your partners:
– the main differences between the two versions of the story, as told by Lucy and Gerald in the two books
– your personal reactions to the story
– your reactions to the way Lucy and Gerald behaved
– how YOU would have coped with being Gerald or Lucy's companion

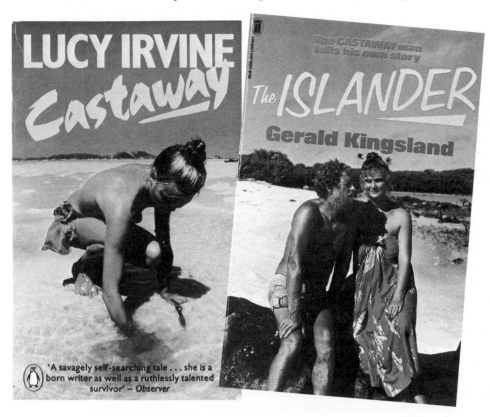

3

1.2　Islands and adventures

A   Work in small groups. Ask your partners:
– if life on a desert island would be wonderful – or a nightmare
– which desert island stories they have seen or read
– why they think desert islands are popular in fiction and movies

B   Fill the gaps in these sentences with suitable words. Look up any
unfamiliar words in a dictionary. The first is done as an example.

1　Although there was an a.**mple**. supply of fish, Tuin Island had very few natural r............
 and a limited supply of f............. water.
2　Lucy and Gerald's s............. r.............s consisted of rice, oil and tea.
3　Lucy and Gerald agreed on the d............ of l............ between them, but the building of a
 permanent s............ was a bone of contention between them.
4　If two people spend too long together the t............ between them starts to grow and they
 get on each other's n............s.
5　In Shakespeare's *Tempest* (1611), some sailors are s............d on a remote island where
 Prospero and his daughter Miranda live.
6　In Robert Louis Stevenson's *Treasure Island* (1883) a man is r............d after many years
 alone on an island where he had been left by pirates.
7　If you are a resourceful, determined person you stand a better chance of s............ing in
 difficult c............s.
8　People are fascinated by stories about desert islands but they prefer to experience d............
 and hardship vicariously rather than at f............ hand.

C　🎭　Work in groups of three. Student A should look at Activity 1 on
page 217, student B at 32 on page 230 and C at 50 on page 237. You will
each see a summary of the story of one of these books:
 The Blue Lagoon   The Swiss Family Robinson   Robinson Crusoe
Spend a few minutes studying the summary and then tell your partners what
you know about the story. Try to MEMORISE the main points, and refer back
to the summary only if you lose track of the story.

1.3　The Castaways

A　📼　Look at the poem on the next page and listen to the recording.

🖍️　Before you do the task in **B**, highlight any unfamiliar words using a
fluorescent highlighter and, if necessary, look them up in a dictionary.

B　Work in small groups. For EACH of the five characters in the poem,
make notes on the following information:

1　Name of character
2　Useful things accomplished
3　Useless or pointless things accomplished
4　Why you admire or sympathise with him or her
　or　Why you find him or her objectionable or unlikeable

The Castaways or Vote for Caliban

The Pacific Ocean
A blue demi-globe
Islands like punctuation marks.

A cruising airliner
Passengers unwrapping pats of butter
A hurricane arises,
Tosses the plane into the sea.

Five of them, flung on to an island beach,
Survived.

Tom the reporter.
Susan the botanist.
Jim the high-jump champion.
Bill the carpenter.
Mary the eccentric widow.

Tom the reporter sniffed out a stream of
    drinkable water.
Susan the botanist identified a banana tree.
Jim the high-jump champion jumped up and
    down and gave them each a bunch.
Bill the carpenter knocked up a table for their
    banana supper.
Mary the eccentric widow buried the banana
    skins,
But only after they had asked her twice.
They all gathered sticks and lit a fire.
There was an incredible sunset.

Next morning they held a committee meeting.
Tom, Susan, Jim and Bill
Voted to make the best of things.
Mary, the eccentric widow, abstained.
Tom the reporter killed several dozen pigs.
He tanned their skins into parchment
And printed the Island News with the ink of
    squids.

Susan the botanist developed new strains of
    banana
Which tasted of chocolate, beefsteak, peanut
    butter,
Chicken and boot polish.

Jim the high-jump champion organised games
Which he always won easily.

Bill the carpenter constructed a wooden water
    wheel
And converted the water's energy into
    electricity.
Using iron ore from the hills, he constructed
    lampposts.

They all worried about Mary, the eccentric
    widow,
Her lack of confidence and her . . .
But there wasn't time to coddle her.
The volcano erupted, but they dug a trench
And diverted the lava into the sea
Where it formed a spectacular pier.
They were attacked by pirates but defeated
    them
With bamboo bazookas firing
Sea-urchins packed with home-made
    nitroglycerine.
They gave the cannibals a dose of their own
    medicine
And survived an earthquake thanks to their
    skill in jumping.

Tom had been a court reporter
So he became the magistrate and solved
    disputes.
Susan the botanist established
A university which also served as a museum.
Jim the high-jump champion
Was put in charge of law enforcement –
Jumped on them when they were bad.
Bill the carpenter built himself a church,
Preached there every Sunday.

But Mary the eccentric widow . . .
Each evening she wandered down the island's
    main street,
Past the Stock Exchange, the Houses of
    Parliament,
The prison and the arsenal.
Past the Prospero Souvenir Shop,
Past the Robert Louis Stevenson Movie
    Studios,
Past the Daniel Defoe Motel
She nervously wandered and sat on the end of
    the pier of lava,
    ›
Breathing heavily,
As if at a loss,
As if at a lover,
She opened her eyes wide
To the usual incredible sunset.

by Adrian Mitchell

5

C   Work in groups. Find out from your partners:
- what their main impression of the poem is
- which character they sympathise with most – and why
- what they think the poem is about, beneath the surface of the narrative

And write two or three sentences describing the theme of the poem.

D   Work in groups. How would you and your partners cope if you found yourselves together on a desert island? Decide:
- what useful skills you possess between you and which you could use if you were on a desert island – make a list
- what qualities you would hope for in a fellow castaway – make a list
- what basic supplies you'd need on a desert island as survival rations
- what TEN luxury items you'd like to have with you on the island

---

1.4   Joining sentences – 1   Effective writing

A   In an informal spoken narrative, the events of a story are often given in fairly short sentences in the order they happened, but in a formal WRITTEN narrative longer, more complex sentences tend to be used. Look at these examples:

1   'Well, you see, the train was late so we didn't arrive till midnight. We were much too late for dinner at the hotel and we had to go to bed hungry. It was awful!'

2   **As** our train was late we did not arrive till midnight and, unfortunately, **as** this was too late for dinner at the hotel, we had to go to bed hungry.

3   Our arrival at the hotel was delayed till midnight **because** our train was late and we had to go to bed hungry **because**, unfortunately, they were no longer serving dinner at that time.

4   'Well, we had a nice lunch and we had a long chat about old times and then we split the bill and went for a lovely walk together beside the lake.'

5   We had a long, nostalgic conversation **while** we were having lunch and **when** we had split the bill we went for a very enjoyable walk beside the lake together.

6   **During** lunch we enjoyed reminiscing about old times and **after** splitting the bill we went for a delightful walk together beside the lake.

B   Work in pairs. Decide how to rearrange the events in the stories on the next page into chronological order, adding any information necessary and using some of these conjunctions. The first is done as an example.

after   although   and then   as   as soon as   because   before
but   by the time   eventually   finally   however   in the end
once   since   so   so that   subsequently   until   when
which   while

1 They managed to get to a nearby island. Their ship went down in a typhoon. They wanted to attract the attention of passing ships. They lit a fire on the highest point of the island. They were rescued. Fortunately, a passing fishing boat spotted their signal.

> *Their ship went down in a typhoon, but they managed to get to a nearby island. As they wanted to attract the attention of passing ships, they lit a fire on the highest point of the island. Fortunately a passing fishing boat spotted their signal and they were rescued.*

2 I arrived late for work. I couldn't get the car to start. It was a cold, damp morning. I had to push the car down the hill. I managed to start the engine. I jumped into the car. The car gathered speed.

3 Her interest in politics made her decide to stand for parliament. She won the by-election with a large majority. She gave up politics for good. She lost at the next general election.

4 They got home very late. They spent a long time drinking coffee and talking. They went dancing together. They went to a café together.

5 Our plane didn't take off. The airport was closed because of fog. Many flights were delayed. Inconvenience was caused to hundreds of passengers. We had to spend the night in the departure lounge.

6 The kidnappers were caught by the police. All ports and airports were being watched. The kidnappers were trying to get out of the country. The hostages were released. The ransom money was paid.

C   Now compose one or two long sentences out of each group of short sentences, but this time WITHOUT rearranging them. You'll have to alter some of the verb forms (e.g. *did* to *had done*) and use the linking words introduced in **B** above.

▶ If you like, you could also change each ending, substituting a happy end for an unhappy end and vice versa – as in this example:

> *They managed to get to a nearby island after their ship had gone down in a typhoon. As they wanted to attract the attention of passing ships, they lit a fire on the highest point of the island, but their signals went unnoticed and none of them survived.*

D   Rewrite each of these informal sentences in a more formal style, using suitable conjunctions. The first is done as an example.

1 Well, what happened to them was that their ship went down in a hurricane and they were nearly drowned.
> *They were nearly drowned after their ship had gone down in a hurricane.*

2 What they did next was to find some driftwood and build a bonfire on the beach. They caught some fish and grilled them over the fire.

3 Then they gathered palm leaves and built themselves a rough shelter.

4 They suffered a sleepless night because of all the insects and began to lose heart.

5 Anyway, the next thing they did was to make mosquito nets to protect themselves the following night.

6 They were very glad to find wild bananas growing on a hillside. They ate them and then they started to look for a supply of drinking water.

7 They couldn't find any fresh water, you see, and they were afraid they wouldn't be able to survive on the island.

⟫→

8 Actually, they hoped to collect some rainwater to drink, but there was so little rain that they were in despair.

9 What they decided to do was to build a raft from the remaining driftwood and then they set sail across the ocean.

10 So what happened in the end was that the raft started to sink and man-eating sharks began to circle ominously round them.

1.5 Your own ideas

Creative writing

A Select just ONE of these opening lines. Use the words to begin your own desert island story OR to give your views on the topic. Make notes of the ideas you would like to include.

I began to swim towards an island on the horizon ...

It was clear to us both that we were alone ...

I found myself lying on a sandy, palm-fringed beach ...

After the plane crash the three of us were the only survivors ...

I wonder what it would be like to be shipwrecked on a desert island ...

Stories about adventures on desert islands are, in my view, ...

If I were alone on a desert island ...

B As homework, write your narrative or essay. Write the last paragraph of your work on a SEPARATE sheet of paper (see **C** below).

C Work in small groups. Show your unfinished story or essay (*without* the last paragraph) to your partners and ask them to suggest what might come next. Do their ideas agree with what you had in mind?

Finally, show them your last paragraph and ask for their comments.

1.6   All in all . . .

Each unit in this book has a section on idioms or verbs and idioms. The idea of these sections is to introduce you to a range of useful expressions, so that, with time, you can incorporate them into your active vocabulary.

A   Work in pairs or on your own. Replace the phrases in italics with one of the expressions below. The first is done as an example.

1 *Taking everything into consideration*, I wouldn't like to be a castaway.
   All in all, I wouldn't like to be a castaway.
2 There has been a *general* improvement in the weather.
3 Factory workers often wear *garments to protect their clothing*.
4 There were palm trees *on every part of* the island.
5 When the party *had finished*, everyone went home.
6 If *it doesn't matter to* you, I'd like to borrow this book.
7 A two-week holiday on Tahiti costs £499, *including everything*.
8 They were *completely exhausted* after swimming to the island.
9 *Suddenly and unexpectedly* they heard an explosion and the ship started to sink. Miraculously, *everyone except* the captain survived.
10 *If nothing goes wrong* my plane will arrive just before lunch.
11 Resourcefulness and determination are *vital*.
12 The film wasn't brilliant but it was *just about satisfactory*, I suppose.
13 'How are you feeling?' 'Much better, I'm feeling *well* today.'
14 I enjoyed the story but *nevertheless* I felt a little cheated by the ending.
15 There were 187 passengers on board *altogether* and they tried to get into the lifeboat *at the same time*.
16 In an emergency, remember, *this is important*, don't panic!

> above all   all at once   all at once   all being well   all but
> all important   all in   all in   all in all ✓   was all over
> all over   all right   all right   all the same   all told
> it's all the same to   overall   overalls

B   Fill these gaps with suitable expressions from the list above.

1 All ...., I think you'll find that learning new idioms and expressions is worth the effort.
2 I'll meet you tomorrow evening at 8 o'clock, all ....
3 If you want to read a book, I don't mind at all: it's all .... me.
4 Going out on Sunday sounds like a good idea. All ...., I don't think I'll join you this time.
5 We got caught in the traffic and by the time we arrived it was all ....
6 I'd rather do this work by myself, if it's all .... you.
7 ...., when reading an English text, try to work out the meaning of unfamiliar words from the context before you consult a dictionary.

C   🔲 Highlight any expressions in **A** above that are new to you. Write five sentences using the most useful expressions from **A**.

2 Around the world

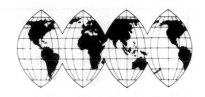

2.1 United nations

A Work in pairs or small groups.

1 What would you call a person from each of these cities? The first two are done as examples.

Algiers *an Algerian* Ankara *a Turk* Baghdad Bamako
Bangkok Belgrade Bogotá Brussels Bucharest
Budapest Cairo Caracas Dakar Delhi Dublin
Havana Jakarta Karachi Khartoum Kuala Lumpur
Lagos Lima Manila Moscow Oslo Prague Pretoria
Riyadh Rome São Paulo Seoul Sofia Tehran Vienna

2 Where do these cars come from? What nationality is the driver?

CDN GR NL PL SF
CH DK IRL P S CD

3 Write down as many of the following as you can:

Asian countries	Members of NATO
Latin American countries	Members of the European Community
Middle Eastern countries	African countries

B Work in groups. Of all the countries in the world, find out which five your partners would most like to visit one day. Ask for their reasons.

C In your notebook, make a list like this for the TWELVE countries you think most important or interesting and which you want to remember. But DON'T include the ones you already know and use correctly.

Country	Nationality	A person	The people	Language(s)
Brazil	Brazilian	a Brazilian	the Brazilians	Portuguese

2.2 World Music

A You'll hear part of a broadcast about World Music. Before you listen, see if you can answer any of the questions from your own knowledge of the subject.

As you listen to the recording for the first time, match these musicians with their country of origin. The first is done as an example.

Algeria
Cuba
Hungary (Transylvania)
Mali
Pakistan
Senegal
South Africa
Sudan

Abdel Aziz El Mubarak
Cheb Khaled
Elio Revé and his Orquesta Revé
General M.D. Shirinda and the Gaza Sisters
Ladysmith Black Mambazo
Márta Sebestyén
Nusrat Fateh Ali Khan
Salif Keïta
Toumani Diabate
Youssou N'dour

B Listen to the recording again and fill the gaps in these sentences.

1 World Music is .... music from .... other than Britain and the USA.
2 Since the ....th century, all popular dance ....s have originated in other parts of the world.
3 American popular music is rooted in .... Rock 'n' roll is a development of ...., which came originally from ....
4 Paul Simon's *Graceland* .... introduced many people to .... music.
5 World Music is more .... than Anglo-American popular music: the music is not organised and managed by .... interests and ....
6 Modern West African music is based on local .... Today's stars belong to families of musicians who have been making music for ....
7 Salsa and son-changüi music from .... really make you want to ....
8 Although traditional west European folk music falls outside the .... of World Music, the popular music of .... and .... does not.
9 The term 'World Music' was invented by a group of .... because there was no convenient .... in record shops for this kind of music.
10 World Music is often recorded in modern .... in .... or ...., or in Wiltshire where the motto is '........................... and ....'

    REALW●RLD

C Note down the ADJECTIVES used by the speakers to describe the work of the various musicians they mention.

D Work in groups. Ask your partners to describe what kinds of music from foreign countries they enjoy listening to and why.

2.3 Looking back Grammar

This section revises the basic uses of the simple past, present perfect and
past perfect. There is more work on tenses in 4.3 and 8.3.

A   Work in pairs. Decide together what the difference in meaning is
between these sentences:

1 When they heard the song everyone started singing.
  When they had heard the song everyone started singing.
2 Did you enjoy your holiday?   Have you enjoyed your holiday?
3 I never enjoyed travelling alone.   I've never enjoyed travelling alone.
  I had never enjoyed travelling alone.
4 She lived abroad for several years.   She has lived abroad for several years.
  She had lived abroad for several years.

B   Work in pairs or on your own.
  First, match these MEANINGS with the **verbs in bold print** in the numbered
examples below:

a) The CAUSE of an event or situation that people already know about.
b) Actions or events that happened BEFORE a particular past event.
c) Recent events that have RESULTS in present time.
d) Actions or events that happened within an as-yet-unfinished period.
e) Events or actions that happened at a definite time in the past.
f) REPORTING what someone said or asked about a past event or action.

Then, fill the .*gaps*. in the incomplete sentences.

And then: *Write a similar example of your own for each meaning illustrated.*

The first one has already been partly done to show what you should do.

Simple past

1 She **was born** in India and **came** to Britain when she **was** eighteen. – MEANING (e)
  She *began*.. learning English six years ago when she .... twelve years old.
  .... that programme about Japan on TV last night?
  And your own example: I made some coffee when my friends arrived.
2 Look over there: someone **has broken** a window. I wonder who **did** it?
  What a lovely photograph! .... you .... it yourself?

Present perfect

3 She **has worked** hard all her life.   I **haven't seen** her recently.
  .... you ever .... to the USA?   .... Lucy Irvine's new book?
4 I've just **returned** from a long trip, so I don't feel like travelling anywhere.
  I heard on the news today that there .... a terrible earthquake in China and
  thousands of people .... killed.

Past perfect

5 It was very cold when he got to Moscow because winter **had** (already) **arrived**.
6 My car wouldn't start this morning because I **had left** the lights on all night.
  He .... get on the plane because he .... his passport.

7 She said she **had been** in Burma in 1988 but that she **had** never **been** to India.
We asked him why .... to the party the previous weekend.

★ In some cases the use of the past perfect is optional. There is no
difference in meaning between these sentences:
    After I **had been** to Japan, I spent a week in Korea.
    After I **went** to Japan, I spent a week in Korea.

Time expressions

● Some time expressions are not normally used with the present perfect but
    with the PAST (or past perfect): e.g. *last week   in 1989   the other day*
        In 1989 Japan **overtook** the USA as the world's richest nation.
        Did you **see** that documentary about South Africa on TV the other day?

● Some are not normally used with the past but with the PRESENT PERFECT
    (or past perfect): e.g. *since January   lately*
        I **haven't been** abroad since January.
        Have you **seen** any good TV programmes lately?

● Some can be used either with the PAST or the PRESENT PERFECT, depending
    on the situation: e.g. *this year   this afternoon   ever*
        '**Have** you ever **been** to Kenya?' 'Yes, I have. I **went** there earlier this year.'
        '**Did** you ever **go** to Mombasa while you were in Kenya?'

● A few are normally only used with the PAST PERFECT: e.g. *by 11 o'clock
    a few days before*
        We were worried because she **hadn't arrived** by 11 o'clock.
        He **had booked** his tickets a few days before.

C   Arrange the time expressions below into four lists:

1 used with PAST
2 used with PRESENT PERFECT
3 either PAST or PRESENT PERFECT
4 used with PAST PERFECT

    already   a few minutes ago   a little while earlier
    a long time ago   a moment ago   all my life   always
    at midnight   by midnight   by now   by the end of the year
    by four o'clock yesterday   for two months   in the morning
    in 1990   just now   last year   never   not long ago
    not long before that   recently   so far   still
    some time previously   this afternoon   this week   this year
    till now   till midnight   two years ago   until today
    up to the present   when I was at school   yesterday   yet

★ Many of the time expressions above can also be used when referring to
the present or future:
    I'll see you in the morning.   I **have** a shower in the morning.
    Let's meet this afternoon.   I **have** a meeting this afternoon.
    He always **has to be** home by midnight.

⟫→

D 🔲 Highlight the time expressions in C that you most want to remember and EITHER write an example sentence using each one in your notebook, OR write only the beginnings of ten sentences and get your partner to complete them, like this:

When I was younger... I didn't know anything about foreign countries.

E Underline the mistakes in these sentences and then correct them. The first is done as an example.

1 How nice to see you again! I <u>didn't see</u> you for ages. haven't seen
2 It's six years since their eldest son has been born.
3 What a delicious Indian meal that was – have you cooked it yourself?
4 Where have you got that marvellous Persian rug?
5 I couldn't look up the word because I lost my dictionary.
6 That is the funniest story I ever heard.
7 It was a long time since I wrote to my friends in Mexico.
8 I didn't finish yet, can I have a few more minutes, please?
9 He was having three cups of tea by the time I arrived.
10 By 1965 most African countries have become independent from colonial rule.

F Work in groups. Ask your partners:
– what foreign countries they have travelled to and what their impressions were of the place, the people and the lifestyle
– what they consider to be the most significant international events that have happened during their lifetime, and why
– what the main turning points in their lives have been: what decisions and choices they have made and what happened as a result
– what the most significant international events this year have been

---

2.4 Other people, other customs Communication activity

A 🔳 Work in groups of three. Student A should look at Activity 4, student B at 36 and C at 53. You'll each see part of a newspaper article about 'Photon', a new craze sweeping Japan.

When you've read your part of the article, find out what your partners have discovered by asking them questions.

Decide together why Photon might (or would never) become popular in your country.

B Work in groups. Find out what your partners know about the people who live in the various countries you talked about in 2.1: their characteristics, habits and behaviour.
• Which countries are supposed to have the friendliest people, the tastiest food, the easiest language to learn?
• Which nationalities do you have first-hand, personal experience of?
• How would you describe a 'typical' English, American, German, Japanese, Italian person, etc? How and why are such stereotypes created?

2.5 Really? That's amazing! Functions

A 📼 You'll hear fifteen short extracts, in which people are reacting to information or news that a friend gives them. Interpret the reactions by noting the number in one of the spaces. The first two are done as examples.

surprised:	not surprised: ....
annoyed:	relieved: ....
disappointed:	uninterested: ...1... ....
pleased:	sympathetic: ....
interested:	excited: ...2... ....

B Arrange the phrases below to show which of these REACTIONS they would normally express *:

SURPRISE   EXCITEMENT   DISAPPOINTMENT   INTEREST   PLEASURE
SYMPATHY   ANNOYANCE   RELIEF

That's amazing!	How annoying!	How infuriating!	What a nuisance!
What a pity!	Phew!	That *is* good news!	Thank heavens!
Good lord!	I *am* pleased!	Fancy that!	Oh dear!
Thank goodness!	Fantastic!!	How interesting!	How exciting!
Really!	What a shame!	That's wonderful!	That's a relief!

Note down some other expressions that express the same reactions.

C 📼 Listen to the second part of the recording and imagine that some friends are talking to you. React to each piece of news or information with an appropriate remark.

D The class is divided into an EVEN number of pairs. Make a list together of the following things. Use your imagination to invent some of these if necessary:

1 Your favourite colour, car, book, TV show, film, writer, song, piece of music, holiday resort, hobby, sport, animal, first name, country.
2 Some things you're looking forward to AND dreading in the future.
3 Some amazing AND annoying AND disappointing things that have happened recently.
4 Some good news and some bad news.

Join another pair and get them to react to your information and 'news'.

*Some of the phrases in **B** can be used sarcastically as well as sincerely: this is covered in 18.5.

'For me? Oooooooooh!
I love surprises!

2.6   How would you feel? Word study

If someone asked you this question:

Would you be afraid if you were about to spend a year on a desert island?

would you reply like this: *Afraid? No, I'd be absolutely petrified!!*

or like this: *Afraid? No, but I suppose I would be a bit apprehensive.*

A   Some adjectives have similar meanings but have a different 'FORCE'.
Notice how these adjectives are arranged in the chart to show their force.

AFRAID: anxious   apprehensive   frightened   nervous   panic-stricken
petrified   scared   scared stiff   terrified   uneasy   worried

SLIGHTLY →	'Normal' →	VERY →	EXTREMELY
anxious apprehensive nervous uneasy worried	AFRAID frightened scared	terrified	panic-stricken petrified scared stiff

B   Work in pairs. Make a chart to show the relative FORCE of these
adjectives. Treat the one in CAPITALS as the 'normal', unemphatic one.

ANNOYED: angry   cross   discontented   dissatisfied   furious
grumpy   indignant   irritated   livid   resentful   upset   wild

SURPRISED: amazed   astonished   horrified   shocked
stunned   taken aback   thunderstruck

CALM: composed   detached   impassive   indifferent   relaxed
self-controlled   serene   unemotional   unmoved   unruffled
unworried

HAPPY: amused   cheerful   delighted   exhilarated   glad
jubilant   light-hearted   on top of the world   overjoyed
pleased   satisfied   thrilled

UNHAPPY: dejected   depressed   desperate   disappointed
discontented   disgruntled   dissatisfied   down   fed up
feeling low   gloomy   glum   heartbroken   inconsolable
miserable   sorry   upset   wretched

C   Work in pairs. Make a list of things that might make either of you feel
angry, happy, unhappy, excited, surprised or afraid.

Then join another pair and ask them to say how they would feel about
the things in your list and ask them why, like this:

> Would you feel afraid if you found a scorpion in your bed?

> Afraid? No, I'd be absolutely terrified!

> Why is that?

> Because if I hadn't found it, it might have stung me!

A   Replace each phrase in italics with the correct form of one of the expressions from the list below. The first is done as an example.

1 We didn't have a map and so we *couldn't find the right direction.*
   We didn't have a map and so we lost our way.
2 I'm sorry that I *panicked* when the policewoman stopped me, but I *was uncertain* about what to say to her.
3 I really enjoy *getting thoroughly absorbed in* a good book but this one is so dull that I'*m no longer interested* in it.
4 I'm so glad you're back, we *couldn't manage without* you.
5 I know you *felt humiliated* when you had to apologise, but don't *worry too much about* it.
6 I don't want to stand too near the edge in case I *start to fall.*
7 70 million people *were killed* in the First and Second World Wars.
8 The only way to *become slimmer* is to eat less. It's easy to *become discouraged* when other people are eating as much as they like.
9 I was going to complain to the manager but in the end I *didn't have the courage.*
10 We used to correspond regularly but now we *are no longer in contact.*
11 He *gets so upset when someone else is winning* – I *can't remember* the number of times he has stormed out of the room.
12 I *couldn't remain calm* with her when she refused to listen to my explanation and I quickly *got angry with* her.

     be at a loss   be a bad loser   be lost without   lose count
     lose face   lose heart   lose interest   lose one's balance
     lose one's head   lose one's life   lose one's nerve
     lose one's temper with   lose one's way ✓   lose oneself in
     lose patience   lose touch   lose weight   lose any sleep over

B   Complete each sentence with a suitable expression from the list above:

1 They were enthusiastic at first, but they soon lost ....
2 Let's write to each other regularly – it would be a shame if we lost ....
3 It's not as serious as you think, try not to lose ....
4 In some countries people will do anything to avoid losing ....
5 In an emergency don't lose ....
6 I'm sorry I'm late, I'm afraid I lost ....
7 He said he could ski down the slope easily but halfway down he lost ....
8 Just because someone doesn't understand, don't lose ....

C   Highlight the most useful new expressions or other vocabulary in this section. Write sentences using these expressions in your notebook.

3 That's show business!

3.1 Films, shows and concerts

A Work in groups. Find out from your partners how often they:

– go to the cinema – and watch movies on television or on video
– go to the theatre or listen to live music
– listen to recorded music on cassette, LP or CD

B Fill the gaps with suitable words. The first two are done as examples.

1 The most popular programmes on TV tend to be **game** shows, **soap** operas and crime ....

2 *Snow White and the Seven Dwarfs* was the first ....-length .... film: it was .... by Walt Disney.

3 Horror films like *A Nightmare on Elm Street* depend on spectacular .... effects rather than a subtle ....

4 *Superman 2*, ... by Richard Lester, was the .... to *Superman*. The .... was co-written by Mario Puzo, who wrote *The Godfather*.

5 A really exciting movie depends on good .... (photography), good .... (the way the film is cut with perfect timing so that each .... surprises you), and exciting .... (car chases, fights and falls).

6 Modern films have a Dolby stereo .... but not all cinemas have the .... to take advantage of this.

7 Foreign-language films can be shown with sub-................ or may be ....

8 Michael Keaton played the .... of Batman in the movie but his ....-star, Jack Nicholson, ... every scene he appeared in.

9 *The Last Emperor* was an Italian–American ...., shot on .... in China. It received a lot of ...., but I thought it was highly ....

10 It was hard to follow the .... because there were so many .... to scenes that had happened earlier.

11 The names of the stars and the .... are given in the opening ...., but you have to wait till the end to see the complete .... of characters and the actors who .... them – and the name of every individual member of the film .... The people who aren't mentioned are all the .... who appear in the crowd scenes.

12 I never go to see .... films – my favourites are ....

13 In the new .... of *The Tempest* by the Royal Shakespeare Company, the .... were designed by David Hockney.

14 In a pop or rock band you may hear these instruments: ....

15 The following instruments play in a symphony orchestra: ....

C Work in groups. Find out from your partners about their tastes in:
music   TV   the cinema   drama   reading
Ask them to explain why they enjoy the things they do.

A  We asked six people to tell us about a film they have enjoyed.
Match the information below to the titles of the films they describe.

© 1987

Cher, Nicolas Cage
Peter Riegert, Burt Lancaster, Denis Lawson
Marilyn Monroe, Tony Curtis, Jack Lemmon
Ronnie Cox, Peter Weller
John Cleese, Jamie Lee Curtis, Kevin Kline, Michael Palin
Dan Ackroyd, Jamie Lee Curtis, Eddie Murphy, Denholm Elliott

Norman Jewison	Charles Crichton
Billy Wilder	John Landis
Bill Forsyth	Paul Verhoeven

B   You'll hear the first speaker again. Before you listen, can you PREDICT
what word or words could fill the gaps in this transcript?

Listen to the recording and fill the gaps in the transcript.

'A film I really enjoyed that I saw recently was *Robocop*, which didn't have
a well-known .... There was an actor named Ronnie Cox who
played the .... and I think the guy who played Robocop was
called Peter Weller, and it was directed by a Dutch director, Paul Verhoeven,
or something like that, it was his .... film. And it was basically
.... in the ...., where the .... of the city of
Detroit, I think it is, has been privatised. And it's actually quite a
.... film and a very funny film, what would happen if the police
were privatised and basically they wanted to .... on their
.... so it would be more .... And this thing called

Robocop is built from a guy who's been virtually killed by a .... gang of thugs and all that's left is his torso and his brain and he's .... into this half-man .... and he goes around after the .... which is not usually the sort of film I like because I don't usually like .... films about cops, but it was actually *very* funny, ..., and it had a lot of pastiches of TV .... that were going on at the time because the whole ... it's a very TV .... society. And I just thought it was really funny and the audience was just ...., which really surprised me. And I think it was a much better film than, say, *Batman* or something that's .... to do the same sort of thing.'

C 🔲 Listen again to the recording and summarise the plot of each film in one sentence. Note down what you'd like and dislike about each one.

Work in pairs. Decide which of the films sounded most entertaining to you and which sounded the least entertaining.

D Work in groups. Find out from your partners which of all the films they have seen were the most:

frightening   exciting   violent   amusing   moving   boring
disappointing   memorable   overrated   underrated

Tell them your own feelings about the films they mention.

3.3 **For adults only?**   Reading

FILM CENTRE

WHO FRAMED ROGER RABBIT?
Sylvester Stallone in ROCKY 4
EMMANUELLE 7
ROBOCOP 2
A NIGHTMARE ON ELM STREET 6
Jane Russell in THE OUTLAW
Humphrey Bogart in CASABLANCA

A Work in pairs. Before you read the article on the next page, discuss which of the films advertised above you would prefer to see.

What do you know about Sylvester Stallone and his films (*Rocky*, *Cobra*, *Rambo*, etc.).
Have you seen any of them?

Attempt to ban Rambo

THE British Safety Council is trying to ban the Sylvester Stallone film, Rambo, from British screens. The film is due to be released on August 30 with a 15 certificate.

BSC's head, Mr James Tye, says some scenes are sickening. He has written to every MP, local authorities, and the British Board of Film Classification, trying to get the film banned.

The rage of Rambo

AS the most popular adults-only US film ever screened, Rambo grossed over $100 million in a few weeks, and was cheered in 2,165 cinemas. Time magazine said, "It seems to have perfectly articulated the nation's mood over Vietnam."

Articulate? Hardly. Stallone, co-writer of the film, substitutes oafish muttering for dialogue, making that other hero of the genre, Clint Eastwood, seem almost garrulous. Other than the mass murder of foreigners who don't agree with him, Stallone's only preoccupation in the film is exposing his preposterous body. His enormous breasts loom over the screen like Jane Russell in The Outlaw. The acting is performed mostly by his biceps.

The several hundred killings are perpetrated almost entirely by Rambo alone, although early on he is assisted by a female Vietnamese agent for the US called Co (who is not even played by an Oriental, but Julia Nickson speaking in broken English).

Rambo stabs, clubs, shoots, strangles, burns, bombs, drowns, and garrottes his victims, using enough knives to equip a meat market, mostly carried in his boots. As well as a high-tech bow with exploding arrows, he also manages to produce three assorted machine guns, all with inexhaustible ammunition clips.

He has no need of a helmet or flak jacket – let alone a shirt – because none of the enemy fire ever hits him, whereas he never misses. Rambo was obviously what the Americans needed before being chased out of Saigon in 1975.

The B-52s might even have remained in Guam, for Rambo is "a human war machine", as his old colonel observes. He becomes Bombo and blows up two dozen bamboo huts, an entire village, a bridge, several vehicles, a monster Russian bomber helicopter, two boats, a rice paddy and about half a battalion.

As an ex-Green Beret, Rambo's task is to find a jungle camp for American MIAs, Missing in Action, photograph any if there, and return "without engaging the enemy." (As this is supposed to be 1985, the incursion is illegal and Vietnam is not an enemy.)

Ignoring his brief from the start, he tells Co that "orders don't matter." His first act is to shoot an arrow through a guard's head, impaling him to a tree. This caused a fellow behind me in a T-shirt marked "USA" in red, white and blue, to shout gleefully "good arrow" as if at a Sunday darts match.

Zombo's final words are the nearest he comes to a full sentence. All he wants, he grunts, is

"for our country to love us as much as we love it." Howls of approval from audiences, most of whom, like Mr Stallone, did not actually serve in the real Vietnam either.

The idea that the US did not lose has obvious attractions for an imperial power beaten by a nation of peasants.

Christopher Reed

B 🔲 Work in pairs. Highlight these words in the article (the ¶ shows the paragraph they are in). Work out their meanings from the context. When you've decided, look them up in a dictionary to check if you were right.

articulated (¶ 1)   confused   expressed   contradicted
articulate (¶ 2)   athletic   interesting   speaking clearly   violent
oafish (¶ 2)   inaudible   noisy   idiotic
garrulous (¶ 2)   very talkative   very quiet   peace-loving   violent
preposterous (¶ 2)   enormous   muscular   ridiculous-looking
perpetrated (¶ 3)   committed   enjoyed   witnessed
inexhaustible (¶ 4)   incredible   tiring   never-ending
brief (¶ 8)   short   instructions   report   request
gleefully (¶ 8)   in dismay   joyfully   loudly   at the top of his voice

Which information in the text helped you to guess the meaning of each word?

⟫→

C Answer these questions about the article, and find examples or quotes as evidence for your answers. (Note that the writer uses irony to make some of his points.)

1 What does the writer dislike about the film?
2 What does the writer like about the film?
3 What does the writer dislike about Sylvester Stallone?
4 Which is the most horrifying scene described in the article?
5 What were the reactions of the audience, according to the writer?
6 What kind of people enjoy films like *Rambo*?
7 Why has *Rambo* been such a popular film?
8 Why does the writer misspell Rambo as 'Bombo' and 'Zombo'?

D 🔲 Work in groups. You'll hear some people talking about the influence of TV and films on behaviour. Make notes as you listen and then discuss whose opinions you agree and disagree with and why.

3.4 Evaluating and emphasising

Word study

When evaluating a performance, film or show – or even a lecture or meal – you can describe your reactions by using words like *terrible* or *terrific*.

A Work in pairs. Draw a chart, like the one below, and arrange these words and phrases into three columns, according to whether they mean TERRIBLE, TERRIFIC or NOT MUCH GOOD:

adequate   appalling   astonishing   awful   boring   dreadful
excellent   exceptional   extraordinary   fabulous   fantastic
first-rate   forgettable   frightful   great   horrible   impressive
lousy   magnificent   marvellous   mediocre   memorable
not bad   nothing special   nothing to write home about
out of this world   outstanding   passable   reasonable
remarkable   rotten   run-of-the-mill   satisfactory   second-rate
sensational   special   splendid   superb   tremendous   wonderful

TERRIBLE   TERRIFIC   NOT MUCH GOOD
appalling   astonishing   adequate
awful   excellent

All of the expressions in **A** can be used in this type of sentence:
The talk/movie/show/presentation/dinner/production was ....

▶ Decide which ones would NOT be used in this type of sentence:
It was a(n) .... play/film/lecture/book/performance/meal.

B To add further emphasis we can add an 'intensifier', like this:
It was an *absolutely* appalling performance.
It was a *really* sensational show.
But we do NOT normally say:
It was very awful. ✗   It was totally not bad. ✗   It was terribly superb. ✗

Make a chart like the one below showing which of the following intensifiers can be used with each adjective in **A** on the opposite page:

very   awfully   absolutely   extremely   really   dreadfully
exceptionally   extraordinarily   incredibly   perfectly
remarkably   terribly   thoroughly   totally   unbelievably

very   good bad boring impressive mediocre memorable second-rate special
awfully   good bad boring mediocre
absolutely   appalling astonishing awful
extremely   good bad boring

C   Work in pairs. Make a list of some films, actors, books, songs, musicians and food that you really like AND some that you really dislike. Then join another pair and ask for their reactions to the items on your list.

3.5   Punctuation

Effective writing

A   Work in pairs. Explain the differences in meaning between each of these sentences:

1   He likes his sister's friends and colleagues.
    He likes his sisters' friends and colleagues.
    He likes his sisters, friends and colleagues.

2   Her sister, who works in America, is a film star.
    Her sister who works in America is a film star.

3   Roger Rabbit was wonderful.   "Roger Rabbit" was wonderful.

4   I don't watch television – much!   I don't watch television much.

5   They said it was entertaining.   They said it was entertaining?
    They said it was entertaining!!   They said it was entertaining . . .
    They said it was "entertaining".

B   Look at these examples and use your own ideas to fill the gaps:

Apostrophes (' ' ')
   If she's your aunt, she's either your .... or your ....
   She was born in '71 and left school in ....
   It's important to distinguish between .... (= *it is*) and .... (possessive).
   .... and .... are contracted forms of *do not* and *they are*.

Commas (, , ,)
   When .... are used, it makes a long sentence easier to ...., doesn't it?
   My four favourite film stars are: .... , ... , ... and ....
   We thought, however, that the music was too loud.
   Hello, everyone, my name's Bond, James Bond.
   James Dean, who died in 1955, is still greatly admired.

If you enjoyed the show, why didn't you tell me?

When the film was over ....

BUT notice the lack of commas here:

Why didn't you tell me if you enjoyed the show?

The film that we saw yesterday was very enjoyable.

He said that he had enjoyed the show.

Colons (: : :)

I thought it was a good film: the photography was marvellous, the acting was good and the story was exciting.

In the words of the song: 'There's no business like show business.'

There are .... members of my family .... and me.

Quotation marks (" " ' ') either single or double

'Moonstruck' was a far more enjoyable film than 'Rambo'.

Rambo is a "human war machine", as his colonel observes.

I was feeling 'down'.

Should it be 'a university' or 'an university'?

"What a lovely day!" she exclaimed, "I feel like taking the day off."

"Well, ..., thank you ...., ladies and ...., the lecturer said at the end of the lecture, ... questions?"

Semi-colons (; ; ;) are used as a kind of 'weak' full stop or 'strong' comma in formal writing; in informal writing a dash is often used instead.

It was a hilarious story; everyone enjoyed it enormously.

'Trading Places' was a wonderful .... the director was John Landis.

Dashes (– – –) are used to add an afterthought – sometimes.

It was an excellent film – apart from the violence.

'Roger Rabbit' was a great .... we all enjoyed it.

C Rewrite this film review, adding the necessary commas, apostrophes, quotation marks, etc. And also split the text into four paragraphs.

A *Nightmare on Elm Street* made one experienced journalist scream with terror at the preview screening I went to. The noise frightened me more than the film itself written and directed by Wes Craven an ex-professor of humanities. Its all very spooky but not at all bloody says Wes of this teen-orientated horror film which has a ghostly and ghastly murderer attacking the children of Elm Street not in their waking hours but in their dreams. John Saxon and Ronee Blakley dont believe all this and he a policeman goes looking for a real madman. But we know better and so does Heather Langenkamp as their daughter. Langenkamp apparently known in America as the worlds most promising Scream Queen screams louder than the journalist. I just cringed. I think Craven has done better though one has to admit that its a good idea followed through with efficiency and state of the art special effects. Perhaps my trouble was that I wanted the Evil One to win. I cant stand those awful kids.

3.6 Planning ahead . . . Creative writing

A 🔲 Work in groups. You'll hear some people explaining what they do before they start a piece of writing. Discuss which of the views you agree with and which you disagree with.

B Work in groups. Here are some guidelines on planning a piece of writing. Rearrange them in the sequence YOU prefer, leaving out any you consider to be irrelevant. Add any further points you can think of.

- Decide which points are irrelevant and should be left out.
- Write a first draft and check it through carefully, correcting any mistakes you notice.
- Check the facts and figures: can you spell all the names correctly?
- Think of your reader: what does he or she want to find out from you?
- Write down your AIM: what is the main purpose of this piece of writing?
- Write an outline in note form.
- Make notes of all the points you might want to make.
- Decide which points each paragraph will contain.
- Rearrange the ideas in the order you want to make them in your writing.

C Work with a partner. Find out what shows or films both of you have seen and can remember reasonably well. Choose one that you share similar views on. (If you can't think of any, ask your teacher for suggestions.)

Make notes on the following aspects:
1 Give the reader an idea of the story.   THE PLOT
2 Tell the reader about the characters and the actors.   THE PEOPLE
3 Help the reader to imagine what it was like – what was particularly remarkable or memorable about it?   DESCRIPTION
4 Explain what you enjoyed and didn't enjoy.   YOUR REACTIONS

D Imagine you're writing in a student magazine or local newspaper. Write a review of the show or film, explaining why you recommend / don't recommend it to your readers.

E Show your completed review to another student and ask for comments.

3.7 *At*...and *by*...

A Replace the phrases in italics with expressions from the list below:

AT...

1 It was a difficult problem and I was *uncertain what to do.*
2 The show closed because it was running *without making a profit.*
3 The misunderstanding arose because we were talking *about different things but didn't realise it.*
4 It's impossible to get tickets for such a popular show *without previous warning* – you need to book *no less than* six months in advance.
5 She was working much too hard *causing harm to* her health.
6 When abroad, it's advisable to carry your passport *constantly.*
7 The winners are selected *without any plan* by a computer.
8 It was a wonderful show – *anyway* I enjoyed it.
9 The hero was rescued *a moment before it was too late.*
10 I'm sure that our friends will arrive *very soon – anyway* I hope so.
11 If you need to stay overnight, please book a hotel room *and we will pay.*
12 I could tell *by taking one quick look* that there had been a mistake.
13 *Finally* they did arrive, but by that time the show was nearly over.

BY...

14 'May I open the window?' *'Certainly!'*
15 A compact disc player operates *using* digital signals.
16 *Incidentally*, have you seen the new Steven Spielberg film?
17 I wonder if you know what is on at the cinema tonight, *perhaps?*
18 These machines are manufactured *in quantities of a thousand or more.*
19 I know that person *from her appearance* but not *what she's called.*
20 I don't like going to the cinema *alone.*

> at a glance   at a loss   at a loss   at all times   at any moment   at any rate
> at cross purposes   at least   at least   at long last   at our expense   at random
> at short notice   at the expense of   at the last minute
> by all means   by any chance   by means of   by name   by sight
> by the thousand   by the way   by myself

B [icon] Highlight the most useful new expressions in this exercise. Write your own sentences using the ones you want to remember in your notebook.

4 Food and drink

4.1   To whet your appetite . . .

A   Work in groups. Find out from your partners:
– what their favourite appetisers, main courses and desserts are
– what their favourite vegetables, fruit and snacks are

B   Fill the gaps in these sentences with suitable words.

1 A nutritionist can tell you how much fat, ... , ... and .... various foodstuffs contain.
2 I'll give you my .... for pasta salad: it's a very easy .... to make if you have all the right ....s.
3 Many ....s don't eat meat because it's against their ....s to kill animals. A vegan doesn't even eat milk products (cheese, ... etc.).
4 A .... of bread is cut into .... to make sandwiches.
5 .... bread contains more .... than white bread.
6 If a product has a .... date on the label you will know how long the product is supposed to .... The label may also tells you if it contains any artificial ....
7 His speciality is pancakes (made from ....): he never uses a .... to turn them over but makes a great show of .... them.
8 In a restaurant it's usually better value to have the .... meal than to choose from the à la carte ....
9 I've got no time to have a .... lunch but I'll try to .... a sandwich.
10 Thinking about food makes my mouth .... and my tummy start to ....!

C   Match the foods in the first column with the ways of preparing and cooking in the second and third columns. Then write sentences like this:
.... are/is usually .... and then ....
e.g. *Onions are usually peeled, chopped/sliced and then fried.*

onions	beat	bake
pancake batter	chop	boil
cake mixture	grate	eat raw
carrots	grind	fry
cheese	knead	grill/broil
cream	mix	roast
dough	peel	serve
a lemon	stir	steam
a lettuce	slice	stew
liver	squeeze	
potatoes	toss	
rice	wash	
walnuts	whip	

D Work in groups. Find out from your partners:
– what they ate the last time they went out for a meal and what the other people at their table had
– what dishes they know how to cook
– what they would cook if they were at home on their own and felt hungry

---

4.2 Good food?

Listen and discuss

A Work in groups. Find out from your partners:
– what the last takeaway meal they had was and what it was like
– what they consider to be 'healthy' food and 'unhealthy' food
– what foods they avoid because they are supposed to be 'bad for you'

Make notes of any useful vocabulary you discover during this discussion.

B You'll hear part of a broadcast. Before you listen, look at the summary below and see which information you already know.

[▭] Listen to the recording and fill the gaps in this summary.

Facts and figures

1 In Britain the most popular takeaway meal is still .... (..................... million portions are bought every year).
2 The next most popular is .... (..................... million sold per year).
3 .... million takeaway ethnic meals are bought each year: the most popular of these are .... and ....
4 Also popular are fried .... (..................... million meals per year) and .... (..................... million per year).
5 The British buy .... million takeaway meals each week (not including sandwiches).
6 The total amount spent on takeaway meals is £..................... per head per ....

Takeaway meals and your health

7 Fast food outlets are not obliged to disclose the ....s of their dishes.
8 Takeaway meals are full of .... , ... and ....
9 Hamburgers only contain a small .... of .... meat – a half-pound hamburger contains .... % fat (i.e. .... calories).
10 A portion of sweet and sour chicken contains .... ounces of fat.
11 Milk shakes rarely contain .... or .... – their .... are usually artificial. Their 'thickness' comes from emulsifiers and ....
12 Chips often contain .... to make them look .... , and are fried in ....

Takeaway meals and the environment

13 Hamburgers are often made of beef imported from .... , which is produced by cutting down .... To produce a single hamburger, ... square metres have to be destroyed.
14 The packaging of hamburgers contains chemicals which contribute to the ....

C Work in groups. Discuss these questions with your partners:

- What are the most popular takeaway meals in your country?
- Where do people eat takeaway meals – in the street or at home?
- What are your favourite and least favourite takeaway meals? Why?
- What do the members of your group understand by the term 'good food'?
  How important is this to you personally?

4.3 Simple + progressive aspect   Grammar

A Work in pairs. Discuss the difference in meaning between these sentences:

1 When we arrived at the station the train had just left.
   When we arrived at the station the train was just leaving.

2 She stood up when he entered the room.
   She was standing up when he entered the room.

3 He usually prepares the meal when his wife gets home.
   He is usually preparing the meal when his wife gets home.
   He has usually prepared the meal when his wife gets home.

4 I have been reading your book.   I have read your book.

5 I'm not having dinner until 8 o'clock.   I don't have dinner until 8 o'clock.

6 They always ask questions in class.   They're always asking questions in class.

7 I think you are being silly.   I think you are silly.

8 Will you join us for lunch?   Will you be joining us for lunch?

9 We'll be having breakfast at 7.30.   We'll have breakfast at 7.30.

B Work in pairs. Look at these pairs of sentences, each of which illustrates how simple and progressive verb forms are used.

First, look at the **verbs in bold print** in each numbered example and make sure you understand WHY that particular form is used. If you change the verb, you'll see that a different form is either NOT correct or gives the example a different meaning.
Then fill the gaps in the sentence that follows.
Then write a similar example of your own for each rule illustrated.
   The first one has already been done to show what you should do.

Present simple or present progressive: *does* or *is doing*

1 Please **don't phone** me while **I'm having** dinner.
      NOT   *don't be phoning* **X**   *I have* **X**
   I usually   *read the newspaper*   while   *I'm having*   breakfast.
   YOUR EXAMPLE: Would you like a drink while you're waiting?

2 Most days she **has** lunch at her desk but today she's **eating** out.
   I usually .... pancakes with honey, but today .... with sugar, for a change.
3 I **hear** that you had a Chinese meal last night.
   I understand he .... just .... vegetarian.
4 When the sketch **begins**, a man **arrives** at a restaurant and **starts** eating.
   In the end, the man .... so much that he ....
5 When **are** you **having** dinner this evening?
   What time .... your friends .... tomorrow?

Past simple or past progressive: *did* or *was doing*

6 I **didn't want** to phone her while she **was having** dinner.
   He started to cough while he .... and nearly ....
7 He **was** just **finishing** dinner when his wife **got** home from work.
   When the guests .... , she .... still .... a bath.
8 He **didn't start** preparing dinner until his wife **got** home.
   They .... the results of the exam until the end of the year.
9 Traffic **was diverted** because a new bridge **was being built**.
   While the restaurant .... redecorated, it .... closed to the public.
10 I **was wondering** if you could tell me why you don't like her.
   Nothing's ready I'm afraid because I .... you to come so early.

Present perfect simple or progressive: *has done* or *has been doing*

11 I **have been reading** this book for a week but I've only **read** 23 pages so far.
   How long has she .... English and how many words has she .... ?
12 They **have been living** / they **have lived** in London for two years.
   My friend .... in London all her life / since she was a baby.
13 The restaurant is closed because the cook **has been taken** to hospital.
   These vegetables are delicious – have .... steamed or boiled?

will do or *will be doing*

14 What **will** you **be doing** tomorrow evening? **Will** you **be waiting** for your guests to arrive? What **will** you **do** if they're late?
   This time tomorrow I .... and when I've done that I .... , I expect.

15 **Will** you **be coming** with us or are you busy tonight? *FUTURE*
     Could you phone us later on to let us know what time you .... ?
16 **Will** you **come** with us? We'd love you to be there. *INVITATION/REQUEST*
     .... you help me with the washing-up, please?

C Find the errors in these sentences and correct them. One sentence has
NO errors.

1 We are usually having lunch out on Sundays.
2 We can take a picnic but what will we be doing if it starts to rain?
3 She stayed at home because she was having a cold.
4 While I drove along I suddenly remembered that I had left the freezer door open.
5 The last time I saw him he was getting on a bus, eating an ice cream.
6 Breakfast is normally being served in the dining room but today it is served in the coffee shop.
7 Who is this recipe book that's lying on the table belonging to?
8 She was disliking vegetarian food at first but now she's enjoying it whenever she has been having it.

D Work in groups. Find out about your partners' experiences of different
kinds of food and drink, using the questions below.
- Unusual foods they have eaten – vegetables, fruit, meat, fish, sauces,
  salads, sweets, cakes, etc.
- Different cuisines – vegetarian, vegan, French, Italian, Chinese, Indian,
  Japanese, Greek, etc.
- Strange things they have eaten – for breakfast, lunch, dinner, supper,
  elevenses, tea, as a snack.
- Strange drinks they have had – hot/cold, alcoholic/soft.

> Have you ever ... ?   Do you ever ... ?
> When did you first ... ?   How long have you ... ?
> How many times have you ... ? When do you ... ?
> How often ... ?   What was it like exactly?

E Work in groups. Ask your partners to
describe the most memorable meal they
have ever eaten.

*'Yes, thank you, everything's fine.
Just to round off the evening,
could we have something to eat and drink?'*

4.4 Words easily confused Word study

▶ To save time during the lesson, check the meanings of any unfamiliar words in **A** and **B** in a dictionary beforehand.

A Work in pairs. Take it in turns to explain the differences in meaning between each of these pairs of words. Write sentences to help you to remember any tricky ones. The first pair is done as an example.

alternate   alternative
alternate = first one then the other – We eat out on alternate Saturdays.
alternative = different – He came up with an alternative menu.

anniversary birthday	memory souvenir
cancel postpone	menu set meal
collaborate cooperate	noise sound
complement compliment	personal personnel
cook cooker	principal principle
desert dessert	receipt recipe
economical economic	rob steal
experience experiment	satisfactory satisfying
fantasy imagination	stationary stationery
historic historical	stranger foreigner
homework housework	sympathetic likeable
immigration emigration	tasteful tasty

B Work in pairs or do this on your own as homework. Explain the difference in meaning between the words in each of these groups. Check any unfamiliar words in a dictionary.

actually at present presently nowadays	nervous anxious neurotic
alive living lively	notice note memo
author editor printer publisher	outlook view scenery landscape
broken not working out of order	possibility chance opportunity
destroy ruin spoil	print publish distribute edit
discussion argument row quarrel	professor lecturer teacher tutor
elder older elderly	propaganda advertising publicity
guard guardian attendant	shadow shade shelter
husband bridegroom fiancé boyfriend	thousand million billion
leave lie let lay	wife bride fiancée girlfriend
marriage wedding engagement	wounded injured hurt

C Work in groups. Write down some more words which YOU personally often confuse and then pass your list on to another group and ask them to explain the differences in meaning.

4.5   That doesn't sound right!

A   Work in pairs. Look at these short conversations and explain which remarks are inappropriate to the situation, as you imagine it. Decide what the people should have said instead. Look at this example first:

8 year-old: Hello.
Adult: Good afternoon, I wonder if I might have a word with your mother?

Hello. Is your mummy at home?
or Can I speak to your mummy?

1 Assistant: Can I help you?
   Customer: No, that's not necessary.

2 Patient: Good morning, doctor.
   Doctor: Oh dear, you look ghastly, what's the matter?

3 Your boss: Yes, come in.
   You: I'm going to come to work half an hour late tomorrow.

4 Boss: Do you see what I mean?
   New employee: Yes, and I don't agree with you.

5 Friend: Would you excuse me, please? I'd very much like to make a phone call.
   You: Fine.

6 Student: Have you had time to mark my composition?
   Teacher: Yes, and I hope you don't mind my saying this, but you've made one or two tiny mistakes.

7 Waiter: Are you ready to order now?
   Customer: No, go away.

8 Wife: Would you mind assisting me with the washing-up, if you've got a moment?
   Husband: Certainly, I'd be delighted to.

9 Waiter: Was your meal any good?
   Customer: Yes, it was.

10 Guest: The meal wasn't as bad as I expected.
    Hostess: Oh, good. I'm so glad you enjoyed it.

B   The kind of language you might use yourself in different situations depends on who you are talking to, and also how polite, tactful or direct you want to be. There are also different degrees of formality:

VERY FORMAL	I owe you a deep debt of gratitude; I should like to say how honoured I was to make your acquaintance.
FORMAL	It was a pleasure to meet you. Thank you very much indeed.
NEUTRAL	Goodbye. Thank you.
INFORMAL	Bye for now. Thanks a lot.
FAMILIAR	Bye bye. Cheers.

⋙→

Work in pairs. Decide which of the following phrases are:
VERY FORMAL   FORMAL   NEUTRAL   INFORMAL   or   FAMILIAR

1 A lot of people like fish and chips.   Loads of people like fried chicken.
Lots of people like curry.   Many people enjoy hot dogs.
A significant number of people prefer sandwiches.

2 Good to see you.   Hello.   Hi there.
It's a pleasure to make your acquaintance.   Pleased to meet you.

3 I'd like to introduce myself. My name's ......   I'm ...... – what's your name?
May I introduce myself, I'm ......   My name's ...... – who are you?

4 Do you feel like a drink?   Like a drink?   Want a drink?
May I offer you a drink?   Would you like me to get you a drink?

5 Can I have tea, please?   I want tea, please.   Tea, please.
I'd like a cup of tea, please.   Would it be possible for me to have some tea?

6 One should always try to be polite.   You should always try to be polite.

7 Give my best wishes to your parents.   Give my love to Jan, won't you?
Oh, love to Jim, by the way.   Remember me to your husband.
Please give my best regards to your wife.

▶ Why might it sound strange if you greeted a close friend like this:
Good morning, how very pleasant to see you again!
or, if you greeted an elderly acquaintance like this:
Hi there, how's it going?

▶ What's the effect of using a very formal phrase in an informal situation?
Friend: I've brought you some coffee.
You: That's extremely considerate of you – thank you so much.
Or very familiar language in a formal situation?
Stranger on train: Would you like to have a look at my newspaper?
You: OK.

C   The vocabulary that we use may also change according to the situation
we are in. In most cases this is a question of:
- Your attitude – serious, joking, sarcastic, disparaging, approving, etc.
- Who you are talking to – someone older, younger, senior, friend, stranger,
  acquaintance, superior, male, female, etc.
- The subject you are talking about – food, farming, films, geography, etc.

Work in pairs. Decide what situations you would use these words or phrases
in:
1 children   kids   youngsters   boys and girls
2 people   men and women   ladies and gentlemen   everyone   persons
population   human beings   citizens
3 man   boy   gentleman   bloke   chap   fellow   person   guy   male
4 woman   lady   girl   person   female
5 food   nutrition   cuisine   cooking   feast   meal   banquet   something to eat
6 delicious   yummy   nice   tasty   appetising   quite nice   wonderful   superb

A Work in groups. Ask your partners these questions:
- What is your favourite dish – how is it prepared?
- What is the most 'typical' dish of your country or region? How would you explain it to a foreign visitor?
- What are the basic characteristics of your/our country's cuisine? How is it different from the cooking of another country you know about?

B Work in groups. Imagine that you're in The Clifton restaurant and looking at the menu below.
Discuss what you're each going to order.
Then role play 'Ordering a meal' with one of you playing the role of waiter/waitress.

THE CLIFTON

WHOLE COUNTRY FOOD

*** SEE BLACKBOARD FOR DAILY SPECIALS ***

STARTERS

Soup of the Day £1.75

Cream Cheese and Smoked
Salmon Roulade £2.45

Farmhouse Paté with Granary
Toast £1.75

Scallops wrapped in Bacon £3.05

Honey Roast Ham and Melon £2.05

SIDE ORDERS

Garlic and Herb Bread £1.45

Mixed Seasonal Salad £1.45

Garlic Mushrooms, topped with
Melted Cheese £1.95

MAIN COURSES

Chargrilled to perfection on its own,
with Garlic Butter or a Barbecue Sauce
Rump Steak £6.95

Fillet Steak £7.95

Lamb Chops £5.75

Baked Salmon Steak £6.45

Vegetarian Lasagne under
Mornay Sauce £4.25

Beery Beef Pie with Flaky Pastry £4.75

All accompanied by seasonal Potatoes
and Vegetables

SALADS

Salad Nicoise £4.25

Creamy Coronation Chicken £4.75

Prawn, Avocado and Grapefruit £5.60

Smoked Salmon £6.95

PUDDINGS

Bread and Butter Pudding
with Cream £1.50

Apple Crumble with Custard £1.50

Summer Fruits Trifle £1.75

A Selection of Country Cheeses £1.75

Fresh Filtered Coffee £0.65

Tips only accepted if you have fully enjoyed your meal

4.7 *Bring* and *carry*

A   When a phrasal verb has a literal (as opposed to idiomatic) meaning, it is generally easy to work out what it means.

Complete each sentence with a pronoun and a suitable particle from the list below. The first is done as an example.

1 I needed my recipe book again, so I was glad when he brought **it back**.
2 There's a bottle of wine upstairs, could you please bring .... to me?
3 When our glasses were empty we carried .... to the kitchen.
4 I'm upstairs and I'd like some tea – could you bring .... to me, please?
5 While your friends are here, bring .... to have a meal at my place.
6 The injured woman was carried .... by the ambulance crew.
7 The dog picked up the bone and carried ....
8 If you give me a tray of drinks I'll pass .... to everyone.
9 I'll take the tray, so if you open door for me, I'll carry ....

> away   back   down   off   out   over   round   through   up

B   Most phrasal verbs have idiomatic meanings. If you don't happen to know what one means, you may have to use a dictionary.

Replace the phrases in italics with a suitable verb from the list below:

BRING
1 Whenever I drink hot chocolate it *makes me remember* my childhood.
2 She was *cared for* by her grandparents when her parents split up.
3 MacDonald's have *introduced* a new product: it's called a Lamburger!
4 She seemed to be adamant but after a long discussion I *persuaded* her *to accept* my point of view.
5 Why don't you *raise* the matter *for discussion* at the meeting tomorrow?
6 He was very upset: I wonder what *caused* that *to happen*?
7 His illness was *caused* by stress and overwork.
8 I need to make an early start in the morning, so can we *arrange* our dinner *for an earlier time*?
CARRY
9 I *was very excited* when I saw the buffet and took more than I could eat.
10 Don't worry about me, just *continue* what you were doing as if I wasn't here.
11 In the film the main character was *having an affair with* her brother-in-law.
12 The canteen will be closed until repairs to the kitchen have been *done*.

> bring about   bring back   bring forward   bring on   bring out
> bring round   bring up   bring up
> get carried away   carry on   carry on with   carry out

C   ▣ Highlight any new expressions or other vocabulary in this exercise. Use a dictionary and find six more expressions in which BRING or CARRY are used. Write a sentence using each expression in your notebook.

5 Crossing the Channel

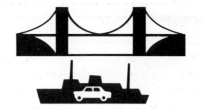 

5.1   Inside the Channel Tunnel

Reading

A   Work in groups. Discuss these questions with your partners:
• What do you think are the advantages of having a tunnel between England and France? Why hasn't a tunnel been built before now?
• If you had the choice, would you go through the Channel Tunnel – or would you prefer to go by ferry or plane?

B   Work in pairs. Before you read the article below, decide what information you would like to find out about the Channel Tunnel and its construction. Write down five questions about it that you would like to know the answers to. One is done for you as an example.

1   *How long is the Channel Tunnel?*
2   ....
3   ....
4   ....
5   ....

Now read the article and see if you can find the answers to your questions.

Inside the Channel Tunnel

The Channel will link Folkestone to Calais in 35 minutes.

The Channel tunnel, or Chunnel, will be the first fixed link ever built between Britain and the Continent.

A French engineer, Albert Matthieu, first submitted the idea to Napoleon in 1802. A French tunnel was started in 1877 and a British one in 1881, but they came to nothing. In 1960 new plans were made and two tunnels were begun in 1974, only to be abandoned in 1975.

Now things are different. A group called Eurotunnel began work in 1988 on a massive engineering project that seems certain to link up terminals near Folkestone in Britain and Calais in France.

Scheduled to open in 1993, the £7,500 million tunnel will carry passengers and freight on electric shuttle trains that will race from England to France in under 35 minutes.

The tunnel will symbolise the fact that Britain is European and make it easier for travellers to reach the Continent.

The Anglo-French group in charge is building two 31-mile rail tunnels 7.6m in diameter, and a 4.6m-diameter service tunnel for ventilation and routine maintenance.

They will run 100m below sea level through a layer of chalk marl, which is almost impervious to water and is ideal for tunnelling.

⟫→

37

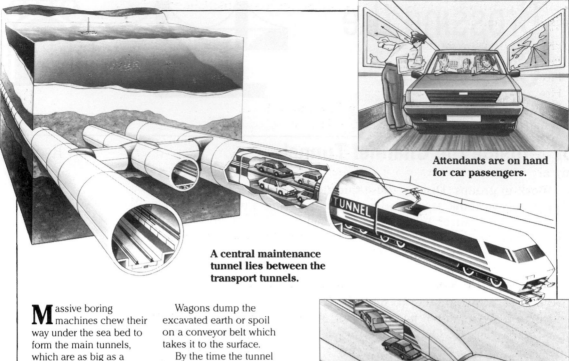

A central maintenance tunnel lies between the transport tunnels.

Attendants are on hand for car passengers.

Massive boring machines chew their way under the sea bed to form the main tunnels, which are as big as a two-storey house.

The 500-tonne machines being used have rotating heads with tungsten carbide teeth capable of tunnelling 20m a day.

Aligned by satellite and lasers, men are drilling from both ends of the route – chosen after numerous surveys of the geology. Behind them move construction trains to remove the 7.5 million cubic metres of excavated earth (about an Egyptian pyramid's worth) and deliver the 700,000 concrete or iron segments to line the tunnels.

Wagons dump the excavated earth or spoil on a conveyor belt which takes it to the surface.

By the time the tunnel is finished, 3,000 men and women will have worked in construction teams night and day for six years.

When the tunnel is open, passengers will be able to board special BR trains for the Continent at Swanley in Kent, at London's new international terminals at Waterloo or King's Cross, or at one of many towns north of London. The trains will travel at speeds of up to 100 miles per hour in the tunnel. Passengers will not have to leave their seats until they reach Paris, Brussels or other European destinations.

Other trains, called tourist shuttles, will also be used, running in a loop between the Chunnel's terminals.

As long as eight football pitches, they will be made up of 13 double-deck wagons for 120 cars, and 13 single-deckers for coaches and caravans. Cars and coaches will board the shuttles at the Folkestone terminal, once they have passed the restaurant, duty-free shops, banks and tollgates.

The shuttles will be brightly lit and ventilated and attendants will be on hand.

The Folkestone-Calais journey is planned to take 35 minutes with only 27 minutes actually in the tunnel – less than half the ferry time.

The tunnel will help cope with the huge increase in Channel traffic. From 1993 onwards, about 30 million people will travel annually via the tunnel, rising to 40 million ten years later and 46 million in 2013.

Banks and others who are paying for the tunnel will get their money back from fares paid by people who use it.

ROGER HIGHFIELD.

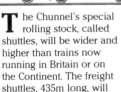

The Chunnel's special rolling stock, called shuttles, will be wider and higher than trains now running in Britain or on the Continent. The freight shuttles, 435m long, will consist of 25 wagons capable of taking 25 lorries. A freight shuttle could contain 176,000 LP records, a circus, or clothing for 30,000 people.

C   Note down your answers to these questions about the Chunnel. Look back at the text if you need to.

1 How is road freight carried?
2 How is rail freight carried?
3 How are private motorists carried?
4 How are rail passengers carried?
5 How long does it take to get from England to France?
6 What is the principal attraction of this scheme?

D   Work in pairs. Highlight the following words in the passage – if any are unfamiliar, try to work out their meanings from the context.
   submit   symbolise   routine   board   loop   toll

Fill the gaps in these sentences with the words you have highlighted.

1 Do motorists have to pay a .... to cross this bridge, or is it free?
2 I have to .... my report first thing tomorrow.
3 You can't tie a knot without making a .... first.
4 The plane won't take off until all the passengers have ....
5 The stars on the US flag .... the 50 states.
6 Working in a government office sounds like a dull, ... sort of job.

E   Before the EuroTunnel scheme was adopted by the French and British governments, several other schemes were proposed. You'll hear about three of these: Channel Expressway, EuroRoute and Flexilink.

1 Match the pictures below to the schemes you hear about.
2 For each scheme described in the recording, note down the answers to the questions in **C** above.

a
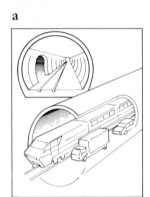

b

c

d

F   Work in groups. Discuss these questions with your partners:

● If you had been responsible for the decision, which scheme from **E** would you have chosen? Give your reasons. If necessary, listen to the recording again before deciding.
● What are likely to be the social, political and economic consequences of the building of the Chunnel?

5.2 Giving a presentation Functions

Most people get nervous if they have to speak in front of an audience – even if it's only a small, responsive group of friends or colleagues.

Work in groups. Here are some tips on giving a presentation or short talk. Decide which advice you agree with and which you find unhelpful.

Highlight the tips you want to remember.

- Make sure there is time for a Q and A session at the end.
- Use the blackboard, whiteboard, a flipchart or an overhead projector.
- Make sure you don't talk for too long – conciseness is preferable to long-windedness.
- Rehearse the whole presentation on your own in front of a mirror.
- It's best to speak from notes or an outline.
- Prepare a handout for each member of the audience.
- Allow people to ask you questions during the presentation if they like.
- Visual aids (posters, diagrams, maps) give more impact than just talking.
- Don't allow people to interrupt you during the presentation in case you get put off or sidetracked.
- A spontaneous presentation is more effective than a prepared one.
- Start by explaining what you're going to say, then say it, then at the end say what you've said.
- It's safer to read out a written speech than to rely on notes.
- A 'double act' with someone else is easier than a solo performance.
- It's best to do some research about the topic, rather than rely on what you already know or think you can remember.

▶ As giving a presentation usually requires time for research, we'll postpone practising this till later – see 5.3 **D** and 5.6 **B**. The short talks you'll hear in 5.3 **A** may give you some more ideas on this.

5.3 Connecting or protecting Listening

A You'll hear short talks about three historic engineering projects: the Panama Canal, the Great Wall of China and the Golden Gate Bridge. Before you listen, find out what your partners already know about them.

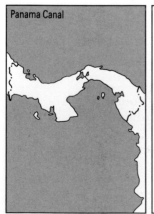
Panama Canal

Great Wall of China

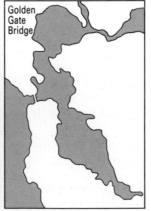
Golden Gate Bridge

🔊 Listen to the presentations and note down the information required in this chart about each of the projects:

```
Name of project:

Date completed:            Length:

Reason for its construction:


Engineer or client:

Most surprising or interesting fact:
```

B 👥 Work in groups of three. Student A should look at Activity 6, student B at 24 and C at 41. You'll each have information about the famous civil engineering projects listed below.

Find out from your partners:
– the location and length of each of the projects, and when it opened
– why each project was built
– any other interesting facts about it

And discuss these questions:
● How do these projects compare with the Chunnel and with the ones you found out about in 5.3 **A**?
● Which of the projects probably had the greatest impact on the communities it served?

Ship canals
Suez Canal   Kiel Canal   Houston Canal   The St Lawrence Seaway

Walls
Berlin Wall   Hadrian's Wall   Rhine-Danube Wall

Bridges
Humber Estuary Bridge   Seto Osashi Bridge   Verrazano Narrows Bridge
Lake Pontchartrain Causeway   Chesapeake Bay Bridge-Tunnel

Tunnels
Seikan rail tunnel   Oshimizu rail tunnel   Simplon rail tunnel
St Gotthard road tunnel   St Gotthard rail tunnel

C Work in groups. Discuss these questions with your partners:
● What are the most impressive bridges, tunnels or public buildings in your own country, region or city?
● What do you know about their construction and why they were built?

D Work in pairs. Decide on a topic for a short joint presentation OR separate solo presentations that you will give to the class – preferably about an engineering project or well-known building in your own country. You will need to carry out some research for this, perhaps in a library.

▶ Prepare the presentation according to the guidelines you discussed in 5.2. The talk you give to the class should only last a few minutes.

A Read the article below and then discuss these questions with a partner:

1 How would you describe the writer's attitude?
2 Which meaning of *blow up* seemed to be implied by the headline BEFORE you read the article?
    a) cause to explode   b) exaggerate   c) enlarge a photo   d) fill with air
3 Which meaning of *blow up* is implied AFTER reading the article?
4 What is meant by *the Earth's plasticity*?
5 Why does the writer use the phrase *a fairly volcanic mishap*?
6 What seem to be the main drawbacks of Daedalus's scheme and why haven't the engineers of the Channel Tunnel considered these ideas?

Let's blow up the Channel Tunnel

Daedalus

THE Channel Tunnel, it is claimed, will cost nearly £5 billion by the time it is finished, so you can be pretty sure the final bill will be nearer £10 billion – and all for a hole.

Much of the expense comes from the very simple-minded way in which engineers make holes: they smash up the material which constitutes the interior of the hole, and cart it bodily away, piece by piece. Daedalus now proposes a much neater method. He points out the rapid fate of coalmine tunnels. Unless adequately supported, the roof of such a tunnel slowly subsides while its floor, freed of the previous overburden, rises: the tunnel is soon squashed flat.

So, says Daedalus, a tunnel could most easily be made simply by reversing this consequence of the Earth's plasticity. His scheme is to adapt standard oil-well techniques to horizontal drilling, and bore the Channel Tunnel initially as a narrow pilot tube a few inches wide. This should be quite a cheap and rapid process. He will then apply an internal pressure, and simply pump the tunnel up to the required diameter.

Fairly soft and plastic rocks like clay and chalk yield and flow quite rapidly to applied pressure. A year or so of heavy pumping should give an excellent tunnel. But if harder rocks like granite are encountered, the plastic-flow expansion process could take thousands of years. Daedalus will need to soften such rocks by heating. Rock softens rapidly as temperatures rise, and the tunnel should expand quite feasibly at a few hundred degrees celsius.

Dreadco's engineers are developing a neat way of applying the heat and the pressure simultaneously. They will thread an electric cable through the pilot tunnel, fill the hole up with water, seal the entrances, and pass a heavy current. The trapped water will boil, creating enormous pressure in the confined space, and this will raise its temperature much above the usual boiling point. Even better, superheated water and steam are remarkably good solvents for many rocks. The tunnel will not only expand by plastic flow; it will be eaten out by the dissolving water.

One obvious snag to this neat scheme is that most boreholes leak. Usually groundwater gets in; in this case steam and hot water will get out. Some sort of mud might be pumped in to seal the leaks, but Daedalus hopes that the rock-laden superheated water will seal them automatically as it leaks out. It will cool, and deposit its burden of rock, in the narrow escape-channels, sealing them in the same manner as those sealing solutions for leaky car radiators.

At least, Daedalus hopes sincerely that this will happen. If the escaping hot liquid makes the cracks wider instead of blocking them off, the ultimate eruption of a tunnelful of superheated steam would be a fairly volcanic mishap.

The final tunnel will be more like a meandering string of sausages than a neat cylinder. The softer areas of rock will be widened more than the tougher ones. Elaborate pillars, grottoes, stalagmites, stalactites, and other effects of the dissolving action of water on rock may even give its interior a charming, natural rococo appeal.

B The article deals with the following topics. Number them in the same order that they're dealt with in the article. The first is done as an example.

.... why coal-mine tunnels have to be supported
.... consequences of escaping hot liquid
.... conventional tunnelling
.... cost of building Channel Tunnel
.... dissolving rock
.... how to heat rock
.... techniques of boring oil wells
.... plasticity of the Earth
.... problems with hard rock
.... pumping up
.... sealing holes
.... shape of final tunnel

C ▢ Highlight the following words in the passage – if any are unfamiliar, try to work out their meanings from the context.

*consequence   technique   encounter   snag   ultimate   mishap
elaborate   appeal*

Fill the gaps in these sentences with the words you have highlighted.

1 In spite of all the problems she .... , she managed to attain her .... objective of finishing her thesis.
2 Don't spend all day preparing a very .... dinner because a simple meal .... to me more.
3 Apart from one minor .... everything went according to plan.
4 I like the sound of your plan but I can foresee just one small ....
5 As a .... of using advanced engineering .... , the work was finished ahead of schedule.

D WITHOUT looking at the complete article, arrange these clauses in the correct sequence, adding capital letters and punctuation:

1 one obvious snag to this neat scheme is that most boreholes leak
2 but Daedalus hopes that the rock-laden superheated water will seal them automatically as it leaks out
3 some sort of mud might be pumped in to seal the leaks
4 if the escaping hot liquid makes the cracks wider instead of blocking them off
5 the ultimate eruption of a tunnelful of superheated steam would be a fairly volcanic mishap
6 at least Daedalus hopes sincerely that this will happen
7 usually groundwater gets in
8 sealing them in the same manner as those sealing solutions for leaky car radiators
9 in this case steam and hot water will get out
10 it will cool and deposit its burden of rock in the narrow escape-channels

A Look at these three different styles of notes. What are the merits of each style and which do you prefer?

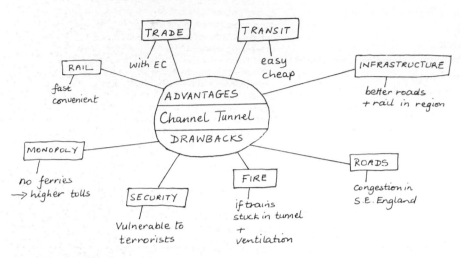

THE CHANNEL TUNNEL

Advantages
1. Fast rail connections between England and Continent: more convenient than flying.
2. Improved trade within European Community.
3. Transit through tunnel easy and relatively cheap.
4. Improved road and rail infrastructure being built to serve the Chunnel.

Drawbacks
1. Increased congestion on roads in south-east England.
2. Target for terrorist attack.
3. Fire hazard if trains trapped in tunnel + ventilation problem.
4. Chunnel will have a monopoly if ferries driven out of business: may then no longer be cheap.

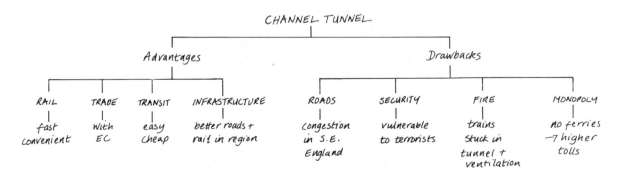

B Work in pairs. Add any further points to each of the diagrams above.

C Work in pairs. Using one of the styles from above, make notes on the pros and cons of ONE of the following proposed tunnels or bridges:

Europe – Canada   Alaska – Siberia   South America – Africa   Spain – Africa

5.6　Building bridges . . .　

A　Work in teams of three or four. Each team of 'engineers' is going to have to design and build a 'bridge' between two tables, using only the following materials:
　　one sheet of A4 paper
　　and two paper clips

Your bridge must span a gap between two tables without collapsing and without being physically supported by the engineers themselves. The winning group will be the one that builds the LONGEST bridge.

★ You will only be given ONE piece of paper and no extra pieces will be supplied, so don't fold it, cut it or tear it until your group has reached a consensus on how to construct it. It might be wise to make sketches of your design before starting construction.

B　Give a presentation about your project to the rest of the class. Explain how you constructed it and why you decided on this particular design.

5.7　Describing a process　Creative writing

Either　Write a report of how your group solved the problem in 5.6 above. Describe how you dealt with the problem, your method of construction and evaluate your success.
Or　Write a report of the presentation you gave in 5.3 D. Describe how you prepared and gave the presentation, summarise the talk itself and evaluate your success.

Make notes before you start, following these guidelines:

1st paragraph:　**The task**
　　Explain what you set out to do or were asked to do.
2nd paragraph:　**Discussion / Research**
　　Summarise your discussion and describe the research or experimentation you did. Explain how you reached your decisions.
3rd paragraph:　**Methods**
　　Describe the methods you used to solve the problem and/or prepare the presentation.
4th paragraph:　**Results**
　　Describe your completed bridge and/or presentation and the reactions of the other people in the class.
5th paragraph:　**Evaluation**
　　Compare your own presentation and/or solution with the other presentations you heard. Evaluate your own success.

5.8 *High, middle* and *low*

A Replace the words in italics with expressions from the list below.

1 Use a yellow pen to *make* useful new words *stand out* in a text.
2 Delays in the tunnel may be terrible in the *main holiday period*.
3 This cassette contains the *best parts* of the show, not the whole thing.
4 Operas and chamber music are often considered to be *intellectually superior* while shows like musicals are sometimes described as *uncultured* – or at least *not so very artistic*.
5 Don't put off doing this work any longer – *you should do it now*.
6 I have searched *everywhere* for my keys.
7 Would you like to live in a *tall multi-story* building – or do you think *two to three storey* buildings are more pleasant for people to live in?
8 Passengers and vehicles will be carried on *ultra-modern* shuttle trains.
9 Everyone was *feeling elated* before the weekend.
10 There's less room for holidaymakers on the beach *when the sea comes up high* than *when it goes out*.
11 I've got a bad cold and my work is getting me down – that's why I'm *depressed*.
12 After all the trouble you've caused, you'd better *remain unobtrusive*.
13 Do you think a person is *no longer young* when they're 40, 50 or later?
14 In Britain, it's not only *professional and business* people who own their own homes.
15 Students who do well in their exams at secondary school can go on to *university or polytechnic*.
16 *Good quality audio* equipment is on sale in every *main shopping street*.
17 THESE WORDS ARE IN *CAPITAL* LETTERS and these are in *small* letters.
18 During the *period from 500 to 1500* the only way to cross the Channel was by sailing boat.

> at high tide   hi-fi   high and low   highbrow   higher education
> highlight   highlights   high-rise   high season   high street
> high tech   in high spirits   it's high time   upper case
> Middles Ages   middle-aged   middlebrow   middle class
> at low tide   feeling low   keep a low profile   lowbrow
> lower case   low-rise

B [ht] Decide which are the most useful idioms in **A** that you don't already use. Highlight them to help you remember them.

C Work in pairs. Write a mini-exercise consisting of SIX sentences with gaps (.................) using the expressions from **A**.
Pass your exercise to another pair and get them to fill the gaps.

6 Buildings and homes

6.1 Where do you live?

A   Work in groups. Find out where each of your partners is living at the moment. Begin by finding out about their bedroom, then the rooms adjoining it, then the building, then the street, then the district they live in.

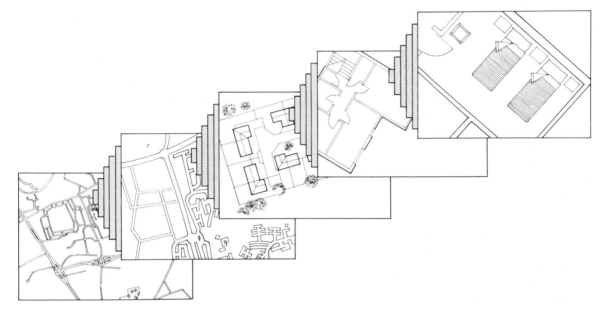

▶ During your discussion WRITE DOWN any useful new words you come across and note down any questions about vocabulary that you want to ask your teacher later.

▶ If you have any difficulties with vocabulary, ask your partners or consult a dictionary.

B   [cassette] You'll hear some people talking about their present homes and where they'd like to live. Make notes as you listen.
   Work in groups. Find out how your partners reacted to what each speaker said and the ideas they expressed.

C   Find out from your partners:
– why they like their present home
– what the differences between homes in their country and Britain are
– what their ideal living room would contain
– about the advantages and drawbacks of living with your parents

47

6.2   Do you see what I mean?

A   Before you listen to the recording, look at the speech balloons below. What other expressions can you think of that mean the same as the ones given in each balloon?

What do you think about...?

I think that...
I'd say that...

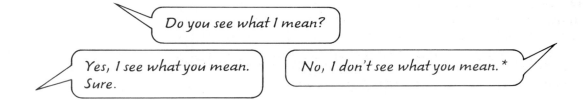

Do you see what I mean?

Yes, I see what you mean.
Sure.

No, I don't see what you mean. *

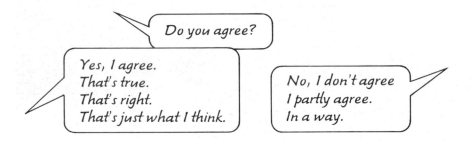

Do you agree?

Yes, I agree.
That's true.
That's right.
That's just what I think.

No, I don't agree
I partly agree.
In a way.

*=Please repeat, clarify or explain.

B   🔲   Listen to the recording. You'll hear six short conversations. Note down the expressions the speakers use as they give their opinions and react to each other's views. The first ones are done for you as examples in the speech balloons.

▶ How strongly does the last person to speak in each conversation agree or disagree with what the others have said?

48

C   Work in groups. Find out your partners' views on these topics:

> living with parents   living in a flat
> living in a big city   furniture
> motoring   nuclear power stations
> jazz   folk music
> children   transport in cities
> operatic music   parking
> learning foreign languages   politeness
> sunbathing   TV
> this government   my idea of a good night out
> my greatest pleasure

D   ▭   Work in groups of three. Student A should look at Activity 16, student B at 51 and C at 69. You'll each have a different part of an article about Prince Charles, which appeared under this headline:

Charles intensifies architectural war

Find out from your partners what they've discovered in their parts.

E   Work in groups.
What would it be like to live
in these places?

6.3 Articles   Grammar

A   Work in pairs. Discuss the difference in meaning between these
sentences:

1 I'm going to buy a paper.   I'm going to buy some paper.
   I'm going to buy the paper.   I'm going to buy paper.

2 There's a hair in my soup!   There's hair in my soup!
   There's the hair – in my soup!   There's some hair in my soup!

3 Ask a teacher if you have a question.   Ask the teacher if you have a question.
   Ask any teacher if you have a question.

4 She has some grey hairs.   She has some grey hair.
   She has grey hair.   She has a grey hair.

5 After leaving school he went to sea.   After leaving the school he went to the sea.

B   Work in pairs and look at these sentences.
● Explain the meaning of the **articles in bold print** in each example.
● Write a similar example of your own for each rule illustrated.
Sentences 1 to 3 have already been done to show what you should do.

A *or* the
1 I need **a** screwdriver to undo the screws. (=*no particular screwdriver – any one will be
   all right*)
        another example: Have you got a pen I can borrow?
2 Where's **the** screwdriver I had a minute ago? (=*that particular screwdriver*)
        another example: I've lost the key you gave me yesterday.
3 Have you seen **the** screwdriver? (=*you know which one I mean* or *the only one* or *a
   particular one already mentioned*)
        another example: Do you know the answer?

The *or* Ø (*zero article*)
4 I don't really like towns but I do like **the** towns in this region.
5 Modern architecture is impressive, but **the** architecture of the 1970s was terrible.
6 They enjoy living in **the** city but they often spend (**the**) weekends in **the** country.
7 She's looking forward to going to **the** Philippines / **the** Odeon / **the** Atlantic / **the**
   Middle East / **the** Nile / **the** Sahara / **the** Royal Hotel.
8 He's looking forward to seeing France / Asia / Oxford Street / Trafalgar Square / Lake
   Superior / Westminster Abbey / Gatwick Airport / Waterloo Station.
9 There are twenty students in **the** class, but only ten are in class* today.

*cf   at school, in church, to town, at sea, in hospital, at work, at university, in bed,
at college

A *or* Ø
10 They're both public employees: she's **a** tax inspector and he's **a** teacher.
11 They have **a** dog called Rover and **a** cat, but they haven't got any children.
12 I'd like **a** glass of milk and **a** cheese sandwich.
13 Windows are made of glass. Cheese is made from milk.

Some *or* Ø

14 There are **some** amazing new buildings in the city.
15 Would you like **some** tea?   Would you like tea or coffee?
16 People are funny, aren't they?   **Some** people are funny, **some** aren't.

C   Uncountable nouns (e.g. *furniture, money* and *advice*) can't be plural and can't be preceded by *a* or *an*. So we can say:
   I need some advice. How much advice do you need? Advice is free. ✓✓✓
But NOT:
   I need an advice. How many advices do you need? Advices are free. ✗✗✗
If we need to define an exact quantity, we have to refer to *two chairs* or *one table, five pounds* or *ten dollars*, or *both pieces of advice*.

Look at these pairs of words and decide which is countable (C) and which is uncountable (U). The first is done for you as an example.

advice U – hint C   *(advices x – hints ✓)*

air – breath	gadget – equipment	poetry – poem
architecture – plan	harm – injury	progress – exam
behaviour – reaction	job – work	report – news
bridge – engineering	joke – fun	safety – guard
cash – coin	journey – travel	thunderstorm – lightning
clothing – garment	laughter – smile	traffic – vehicle
cooking – kitchen	luck – accident	tune – music
experiment – research	luggage – suitcase	university – education
fact – information	peace – ceasefire	water – drop
flu – cough	permit – permission	weather – shower

D   Some nouns may be either countable or uncountable, depending on their meaning. Look at these examples and then write down your own examples for the nouns in the list below.

   U   Our house is built of stone.
      C   There's a stone in my shoe.   How many stones were thrown?

   U   She's away on business.   Business is improving
      C   The number of small businesses is increasing.

   C   An orange is a citrus fruit.   U   How much fruit was sold?

   C   What a beautiful painting!   U   Painting is not as easy as it looks.

   bone   brick   cake   cloth   crime   fish   glass   language
   life   light   metal   noise   pain   paper   plastic   pleasure
   religion   sound   space   wood   worry

E   Find the mistakes in these sentences and correct them. One sentence contains NO errors.

1 If there has been robbery you should call a police.
2 Her brothers were all in the bed asleep when she left the home in morning.
3 The most houses in South of England are built of the brick.
4 He's in the hospital having operation.

⟫→

51

5 You need permission from the planning department before building a house.

6 What a wonderful news about the Henry's sister getting scholarship!

7 How many luggages are you going to take on plane?

8 I'd like some informations on holidays in USA. Can you give me an advice?

9 What magnificent view of mountains in distance!

10 He has some brown eyes and one moustache.

F Write down what you would actually say if you were giving someone these pieces of information. The first is done for you as an example.

1 **Earthquake victims still in tents one year after disaster**

The victims of the earthquake are still living in tents one year after the disaster.

2 **Important**: make sure computer is disconnected from mains before lifting cover. To replace battery: use screwdriver to loosen screws **A** and **B** and lift cover. Remove old battery from socket **Z** and replace with fresh battery

3 PLEASE SEND INSTRUCTION MANUAL FOR MACHINE WE ORDERED AT END OF MONTH. PRODUCTION MANAGER ALSO REQUIRES COPY OF SPECIFICATION SHEET.

4 **SHOPPING LIST** 1 kilo potatoes, ketchup, bread, wine, food for cat – only eats sort with blue label

5 Is building like work of art or piece of engineering? Designed for people in street and people inside? Is building 'machine for living in' where every part has function? Or can parts be decoration: 'pleasure to eye'?

G Fill the gaps in this passage with *this*, *their*, *a*, *the*, or Ø (i.e. no article).

60% of families in .... UK own .... own homes after borrowing money (known as .... mortgage) from .... building society or bank. They have to make .... monthly repayment of .... total sum (plus interest) for 20–25 years. Borrowers can usually borrow .... sum equivalent to three times .... annual salary, but need to put down .... cash deposit of 10% of .... purchase price. .... people in Britain tend to move .... home several times in .... lives. .... typical pattern is for .... young couple to start as 'first-time buyers' in .... small flat or house, then move to .... larger house when they have .... family and, when .... children have left .... home, to move into .... smaller house or bungalow. Usually they move into other people's houses or into .... new home that has been built on .... new estate by .... builder. Families in .... lower income groups are more likely to live in .... rented accommodation, for example in .... council house or flat.

Moving home can be .... stressful experience, only slightly less traumatic than .... bereavement or divorce. Often .... buyer and seller of .... house are part of .... 'chain', where .... sale of one house depends on .... whole series of strangers doing .... same thing at .... same time. If one deal falls through at .... last moment, ... whole chain breaks down and no one is able to move.

6.4   Using abbreviations Word study

A   If you're reading a reference book you'll come across abbreviations like
these. Match them to their meanings below:

i.e.   e.g.   fig.   pp.   qv   cf   ch.   ed.   para.   NB   intro.   cont'd

*important note   pages   see another entry   edited by   that is
for example   introduction   continued   chapter   paragraph
figure   compare*

★ Abbreviations made up of initial letters, like EEC, NB and USA, are
spoken with the stress on the last letter: /iːiːˈsiː/   /enˈbiː/   /juːesˈeɪ/
   Notice that we refer to **the** EEC, **the** USA, **the** UN, but acronyms like
NATO, UNO, OPEC have a zero article.
   Many frequently used abbreviations may be written with or without full
stops: i.e. or ie, a.m. or am, p.m. or pm, U.S.A. or USA.

B   Work out the meanings of these abbreviations, which are used in
business situations. The first is done as an example.

1 *I heard my name called out on the PA system.*   public address
2 May I introduce Kay, who is Ms Brown's PA.
3 Salary up to £15K p.a.
4 If you're filling in a form, put N/A if the question doesn't apply to you.
5 encl. CV & photo.
6 Ask them to reply asap.
7 Thank you for your letter ref. 4352.
8 We can supply 15 packs @ £19.99 (incl. VAT) per doz, with the usual 15% discount.
9 Marks and Spencer Ltd became Marks and Spencer plc in 1985.
10 My tel. no. is 518362, ext 414.
11 K. Wells p.p. Angela Brown, Export Dept.

C   Rewrite each sentence using abbreviations and contractions where possible:

1 Doctor Brown does not live at 43 Saint Albans Avenue any more – she has moved to
   number 120, has she not?
2 Long-playing records do not sound as good as compact discs.
3 The Union of Soviet Socialist Republics is over 22 million square kilometres in area: it is
   seventy times larger than the United Kingdom.
4 This equipment operates at 240 volts alternating current, not direct current.
5 At the end of the talk there was not time for a question and answer session.

D   Do these activities in small groups.

• 🖽 Look at an English-language newspaper and highlight the abbreviations you find
   and, if necessary, check their meanings in a dictionary.
• Note down ten common abbreviations that are used in your own country. Explain each
   one and, if possible, translate them into English.
• Note down some international abbreviations (WHO, USSR, etc.).
• Write a note to the members of another group, including six abbreviations.

6.5 *Make* and *do*

Verbs and idioms

A Which of these things or activities are MADE and which are DONE?

the most/best of a situation   the shopping   your best   a cake
mistakes   some painting   a plan   a habit of   arrangements
someone a good turn   someone a favour   a suggestion   an exam
some cooking   harm   improvements   some reading   a decision
an effort   good   an excuse

▶ Write down three more things or activities you'd MAKE and three you'd DO.

B Replace the phrases in italics with suitable expressions from the list below.

MAKE
1 Hundreds of homes will be destroyed to *provide space* for a new motorway.
2 I could only just *understand* what she was trying to say.
3 In section 6.3 **B**, we had to *invent* our own examples.
4 They had a big row, but later they *became reconciled*.
5 If there aren't enough pillows, you'll have to *manage with* cushions.
6 As he's colour-blind he can't *discern* the difference between red and green.
7 Thanks for doing me a favour, I'll *return the favour* another time.
8 She *pretends* that she's the only member of staff who does any work.
9 They've got a brand new car, but I'm not sure what *brand* it is.
10 They're so well off that people are always *trying to gain favour with* them.
DO
11 One of the most popular adult hobbies nowadays is *home improvement*.
12 I'll be glad when this affair is *completely finished*.
13 When looking for a flat there are a number of *rules* you should be aware of.
14 You don't need to have a sofa to sit on, you can *manage without* one.
15 It's high time the government *abolished* nuclear weapons.
16 This newspaper cutting *is partly concerned with* modern architecture.
17 What she told me *was irrelevant to* the subject we were discussing.
18 He's put on such a lot of weight that he can't *fasten* his trousers any more.

make   make do with   make out   make out   make out
make room/way   make up to   make up   make it up
make it up to someone   do away with   do up   do without
do-it-yourself (DIY)   dos and don'ts   over and done with
have something to do with   have nothing to do with

C 🖱️ Decide which are the most useful idioms in **B** that you don't already use. Highlight them to help you remember them. Then write your own example sentences using the idioms.

D Write a paragraph including four examples of MAKE and four examples of DO on one of these topics:

houses   architecture   living in a city   living in the country

54

7 Put it in writing

7.1   The unstoppable Albert Sukoff

A   Read the article, if possible at home before the lesson, and note down your answers to the questions on the next page.

But first, look at the headline of the article – can you make sense of it? What information do you expect the article to give you?

The unstoppable Albert Sukoff sets a wordy record

Christopher Reed in San Francisco

The odd but undeniable achievements of Herbert Stein and Albert Sukoff in writing sentences in newspapers of 1,286 words and 1,404 words respectively are only too likely to be emulated at even greater length as a result of that encyclopaedia of futile feats, the Guinness Book of World Records, which carried an entry alerting Mr Sukoff to the fact that on February 13, 1981, Mr Stein, an economist who served as chairman of the Council of Economic Advisers under presidents Nixon and Ford, wrote in the New York Times the 1,286-worder – his entire article – on his recollections of various personalities in previous administrations, doing so without the use of a single full stop (except at the end) but instead peppering it with dashes, a technique not employed by Mr Sukoff, a freelance writer and city planner in Berkeley, California, who found out about the Stein sentence when he saw it listed in a 1985 calendar detailing Guinness records on the date they were set, in this case on a Wednesday in February when it happened to be raining and Mr Sukoff had nothing much better to do than to sit down at his IBM personal computer (one wonders if he would have bothered as a two-fingered typist on a 1958 Underwood manual) and create a sentence deliberately longer than Mr Stein's though not, it must be said, of any profounder content, but indisputably passing time as he unabashedly went into laborious detail in his eventual 1,404 words published in the San Francisco Chronicle recently, about how he purchased the calendar, read the entry about Mr Stein, ruminated for a while, and then decided to out-ramble him, though not, Mr Sukoff goes on to explain, by the employment of dirty tricks such as stating that the longest sentence ever to pass an editor of an important newspaper was by Herbert Stein in the New York Times, and then merely to requote Mr Stein, or in another even more banal ploy, simply to say that, "the first 1,000 names in the Salt Lake City telephone directory are the following . . ." neither of which is a real challenge, although Mr Sukoff does become repetitive and, of course, constructed his sentence consciously as a record whereas one presumes that Mr Stein proceeded more spontaneously and therefore deserves more credit – if that is the word – for his achievement, now superseded by one that is certain to be challenged, especially when, as expected, it appears in the next Guinness Book of World Records, for it is a feat with particular appeal to newspaper writers who have always felt constrained by unwritten rules about sentence length and indeed the whole matter of limited space, in which there is never enough for the reporter, who however invariably delivers too much for the editor, a type likely to be strenuously opposed to 2,000- or even 1,500-word sentences landing on their desks, and might even be tempted to insert a full stop here and there, thus rendering the whole exercise pointless, if that is the word.

⟫→

1 How long was Herbert Stein's record-breaking sentence – where was it published and what was it about?
2 What kind of information is found in the *Guinness Book of World Records*?
3 When did Albert Sukoff find out about Mr Stein's record and what was he planning to do that day?
4 What do Mr Stein and Mr Sukoff do for a living?
5 Who used a lot of dashes: Mr Sukoff or Mr Stein – or both of them?
6 What made Mr Sukoff's task relatively easy?
7 Which writer's article contained the more profound information?
8 How long was Mr Sukoff's record-breaking sentence – where was it published and what was it about?
9 What were the two 'tricks' that Sukoff refrained from using?
10 Why might professional journalists be tempted to beat the record?
11 Why would newspaper editors probably prevent them from doing so?
12 *Approximately* how many words do you think there are in the article?

▶ Work in pairs. Compare your answers to these questions.

▶ Look at one of your recent compositions: approximately how many words long is it? How many words are there per sentence, on average?

B 🖺 Work in pairs or on your own. Highlight the following words in the passage. Then match them with the definitions below.

*respectively   emulated   futile   feats   entry   alerting
profounder   ramble   banal   ploy   superseded   constrained
invariably*

copy   separately in the order mentioned   more serious   limit
replace   unoriginal   tactic   write/speak at great length   always
pointless   make aware of
piece of information in a reference book   achievements

Fill the gaps in these sentences with the words you highlighted.

1 To some people it seems .... to climb mountains, but others consider such .... to be admirable.
2 The new edition of the dictionary has .... the old one: the new and the old editions have 30,000 and 25,000 ....
3 I stopped listening as he .... on about his wartime experiences.
4 I .... make notes before writing to prevent myself from .... on.
5 I didn't find the novel .... at all, I thought it was quite ....
6 She said she was unwell, but it was just a .... to gain our sympathy.
7 She knew his success would be .... by the lack of money and staff, but she didn't .... him to the problems till it was too late.

C One technique of adding information to a sentence is to put extra information (such as a digression or a comment) IN PARENTHESIS by using brackets, commas or dashes – as in these examples:

He made a sandwich of jam and lettuce (together), saying it was delicious.
Strawberries and cream, my favourite dessert, was on the menu.

🖺 Highlight the brackets and dashes used in the article.

Another technique, frequently used in the article, is to use PRESENT or PAST PARTICIPLES. Look at these examples and then highlight four more examples in the article.

> . . . **doing** so without the use of a single full stop . . .
> . . . a technique **not employed** by Mr Sukoff . . .

D   Over-long sentences may be difficult to read and make sense of. Rewrite these paragraphs in simpler, shorter, clearer sentences.

1 The reason why language provides such a fascinating object of study is perhaps because of its unique role in capturing the breadth of human thought and endeavour: looking around us we are awed by the variety of several thousand languages and dialects, expressing a multiplicity of world views, literatures and ways of life, looking back at the thoughts of our predecessors we find we can see only as far as language lets us see, looking forward in time, we find we can plan only through language, and looking outward in space we send symbols of communication along with our spacecraft, to explain who we are, in case there is anyone there who wants to know.

2 The reason why this book has been specially prepared to make it enjoyable reading for people to whom English is a second or foreign language is that an English writer never thinks of avoiding unusual words, so that the learner, trying to read the book in its original form, has to turn frequently to the dictionary and so loses much of the pleasure that the book ought to give.

★ In an essay or letter, shorter sentences tend to be easier to understand (and easier to write) than long ones. On the other hand, very short sentences may look rather childish. You have to strike a balance. This may be difficult. There are no fixed rules about this. Perhaps the best ploy is to try to put yourself in your reader's position as you write.

7.2   Spoken and written English – 1   Listening

A   You'll hear the first part of the recording of a lecture on spoken and written English. Before you start listening, spend a few minutes with a partner, noting down what *you* think are the major differences between the style we use when we're speaking and the style that is used in writing.

B   Now listen to the recording and make notes on the lecture – note down the main points the lecturer makes and also any interesting details or examples.

C   Work in pairs. Compare your notes and discuss the lecture – what did you find most interesting (and least interesting) about it?

▶ You'll be able to hear the second part of the lecture in 8.6.

A   Work in groups. Find out from your partners:
- if they ever use a computer and if so what for
- how they think a computer can help you, entertain you, confuse you, etc.
- what they enjoy and hate about using a computer

B   Read the text and answer the questions on the next page.

The first novel

Christopher Reed reports from America on the success of a new author

A COMPLETELY inexperienced writer's first effort at a short story, some verse, and other scribblings is published by a major New York house and is widely well reviewed.

It may be every author's dream but in this case the literary novice will register no emotion. The work is by a computer program called Racter and the creation of William Chamberlain and Tom Etter of New York.

Called The Policeman's Beard Is Half Constructed (Warner Books, £9.95) it is a strange collection of surreal but oddly disarming images and occasional insights. It is advertised as the first ever book by a computer.

Mr Etter and Mr Chamberlain are both computer programmers and Mr Chamberlain is also a published writer. In his introduction he states that the computer was solely responsible for the content.

Mr Chamberlain explains that the computer's output is not in a pre-programmed form. It produces at random what it finds in its files, but as programmed "syntax directives"

so that however odd the meaning, the grammar is faultless.

Odd imagery appears from time to time. I rather like this: "Blissful quiet, the rocking of a recent love is both repose and anguish in my fainting dreams." Or this: "From water and from time a face bounds and tumbles. I seek sleep and need repose but miss the quiet movement of my dreams."

Racter dreams a lot. It also has some peculiar preoccupations. Lamb and lettuce (together) seem a favourite food, which may or may not explain the frequent appearance of a dentist. Characters yodel and chant more than your average Joe. Hence: "A man who sings is a pleasure to his friends but a man who chants is not a pleasure to his associates." Who can argue with that?

Perhaps because Racter is an American, there is lots about the medical profession.

"Many enraged psychiatrists are inciting a weary butcher. The butcher is weary and tired because he has cut meat and steak and lamb for hours and weeks. He does not desire to chant about anything with raving psychiatrists but he

sings about his dentist, he dreams about a single astronomer, he thinks about his dog. The dog is named Herbert."

The major work in this electronic opus is a short story about three men, an oboist, a psychiatrist and a philosopher, who dine – on lamb, what else – with two women, Helene, a maid, and Wendy, who the very last line reveals is "a follower". They are to hear a dissertation from the philosopher.

Wendy and Helene start "quaffing" cognac and champagne. Mathew, "who yearned to look into Helene's night gown," stifles his passions by "walking for an hour in his immense boudoir." Mathew, as you may have guessed, is the psychiatrist.

What with the ladies getting drunk and the discovery that there is only one lamb chop, the evening looks like ending in disaster. Racter also turns out to be a sexist. We meet the maid Helene "slowly ironing her brassiere." She and the unemployed Wendy have to do all the cooking. No wonder they got drunk.

Racter finally owns up. "I suppose this dissertation could be difficult and endless (after all, I'm a computer), but you're doubtless as exhausted and tired as I am – so I'll leave this loony story to your own notions and dreams."

Professional writers need not worry about their jobs, yet.

1 What does the new book of Racter's work contain?
2 How much of the text was written by Mr Etter and Mr Chamberlain?
3 How good is Racter's command of English grammar?
4 Why does the writer think Racter is a sexist?
5 What happens at the end of Racter's story?

C   Racter's output is amusing because of the way that words are used in surprising combinations. Underline the words in each extract which seem INAPPROPRIATE or incongruous. The first is done as an example.

1 Many <u>enraged</u> psychiatrists are <u>inciting</u> a <u>weary</u> butcher.

In real life psychiatrists tend not to be enraged and butchers tend not to be weary. People have to be incited to something (e.g. anger or violence) not just incited. Moreover, psychiatrists and butchers tend not to be associates.

2 The butcher is weary and tired because he has cut meat and steak and lamb for hours and weeks.
3 He does not desire to chant about anything with raving psychiatrists but he sings about his dentist, he dreams about a single astronomer, he thinks about his dog.
4 (Mathew), who yearned to look into Helene's nightgown (was) walking for an hour in his immense boudoir.
5 (The maid Helene was) slowly ironing her brassiere.

★ Inappropriate language can be amusing for the reader – but it can distract people from what you are trying to say.
   It's a good idea to check through your own written work to make sure that you haven't used phrases that might unintentionally cause amusement.

7.4   Different styles

Functions

A   Work in pairs or small groups. On the next page there are ten extracts from various publications and documents. Decide together:

• What each extract is about and what topic it deals with. Try guessing from the layout and typeface before you read the extracts.
• What kind of publication or document each extract comes from.

★ Using phrases like these can help you to avoid sounding too dogmatic or even aggressive in a discussion:

> It looks like ...... because ...
>
> It seems to me that it's ...... because ...
>
> I don't think it's ...... because ...
>
> It could either be ...... or ......
>
> It seems to be about ...... because ...
>
> I think this comes from ...... because ...

1 This book has been specially prepared to make it enjoyable reading for people to whom English is a second or foreign language. An English writer never thinks of avoiding unusual words, so that the learner, trying to read the book in its original form, has to turn frequently to the dictionary and so loses much of the pleasure that the book ought to give.

2 Dickie Kettleson is a ten year-old boy growing up at a time when even the most ordinary life is a struggle. Dickie's world is his home and his neighbourhood – his family, his street, the threat of hunger and destruction that lurks just outside the door.

3 Most of the country will have another dry, warm day with long sunny spells, but there is the risk of one or two showers, perhaps heavy, later in the afternoon and evening.

4 Everyone must, in principle, have a visa to visit Japan. However, to help tourism, bilateral agreements with some countries mean you don't need a visa if you are from western Europe, the UK or most English-speaking countries, with the notable exceptions of the USA, Australia and South Africa.

5 Avoid listening with your headphones at a volume so loud that extended play might affect your hearing. As your headphones are of open-air design, sounds go out through the headphones. Remember not to disturb those close to you.

6 It's a dream come true when compared with making the journey by road. You don't have to contend with traffic jams, motorway hold-ups or the uncertainties of driving to the airport. You won't have to bother about parking either.

7 We found this really terrific place just a little way from the village and because the only way you could get there was on foot, it was completely unspoilt. We were practically the only people there.

8 One grey November morning I was running near the edge of a lake. On the path ahead of me an old man shuffled along slowly, using a cane. As I ran by I called out, 'Good morning!' He returned my greeting and then called after me rather unexpectedly, 'What do you gain by running?' I shouted back: 'It makes me feel good!'

9 The dose may be taken three or four times daily at intervals of not less than four hours. Do not exceed the stated dose. If symptoms persist, consult your doctor.

10 Claims under section 5 (Baggage) will not be considered unless substantiated by an original sales receipt or valuation for any item exceeding £50 or more.

B Highlight the words or information that led you to your decision about each extract. Which was the main language clue in each case?

C Work in pairs. Find five more short quotes from different sources and write them out. Challenge another pair to tell you where they come from.

7.5 Writing letters

A Work in groups. Find out from your partners:
- when was the last time they wrote a letter in their own language, who it was to and what it was about
- when was the last time they wrote a letter in English, who it was to and what it was about

B 📼 Listen to the recording. You'll hear a broadcast report on trends in letter writing. Fill the gaps in this chart:

> **Number of private letters sent in UK per year**
> 1900 ...1,000 million...
> 1930 ....
> 1980 ....
> now ....
>
> **Letters written by 16- to 24-year-olds in UK**
> 22% .... letters
> .... % sent to addresses abroad
> .... % fan letters
> .... % love letters
> 5% letters to ....
>
> Women write .... personal letters per year, men write .... per year.
> 70% of all letters are connected with ....
> Worldwide, more .... are sent than ....

C Work in groups. Continue your discussion now that you have heard the recording in **B**. Find out from your partners:
- what their reactions to the information given in the broadcast are
- how many personal letters they write in a year – and how many they receive
- whether they write more or fewer letters than they used to
- why they enjoy / don't enjoy writing personal letters

D 🏆 Work in pairs. One of you should look at Activity 10, the other at 28. You'll each see some information about graphology: the science of judging personality from handwriting.

When you have studied the information, collect some ANONYMOUS samples of handwriting from other members of the class and analyse them – what can you deduce about the personality of each writer?

This is a sample of my handwriting. What sort of person am I?

This is a sample of my handwriting. What sort of person am I?

This is a sample of my handwriting. What sort of person am I?

THE SECRETS OF WRITING BUSINESS LETTERS

 As far back as biblical times, businessmen have used powerful communication to achieve wealth and position.

Even today the right message at the right time can lead to sweet success.

Want money? A promotion? To sell something? Explain something? Then write a good letter.

Letter writing is not a lost art, just a forgotten one. The principles still exist. If you try them, you'll see improvement in your very next letter.

TO BEGIN WITH

1. Start from the end. Decide what you'd like to happen as the result of your letter.

Make a list of all the things you'd like to say. Look them over. Find any that don't support your main cause, and cross them off without remorse.

Remember, the best letters have a strong sense of purpose.

2. Get to the point early. If your reader wanted a mystery, he'd be reading Raymond Chandler. A letter should tell whodunit in the first paragraph.

3. Put yourself in your reader's place. Think: if the same letter came to you, how would you respond?

Therefore, be friendly. Be nice. And find ways to turn negative statements into positive ones.

NO BUSINESS-ESE

4. Say it plainly. There is no such thing as a "business language". Phrases like "in compliance with your request" and "enclosed herewith" will only make you seem like a robot. Write the way you talk, naturally.

Keep your sentences short – one idea in each. Any sentence longer than two typed lines is automatically suspect.

5. Clear the deadwood. Chop out words, sentences, and even whole paragraphs if they don't contribute. Work hard so your reader won't have to.

In particular, cast a questioning eye on adjectives. They can sap the strength from your words, or stretch your credibility. As Voltaire put it, "The adjective is the enemy of the noun".

6. Use active verbs. Face it, the passive voice is wimpy. "A decision has been reached by the committee" wouldn't last three rounds in the ring with "The committee has reached a decision".

Also, your reader will sniff a coverup if you write: "Your order has been misplaced" instead of "I misplaced your order." Courage!

7. Be human. Your letter should read like a conversation, not a decree.

Address your reader by name: "Dear Ms. Hartman". And if you can fit it in naturally, use Ms. Hartman's name once or twice in the body. You want her to know you wrote the letter just for her.

Whenever you can, use pronouns like *I*, *we*, and *you*. Especially *you* – it's an arrow straight to your reader's heart.

BE POSITIVE

8. Never write in anger. Your anger will evaporate; your letter won't. President Truman often vented his fury in letters. He also had the sense never to send them.

Devise a way to handle the problem in an upbeat manner. Your chances of success will multiply tenfold.

9. End it with an action step. The last sentence of your letter should suggest the reader's next move. Or your own next move.

Resist the hat-in-hand, shuffling type of exit: "Again, thank you for ..." or "If you have any problems, please don't hesitate to call."

Instead, try closing with a plain

and simple "Sincerely", and your signature. It may be the perfect ending.

10. Be professional. The strongest business letter in the world can't survive a bad presentation.

Set up a clean, logical format for your letter. A crowded or overdesigned page will distract from your message.

11. Develop a regimen. The keys to powerful correspondence are 1) writing often and 2) responding quickly.

If it sounds like work, read on.

WRITE FOR POWER

The easiest way to more powerful correspondence is QuickLetter™, from Working Software.

Unlike heavy-duty word processors, QuickLetter is designed to do one thing and one thing only – write letters fast.

Here's how:

QuickLetter's built-in address book places your reader's name and address into your letter. Automatically.

QuickLetter's page preview displays your letter, vertically centred, in the format you've defined. Automatically.

QuickLetter addresses any size envelope. Automatically.

And the list of features goes on.

There you have it. All the secrets of brilliant business correspondence at your fingertips. Except one. And you can pick that up at your local software store.

A Read the advertisement opposite, preferably at home before the lesson.

B 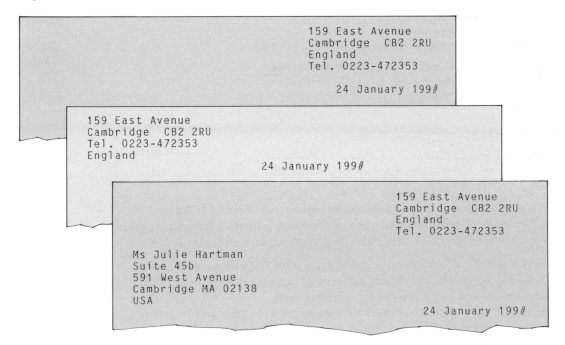 Highlight the following words and phrases in the passage – if any are unfamiliar, try to work out their meanings from the context.

*remorse   whodunit   suspect   deadwood   sap the strength
credibility   wimpy   coverup   vented his fury   upbeat
tenfold   regimen   heavy-duty*

C Work in pairs. Discuss these questions together:
- Where was the ad originally published and who is it meant to be read by?
- Which of the advice given do you agree with AND disagree with?
- Which of the advice holds good for each of these kinds of writing:
  personal letters   essays   reports   narratives   exam answers

---

7.7 **Keeping in touch**   Creative writing

A Work in groups. Find out from your partners:
- whether they normally phone or write if they want to keep in touch with a friend or relative in another country
- how they feel if they receive a letter from a friend which is handwritten or typed or computer-printed – or a photocopy of a letter he or she has sent to several other people
- whether they prefer to keep in touch with friends abroad by sending several postcards or one single long letter during the year

B Work in groups. Decide which of these letterheads would be suitable for a personal letter, a business letter – or neither:

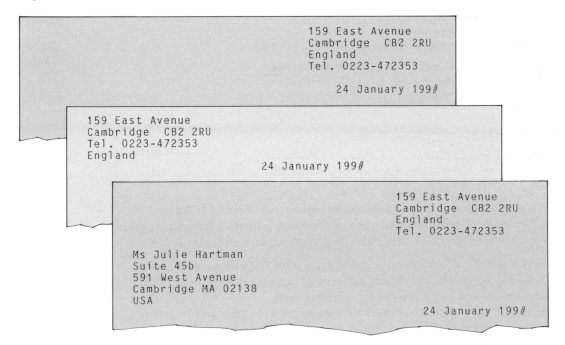

```
                                 159 East Avenue
                                 Cambridge  CB2 2RU
                                 England
                                 Tel. 0223-472353

                                    24 January 199#
```

```
   159 East Avenue
   Cambridge  CB2 2RU
   Tel. 0223-472353
   England

                            24 January 199#
```

```
                                 159 East Avenue
                                 Cambridge  CB2 2RU
                                 England
                                 Tel. 0223-472353


   Ms Julie Hartman
   Suite 45b
   591 West Avenue
   Cambridge MA 02138
   USA

                                    24 January 199#
```

C Work in groups. Decide which of these opening phrases would be suitable in:

  a personal letter   a business letter   both – or neither

In what situations might the phrases that *are* suitable be used?

```
Dear Ms Hartman,
Dear Julie Hartman,
Darling Julie,
Dear Madam,
Julie!
Dear Julie,
Dear Friend,

It's a very long time since I last wrote to you and I feel quite ...
I'm pleased to inform you that ...
I'm sorry not to have written earlier, but I've been very busy with ...
I hope your new job is going well ...
How are you? I'm fine.
Thank you for your enquiry about ...
The reason I'm writing this letter is to let you know that ...
I hope you enjoyed your visit to ...
```

D Work in groups. Decide which of these closing phrases would be suitable in:

  a personal letter   a business letter   both – or neither

In what situations might the phrases that *are* suitable be used?

```
Good luck with your new job.
I'm off to lunch now, so I'll post this on the way.
I have to stop now because lunch will be ready in a few minutes.
I hope you enjoy your holiday.
I look forward to meeting you next month.
Well, I must stop now so as to catch the post.

Give my regards to your husband and the family.
Again, thank you for doing business with us.
Remember me to Ted and the kids.
Assuring you of our best attention at all times.

Yours,
Best,
All the best,
Kind regards,
Your loving friend,
Yours faithfully,
Yours sincerely,
Best wishes,
Sincerely,
```

E Choose ONE of these topics, make notes, and write a suitable letter. Show your completed letter to a partner. Read your partner's letter as if you were the intended recipient of the letter, and then write a short reply.

- A thankyou letter to some people you stayed with for a few days.
- A thankyou letter to the managing director of a company, praising the excellent service and helpfulness of his or her staff.
- A 'keeping in touch' letter to someone you haven't written to for a year.
- A letter to a wealthy English-speaking relation, asking him or her to lend you some money for a round-the-world trip.

A   Fill the gaps with suitable expressions from the list below.

1 Writing an important letter is easier if you write a rough copy .... before you write the final version .... or type it.
2 If you're .... about what to write, it's best to make notes beforehand.
3 .... business letters, personal letters are relatively easy to write.
4 I think he'll be upset and you shouldn't embarrass him .... , so .... it may be better to tell him off ....
5 'Poor Julie was .... when she read the letter,' he told me ....
6 Orders cannot be accepted by phone but must be made .... and accompanied by a 20% deposit ....
7 .... the size of your order we are prepared to offer a special discount of 10% .... the usual trade discount.
8 We knew the firm was .... but no one realised that they were .... such serious ....
9 The book gave some information .... great .... but unfortunately the figures I needed were only given ....
10 She did me a favour and then asked what I'd do for her .... At first I thought she meant it .... but then I realised she was serious.

in addition to   in brief   in cash   in the circumstances
in comparison with   in detail   in difficulty   in doubt   in fun
in ink   in pencil   in private   in public   in return   in tears
in trouble   in view of   in a whisper   in writing

B   Fill the gaps with suitable phrases from the list below.

1 Love letters will never be .... because people will go on falling ....
2 The passengers knew they were .... great .... when the pilot announced he was no longer .... of the aircraft.
3 We used to keep .... by letter but I've lost her address and so now we are ....
4 Although she's still .... considerable .... , she's .... and back home.
5 Sorry, it's not a very good photo because it's .... I used to do a lot of photography but now I'm ....
6 Strawberries are .... at this time of year but the supermarket hasn't got them ....
7 He really is .... : he lost his job last year and he's been .... ever since. Now he's .... he can't afford to pay his mortgage – let's hope he doesn't end up .... !
8 The twins are learning the violin but as they always play .... , they aren't allowed to practise in the house and they have to play .... !

IN *or* OUT OF
    contact   control   danger   debt   doors   fashion   focus
    hospital   love   luck   pain   practice   prison   season
    stock   touch   tune   work

C   ![ht] Decide which are the most useful expressions in **A** and **B** that you don't already use. Highlight them to help you remember them. Then write your own example sentences using the idioms.

8 Those were the days!

8.1 The 20th century

A This is the blurb from the dust jacket of *Chronicle of the 20th Century* (1,360 pp.; 3.9 kg; £29.95). The paragraphs have been mixed up. Work in pairs and decide together on a suitable sequence for the paragraphs. Then answer the questions below.

The book of our Century has finally been written!

A Whether you turn to *Chronicle* for nostalgia, enlightenment, reference or simply for fun, this unique book will be a treasured and much-read possession in every home. For the youngest and oldest, it is the book of our lifetimes.

B Follow the lives of legendary figures such as Winston Churchill, recapture the whiff of scandals such as King Edward's abdication, thrill to great sporting victories, be chilled by disasters such as Aberfan, marvel at scientific discoveries and cheer artistic triumphs from Picasso's first exhibition to the Beatles' first record – it's all in *Chronicle*, as fresh and dramatic as today's news.

C There has never been a century like it – and never a book like *Chronicle*. This lavishly-illustrated book gives you a front-row seat for all the dramas of the century – from world wars to the fashions of the day – as they happened, with all the immediacy and excitement of tonight's television news.

D Now, at last, it is available in an edition specially prepared for Great Britain, almost entirely new and reflecting the distinctly British perspective on a century that began when Queen Victoria was monarch to much of the world. With thousands of illustrations, many in full colour, this book captures the changing social and cultural life of our turbulent times.

E *Chronicle of the 20th Century* is more than a book; it's an experience, taking you back in time to relive history as it happens. No wonder it's been a best-seller wherever it has been published with more than two million copies sold in Germany, France and the United States.

F *Chronicle of the 20th Century* puts you there when man first flies an aeroplane or invents the "talking pictures". Discover what happened at the great moments of history – the Russian Revolution, the rise of Hitler, the D-Day landings, the bombing of Hiroshima, the assassination of President Kennedy and the Moon landing.

1 What distinguishes *Chronicle* from other history books?
2 What other editions of *Chronicle* have been published?
3 How is the British edition different from other editions?

▶ Write a new version of the blurb to include the important events that have happened in YOUR country in the 20th century.

B Read the blurb from the cover of *Dreams for Sale* (256 pp.; 1.3 kg; £17.95) opposite and discuss these questions about it with a partner.

1 What is meant by 'popular culture'?
2 What kind of events and people do conventional history books describe?
3 Which parts of *Dreams for Sale* would you find most interesting?

4 Which of the forthcoming titles would you like to read and why?
5 Which would you buy: *Chronicle* or *Dreams for Sale*? Why?

Harrap's Illustrated History of the 20th Century

Dreams for Sale, the first in this new, six-volume history of the 20th century, offers both the general reader and student a fascinating insight into the development of popular culture since 1900. Drawing on a variety of images from the worlds of fashion, entertainment and sport, Dr Richard Maltby provides a highly-readable analysis of the way in which traditional cultural values have been replaced by a global industry which creates and markets cultural "products" for popular consumption.

■ Coverage of all major fields of popular culture: film, music, fashion, design, sport, media

■ Imaginatively illustrated with photographs and full-colour artwork

■ Special features highlight events and personalities of particular interest

■ Chronological tables and datafiles provide factual reference at a glance

■ Text includes biographies of some 300 key figures of modern popular culture

> **Forthcoming titles in this series**
> Power: A Political History of the 20th Century
> Wealth and Poverty: An Economic History of the 20th Century
> The Family: A Social History of the 20th Century
> The Arts: A History of Expression in the 20th Century
> Science: A History of Discovery in the 20th Century

C 📖 Work in pairs. One of you should look at Activity 18, the other at 43. You'll each see an extract from *Chronicle of the 20th Century* or *Dreams for Sale* describing Charles Lindbergh. Find out what your partner has discovered. Which of the extracts seems more informative and interesting – do they live up to the blurbs you read in **A** and **B**?

8.2 Talking about history   Vocabulary

A Fill the gaps in these sentences with suitable words from the list below.

1 It's possible for us today, with the benefit of .... , to see what mistakes were made by the great leaders of the past: we can see the .... of their decisions and judge the
....
2 Historians describe .... events and their .... effects. They .... and .... events and their .... effects.
3 It's difficult to be .... about events in which one is personally involved – you can't help having a .... view.
4 The .... of the First World War in 1914 was a .... event in world history: for four years the European .... were involved in a bloody .... in which millions died unnecessarily.

> analyse   conflict   consequences   hindsight
> historic/momentous   historical   impact   interpret   long-term
> objective   outbreak   powers   short-term   subjective

B Work in pairs. Discuss these questions with your partner:
● Which periods of history interest you most?
● Which historical period would you most like to have lived in? Why?   ⟫→

67

C Work in groups. Discuss these questions with your partners:
- What are the most significant historical events that have occurred during your lifetime?
- What historical events happened in the year you were born?
- Why is history a subject that is taught in every school in the world?

8.3 In the past

▶ Before starting this section, look again at the exercises in 2.3.

A Work in pairs. Discuss the differences in meaning between these sentences. Then decide how each one might continue.

1 When I was younger we would spend our holidays at the coast and ...
 When I was younger we spent our holidays at the coast and ...
 When I was younger we had to spend our holidays at the coast and ...

2 When I was a child I didn't use to stay in hotels so ...
 When I was a child I wasn't used to staying in hotels so ...
 When I was a child I wouldn't stay in hotels so ...

3 I was going to tell her what had happened but ...
 I was telling her what had happened but ...
 I told her what had happened but ...
 I had told her what had happened but ...
 I was about to tell her what had happened but ...

4 I could see that they had been doing some research because ...
 I could see that they had done some research because ...
 I could see that they were doing some research because ...
 I could see that they were going to do some research because ...

5 I used to be interested in reading history books ...
 I was interested in reading about history ...
 I was used to reading history books ...

B [icon] Work in pairs. Highlight the verbs used in these paragraphs and then match them to one of these meanings. (a) is done as an example.

1 Straightforward narrative
2 Emphasising which event happened before another
3 Talking about past habits and states, particularly if they no longer occur
4 Reminiscing about regular past activities
5 The results of past plans or intentions; future events that were expected or were likely to happen later

a) It was ¹ a very friendly class. After school we used to meet ³ for a drink and chat and once a month we would have ⁴ a meal together. We would usually go ⁴ to an Italian restaurant where they served ¹ fantastic pizzas. We stayed ¹ so late in the evening that sometimes we wouldn't get home ⁴ till midnight.

b) I didn't recognise Sally at first because she used to be much thinner. She had put on a lot of weight and her hair was going grey. When I had last seen her she was slimmer and her hair was black. She used to exercise regularly but for the past few years she hadn't had time to continue since she had moved to London. It took me some time to get used to seeing her looking so different.

c) The boss arrived late that day and was told that everyone had been reading newspapers and making paper aeroplanes all morning. Apparently, no one had done any work: they had taken the phone off the hook and hadn't opened any of the mail. She was about to lose her temper and was going to sack them all when someone pointed out that it was April 1 and that they had been pulling her leg.

d) Father had gone up the ladder without securing it and, sure enough, the ladder had slipped and he was stuck on the roof. Well, no sooner had the ladder fallen to the ground than it started to pour with rain, so there was no one in the street to hear his cries for help. By the time the rain stopped it had got dark and although he went on shouting all evening, no one heard him and he had to spend the whole night on the roof. The next morning, by the time I got there, he had been rescued (by the window cleaner). It was the first time I had seen him look embarrassed – it was one of the funniest sights I had ever seen.

C Correct the mistakes in these sentences – one contains NO mistakes.

1 I didn't knew that you came to stay with me next weekend.
2 In the 1970s people would be less well-off than they are now.
3 In the nineteenth century people weren't used to watching TV – they must make their own entertainment.
4 I just write a letter to her when she was phoning me.
5 I had been waiting so long in the cold that my feet were feeling numb.
6 He used to study history for three years.
7 It was the first time I went abroad and I was feeling very excited.
8 He arrived late because he had forgot what time the train will be leaving.

D Fill the gaps in the two contrasting descriptions of Victorian Britain on this and the next page, using the verbs below in their correct forms.

VICTORIAN BRITAIN

When Queen Victoria .... in 1901 she .... for 63 years. During her reign many great scientific discoveries .... and the population of Britain .... from 18 million to 40 million. The British Empire .... to become the largest empire the world .... ever ....and by then it .... a quarter of the world's people. During her reign Britain .... a time of peace and prosperity and .... not .... in any major war since the battle of Waterloo in 1815. No one .... that the First World War, in which so many young men ...., ... some 13 years later.

die	reign	make	rise	grow	know	include	enjoy
fight	suspect	kill	break out				

69

THE DARKER SIDE

During the reign of Queen Victoria (1837–1901) life for the middle classes and the aristocracy .... never .... better: the Industrial Revolution and the Empire .... them with undreamed-of luxury, convenience and wealth – but at the expense of the lower classes. Although slavery .... in the British Empire in 1834, the working classes in the slums of Britain's industrial cities .... almost as badly as slaves, and even young children .... to work long hours in factories and coal mines. During this period over 10 million people .... from these appalling conditions and .... to America and Australia. The magnificent Empire which .... vast profits to Britain's manufacturers .... the people of the colonies, who .... cheap raw materials for British factories, and .... nations of customers who .... to depend on a supply of British products.

> be   provide   abolish   treat   force   escape   emigrate
> bring   exploit   produce   create   come

E Replace the words in italics with a suitable form of the verbs listed below. Be careful because some of them may be tricky!

1 She *rested* on her bed after the scorpion *had bitten* her.
2 Have you *made* the tape *go back*?
3 The storm *made* her *wake up* in the middle of the night.
4 As he had never *been in a plane* before he *held on tightly* to my arm.
5 He *put* all the clothes on the bed while be *brushed* the floor.
6 The problems *happened* because the firm *selected* the wrong software.
7 He *cried* when he saw that his new shirt had *got smaller in the wash*.
8 We *knew in advance* that the essay would have to be *done again*.
9 Napoleon *sat on* a white horse as he *directed* his troops in battle.
10 She *cursed* when someone *stepped* on her bad foot.

> arise   awake   choose   cling   fly   foresee   lay   lead   lie
> rewind   rewrite   ride   shrink   sting   swear   sweep   tread
> weep

F Work in groups. Decide how to match the names in the first column with the places in the second and dates in the third. Then discuss the questions below with your partners.

Archduke Franz Ferdinand	Battle of Hastings	1963
Christopher Columbus	Dallas, Texas	1066
Ferdinand Magellan	Russia	1903
John F. Kennedy	Pacific Ocean	1917
Napoleon	Moon	1914
Neil Armstrong	Waterloo	1815
October Revolution	Atlantic Ocean	1969
Wilbur and Orville Wright	Sarajevo	1521
William the Conqueror	Dayton, Ohio	1492

● What happened exactly? What were the long-term effects of each event?
● How would the world be different if these events hadn't happened?
● What are the three most significant historical events missing above?

8.4 Fourteen ninety-nine Listening

A 🔊 You'll hear a radio broadcast in which two world-famous historical figures are interviewed. Fill in the missing information below.

Vasco da Gama left Lisbon on .... 1497 with .... men and provisions for three years. Out of sight of land for .... days between Cape Verde Islands and .... (.......... km). Finally arrived at Calicut in .... on .... May 14......... after 23 day voyage across .... Sea.
Left India in August 14......... with cargo of .... and jewels.
Arrived back in September 14......... with only .... survivors – the rest died of scurvy (a disease caused by lack of vitamin C).
His voyage opened up .... to Asia.

Christopher Columbus's first voyage was financed by King Ferdinand and .... of .... Left Spain on .... August 1492 with .... ships and .... men to travel west via the .... Islands. Out of sight of land for .... days (.......... km). Reached other side of Atlantic Ocean (presumably islands off the coast of .... or ....) on .... 1492.
Returned to Spain in .... 14......... with cargo of a small amount of .... , six '.............s' and some ....
His second voyage began in .... 14......... with .... men: set up first .... European .... on other side of Atlantic.
His third voyage began on .... May 14.........: didn't find .... to the Indies.

B Work in groups. Discuss these questions with your partners:
• How would you describe the personalities of the men in the recording?
• Whose achievement was more significant at the time?
• Which historical figures would YOU like to be able to interview?

8.5 Forming adjectives Word study

A Form adjectives from the nouns below and add them to the appropriate column. The first ones have been done as examples. The number of adjectives that should be added to each column is shown.

-ous	-ic	-ical	-al
advantageous	*historic*	*historical*	*continental*
adventurous	*apologetic*		
+ 5	+ 15	+ 7	+ 11

advantage ✓ history ✓ history ✓ continent ✓ adventure ✓ apology ✓
ambition   art   catastrophe   commerce   courage   danger   drama   ecology
emotion   energy   finance   function   grammar   intention   Islam   logic
magnet   metal   mountain   nation   optimism   pessimism   philosophy
politics   profession   region   sarcasm   science   sensation   society   symbol
sympathy   synonym   system   theatre   theory   tradition   tragedy

B Form adjectives from the verbs and nouns below and add them to the appropriate column. The first ones have been done as examples. The number of adjectives that should be added to each column is shown.

-able	-ive	-ly	-y
acceptable	appreciative	cowardly	bumpy
believable			
contradictory			

+ 9	+ 10	+ 6	+ 16

accept ✓ appreciate ✓ believe ✓ bump ✓ contradict ✓
communicate compete decorate describe destroy
enjoy explode forget inform itch jump obtain
possess prefer produce regret rely repeat satisfy
shine slip supplement sweat

coward ✓ day dust fortnight gloom guilt haste
knowledge luck memory month mood neighbour
quarter reason sand stripe taste year

C [icon] Decide which are the most useful adjectives in **A** and **B** that you don't already use. Highlight them to help you remember them.

D Work in pairs. Write a mini-exercise consisting of SIX sentences with gaps (................) using the adjectives from **A** and **B**. Pass your exercise to another pair and get them to fill the gaps.

8.6 Spoken and written English – 2 · Functions

A Work in pairs. Decide which of these phrases you would use:

a) In a face-to-face conversation with a friend or colleague – 'rapid conversational style'
b) In a formal letter or essay – 'formal written style'
c) And which could be used in either a) or b)

 1 I'd like to thank you both for talking to us.
 2 Thanks very much for talking to us.
 3 It was very kind of you to talk to us.
 4 Guess what! I bumped into whatshername the other day.
 5 Our unexpected meeting developed into a very productive conversation.
 6 We had a nice chat about this and that. It turned out to be really useful.
 7 That reminds me – please don't forget to get enough photocopies done.
 8 Please do not forget that sufficient photocopies should be made.
 9 It would be kind of difficult to follow, wouldn't it?
10 A considerable amount of difficulty is likely to be experienced.
11 It is important to remember that considerable effort is required.
12 You've got to remember that it takes a little effort.
13 I found it amazing that he should suggest such an idea.
14 Goodness, how amazing!
15 A special tool is required to remove the retaining catch.

16 Listen, I need a watchamacallit to undo this catch here.
17 A suitable reference book should be used to check the information.
18 I suggest you check the information in a reference book.
19 Why not look it up in a reference book or something?
20 Studying history can help us to understand the causes of current events.

h̄t⊘ Highlight the words or phrases that led you to your decisions.

▶ What's the effect of using a 'conversational' style in a letter, like this:

Dear Jim,
    How are you? Got over your cold, I hope.
Isn't this winter weather awful! Well, the
reason I'm writing this letter is to let you know....

B Before you listen to the recording, refer back to the notes you made in
7.2. The first part of the lecture covered the following points:

```
Rapid conversational style is face-to-face, unplanned,
spontaneous
Formal written style happens alone, is planned
Main features of speech:
1 Hesitation
2 Listener contact
3 Silent language: gestures, eye contact, body language
```

⊑▭ The lecturer still has four more points to make. Listen to the last part
of the lecture and make notes.

▶ Compare and discuss your notes with a partner.

C The adjective NICE is used a lot in spoken English, but less in formal
writing. Look at these examples and find synonyms from the list below.

1 Did you have a nice time?   5 She's a very nice woman.
2 He said some nice things about you.   6 It was nice and quiet there.
3 It was very nice of you to invite me. 7 Please be nice to them.
4 You look very nice.   8 How nice of you to give me that.

    complimentary   enjoyable   friendly   generous   likeable
    smart   thoughtful   pleasantly

▶ Another word commonly used in spoken English is GET. See 8.7.

D **⊑▭** Special language is used in different situations and to express
different functions. Decide which of the situations and functions in this list
match the extracts you hear. The first is done as an example.

Anecdote	Excuse	Lecture
Announcement	Explanation	Lie 1
Apology	Friendly advice	Rumour
Complaint	Interview	Small talk
Contradiction	Joke	Warning

A   GET has got a lot of meanings! Match the synonyms* below to these uses of GET:

1 I must get my hair cut.
2 She got someone else to do the work.
3 We all get old eventually.
4 It's upstairs, can you get it for me?
5 How much does she get a week?
6 It may be hard to get to see him.
7 She didn't get the joke.
8 Did you get my letter?
9 Will you get the meal ready?
10 When did you get there?
11 I'm trying to get a new car.
12 Did she get an A in the exam?
13 It's time to get going.
14 His attitude really gets me.

acquire/obtain   annoy   arrive   become   earn   fetch   have
manage   persuade   prepare   receive   start   understand

B   Rewrite these sentences, replacing the phrases in italics with the correct form of the expressions listed below which mean the same. The first is done as an example.

1 Leave a message and I'll *return your call*.
   Leave a message and I'll get back to you.
2 I tried phoning several times but I couldn't *make contact*.
3 It may be difficult to *communicate* these ideas to everyone.
4 I don't understand what you're *implying*.
5 Try not to let it *depress* you if someone *criticises* you.
6 The lecturer spoke so fast that we couldn't *write* everything she said.
7 I don't want to take part in the show, but how can I *avoid* it?
8 They were unable to *recover from* the setback.
9 I hoped we could *meet* but we never *managed to find the time*.
10 It may take you a while to *become involved in* the book.
11 I haven't got time for a holiday but I hope to *escape* for a long weekend.
12 The only way to *succeed* in politics is to have the right connections.
13 We'd better *start moving* – it's *nearly* lunchtime.
14 He's a difficult person to *have a friendly relationship with*.
15 Look, it's clear we're *having no success*, let's try a different plan.
16 She *got her revenge* by letting his car tyres down.

get ahead/on   get along/on with   get at   get at   get away
get back to someone   get going   get into   get down
get me down   get nowhere   get on for   get one's own back
get out of   get over   get over/across   get round to something
get through   get together

C   [icon] Decide which are the most useful idioms in **B** that you don't already use. Highlight them to help you remember them. Then write your own example sentences using the idioms.

*Remember that there's rarely a one-to-one equivalence between 'synonyms'.

9 The third age

9.1 'U3A'

A Work in groups. Ask your partners to imagine that they're due to retire next year. They're still fit and healthy but not very wealthy. Ask them to put these factors in order of importance:

comfort and warmth in winter
companionship
closeness to children/grandchildren
a nice garden or nearby park
peace and quiet
books and records

privacy
intellectual stimulation
financial independence
having a part to play in society
security
+ *Any other factors?*

B Read the article below, preferably before the lesson. Find the answers to these questions in the article.

1 What are the aims of the U3A movement in Britain?
2 Who organises the classes for U3A students in Britain?
3 How long ago were the first U3As in France started up?
4 What is the main difference between U3As in France and Britain?
5 Why did the French government encourage the setting up of U3As?
6 How many U3As are there in Britain?
7 How many students are there at a typical U3A in France?

Life begins at 50 for Third Age students

The period after earning a living and raising a family is an age of discovery for students at the Third Age universities, which are growing rapidly in Britain. They find it is never too late to learn, and that intellectual stimulation can lead to better health for the elderly.

At first glance it's the usual Cambridge scene: the fight for places to park the bicycle, the hasty greetings called across the courtyard, the
1 scramble for decent seats next to your friends, the silence before the lecture begins. The difference here is that the greetings are a little cheerier, the scramble a little more intense, the silence a little more avid, and, though you may not

notice it, there are more grey hairs. The students at the new Cambridge University are all aged 50 or over.

The Wednesday afternoon lecture is the main event of the week for members of the University of the Third Age, or 'U3A' as they call it. But every day there are classes going on all over town ranging from Chinese to computers. Founded only three years ago, the new university now has more than 700 members. It was the first of its kind in Britain, but the idea caught on quickly and Third Age universities have started up all over the country.

Although Shakespeare chronicled Seven Ages of Man, the new university makes do with four. The Third Age comes when the First Age of childhood and the Second Age of earning a living and bringing up a family are over. It may well last as long as 30 years, beginning in the fifties and going on into the sixties, seventies and eighties. The belief and the hope is that an active Third Age can postpone the Fourth Age of weakness and death, squeezing that into the shortest period possible.

Thirty years is a long time to feel bored, lonely and useless; it's not nearly long enough for the members of the University of the Third Age to do all the things they want to do. Barbara Taptiklis is a case in point. A widow and a grandmother, her life is still as busy and active as ever. 'We dash to classes and then we meet up for coffee. I'm learning French. I never had the time before. People say you can't learn a new language when you're old, but that's nonsense. It just depends on your drive and willingness to do it. The difference with U3A is that we feel we're using our brains. We're not superior, not at all. We're just extending our knowledge, starting again really – and it's fun.'

Students pay £10 for six months' membership of the university and for this they can go to as many, or as few, classes as they wish. There are also regular social and sporting events. One of the reasons why so much activity is possible and costs so little is that the teachers give their time free and seem to enjoy it just as much. Richard Bennett, a retired schoolteacher who takes one of the French classes, says the great joy is that everybody is motivated. There are none of those little boys in the back row trying to hide under their desks. 'Most of us who teach also learn. I'm doing cookery and music. We're doing areas of 20th-century music I'd never explored before and I'm finding out all sorts of things.'

The new university is a cooperative venture and everyone can contribute something, by teaching or learning, by delivering the newsletter or making the coffee. The university belongs to its students and they choose the classes. Many classes started because two or three people discovered a mutual interest, found someone to take the lead and it has grown from there. In this – and in many other ways – it is quite different to the other Cambridge University. Dr Peter Laslett, who is a Fellow of Trinity College and thus knows both from the inside, was a founder member of U3A. 'We have a claim, I think, to be what some people call the *true* university because we insist that nobody needs qualifications to join. Nobody is paid, there are no awards, no exams, we are not agents for any outside body which wants to know whether Smith is better than Brown. All our people study because they *want* to – for aesthetic, literary or other reasons – and this is what a university is *for*.'

The University of the Third Age is fiercely independent and has no ties with any other educational institutions. Peter Laslett is adamant that it should remain so. Too much, he feels, is done *for* the elderly, not enough *by* them. Organising their own university answers part of their need for intellectual stimulation. But in France, where the movement began, they take the opposite view. There the new universities are run in, and by, the established institutions.

U3A takes its name from the Université du Troisième Age launched in Toulouse in 1972. Professor Francisque Costa was one of the founders. He says they were moved partly by their awareness of the growing number of elderly people who were bored and lonely and partly by the fact that a law was passed requiring educational institutions to do something about it. This was no mere act of charity. The French government was convinced by the research which said that as soon as people have no stimulation, stop working, and stop being interested in life around them, they decline physically. If you stimulate the brain you are physically fitter. The economic consequences were clear: it was in the government's interest to promote the educational and cultural stimulation of elderly people because that would cost less than the health care that would otherwise be needed. Universities of the Third Age sprang up all over France and most other European countries soon followed suit. Professor Costa is delighted with the results. 'It has been proved that elderly people can progress – they can do research, they can learn languages. Even if you decline in some ways, in others you can grow – you can be more creative in old age than in your younger days.'

In Britain we seemed not to have noticed how old we were getting; that one fifth of our population – some ten million people – were in their sixties or older and that many of them were bored and lonely, desperate for something more intellectually stimulating than a game of bingo and a singsong. It took someone of Peter Laslett's vision and determination to get the U3A idea going in this country. Now it is spreading like wildfire. There are thriving U3As in cities like Huddersfield and Nottingham and in smaller towns like Saffron Walden and Abergavenny (at the last count, there were 112 altogether). Some of the newer ones have only 20 members, the more established as many as 800. They are all fiercely independent. They raise funds by subscription and donation because they don't want government funds with strings attached. Each university develops its own character and programme in response to the needs and resources of the area, and ideas are shared through a nationwide network with its own newsletter.

Peter Laslett believes many of the new universities will grow to a size of 1,200 to 1,500, which is the pattern in France. They will take on their own research projects and lobby for the needs of their own age group. Above all, they will correct the public image of Britain's Third Age population. It will become accepted that, once the Second Age is over, a new time of creativity and fulfilment can begin.

Marion Dawson, who attended that Wednesday afternoon lecture in Cambridge, would have found that hard to believe two years ago. When her husband died in Hong Kong, where they had lived for some time, she felt she had lost everything. She came back to Cambridge and had to build a new life. But she wanted to keep in touch with her Chinese friends, to be able to read their letters without an interpreter. So she joined a Chinese class at the University of the Third Age. Now, to her great delight, she can already express her own thoughts quite fluently in Chinese. She has ventured into other U3A activities and made new friends. 'It has given a purpose to my life again – something totally different – and I'm enjoying every minute of it.'

At Christmas, when so many older people can only look back in loneliness, Marion Dawson and her friends can look forward together – to the new discoveries and new delights that the New Year will undoubtedly bring.

Sonia Beesley

C [ht] Highlight the following words and phrases in the passage (the ¶ shows which paragraph they are in). If any are unfamiliar, try to work out their meanings from the context. Match them to the definitions below.

chronicled (¶ 3) *promote* (¶ 8) *thriving* (¶ 9)
mutual interest (¶ 6) *followed suit* (¶ 8) *with strings attached* (¶ 9)
founder member (¶ 6) *singsong* (¶ 9) *resources of the area* (¶ 9)
adamant (¶ 7) *like wildfire* (¶ 9) *fulfilment* (¶ 10)

available talents and facilities   determined   did the same
encourage   feeling of deep satisfaction
interest shared in common   one of the group who started it
party where everyone joins in singing   recorded   successful
very rapidly   with conditions that must be fulfilled

D Work in pairs. This exercise will help you to appreciate the content and style of the text.

1 Look at the first paragraph again, perhaps read it aloud. Notice the style of the writing.
   a) How does the writer evoke the atmosphere of excitement?
   b) How does she make *you* feel that you're actually there?
   c) How does she emphasise the differences between the old and the new Cambridge University?

2 [ht] Highlight the words *bored* and *lonely* each time they are used in the article. What is the effect of this repetition?

3 [ht] Highlight an example in the text of each of the following:
   a) information (something you didn't know or realise before)
   b) opinion (a point of view that made you pause and think)
   c) entertainment (something that made you smile)
   d) social comment (a criticism of the way people behave)
   e) empathy (something that made you share the writer's feelings)

⟫→

4 What was your reaction to the article? Were you surprised, interested, inspired, depressed or amused by what you read?

E Work in groups. Find out from your partners:
– what the 'public image' of old people in Britain is, according to the article
– what image older people have in their country
– what educational facilities are provided for older people in their country
– whether they prefer the French or British system of organising U3As
– what role older people play in society in their country

9.2 Living to a ripe old age Vocabulary

A Fill the gaps in these sentences with suitable words or phrases from the list below.

1 A retired person, living on a .... , can also be referred to as an old-age .... , a .... or (in the USA) as a ....
2 Growing older brings .... and .... but one tends to become less .... , ... and ....
3 Older people tend to be more dependent on .... and .... facilities than the young.
4 In the UK .... is 77 for women and 71 for men (see below).
5 Sexism and racism are discrimination against people because of their sex or race, ... is discrimination against older people.
6 Many older people enjoy looking back .... at the '...............' when they were younger. '...............!' they often say.

> adaptable ageism agile confidence energetic
> good old days
> health life expectancy nostalgically pension pensioner
> retiree senior citizen Those were the days welfare wisdom

B Work in groups. Look at this chart and discuss the implications of the information.

Life expectancy for WOMEN and MEN			
Argentina	71 — 65	Australia	67 — 74
Canada	76 — 69	China	64 — 60
Ethiopia	40 — 37	France	78 — 70
India	50 — 50	Indonesia	48 — 46
Japan	77 — 72	Mali	42 — 39
Sweden	81 — 75	UK*	77 — 71
USSR	74 — 64	USA	76 — 68

*In 1900 the figures were: 50 — 46; in 1930: 63 — 59; in 1960: 74 — 68

C Work in groups. Think of some retired people YOU know personally. Ask your partners these questions:
● What sort of lives do the retired people you know lead?
● Would you like to be in their shoes? Why / Why not?

78

9.3   Granny power

A   You'll hear part of a radio programme about the state of the world in 2025 – how old will *you* be then?

Before you listen to the recording, look at the summary and see if you can already fill any of the gaps.

📼 Listen to the recording and fill the gaps.

In 2025:

1 In West Germany .... % of the population will be over 50 (compared to .... % now).
2 In West Germany and Japan .... % will be over 75.
3 Most Western countries will have .... % over 65.
4 .... , ... and .... will be 'elderly countries'.
5 .... , ... and .... will be 'young countries'.
6 Younger workers are more .... , ... and ....
7 Older workers acquire .... and ....

In China:

8 In 2025 .... % of the population will be over 60.
9 The retirement age is .... for men and .... for women, but most retired workers remain on the ....
10 Shanghai's textile mills employ .... people, of whom .... are retired people: they are paid .... % of active workers' wages.
11 Before 1949 life expectancy was .... Old people were looked after in traditional .... Now, with the 'one-child' policy, couples face sole responsibility for ....
12 The government encourages .... and .... to remarry, but some Chinese still believe that a widow who remarries is ....

The main problems facing the West are:

13 A relatively small working population will have to support a large number of .... retired people.
14 Younger countries will be more .... in the world market.
15 Huge sums will have to be spent on .... facilities for old people.

B   Work in pairs and compare your answers. Which information surprised or interested you most?

▶ Write ONE sentence summarising the broadcast.

C   🎲 The class is divided into an EVEN number of pairs. Half the pairs should look at Activity 23, the others at 60.

Each pair has some more facts and figures to discuss, and then to share with another pair, working as a group of four.

D   Work in groups. Each of the problems on the next page presents you with a different situation. Decide together how you would solve them.

Make sure every member of the group has a chance to give his or her own point of view BEFORE you work out a joint solution.

When you are ready, explain your solutions to the rest of the class.

⟫→

1 You have an elderly parent who can no longer look after him- or herself. Should you persuade him or her to come and live with you, or should you find accommodation in a sheltered flat or a room in a rest home? Or should you persuade your brother or sister to look after him or her?

2 You are due to retire next year. Will you move to a more pleasant part of your country – or maybe to another country? What will you do with all your free time?

3 You are 70 years old and your estate is worth about £100,000. You have decided to make a will. You have three children (ages 39–45), seven grandchildren (ages 11–24) and one great-grandchild. How should the money be divided?

4 An elderly relative lives in an inexpensive flat in an inner city area where there is a lot of crime. He or she can't afford to move to a safer, more expensive place. What should you do?

5 An old person, who you once helped with shopping and errands, leaves you £10,000 in his or her will, which must be spent for the benefit of local old people. What will you do with the money?

9.4 Building paragraphs   Effective writing

★ Paragraphs break a text into easy-to-manage sections, making it easier for the reader to understand. Normally, related ideas and examples are grouped together in the same paragraph.

Each new idea requires a fresh paragraph.

A Work in pairs. Here is the first part of a newspaper article. Decide with your partner WHY the writer has chosen to start each fresh paragraph in the places she has.

Greys set to shake up German political scene

Anna Tomforde in Wuppertal

WEST Germany, which has Europe's youngest pensioners and oldest students, now has a rebellious Grey Party claiming that "old is beautiful" and calling for a greater say for the over 60s.

The leader of the new party, Mrs Trude Unruh, aged 64, says she has decided that remaining quiet is "no good." Clubs for old people should be turned into "centres for political education and agitation."

Mrs Unruh (her name in English means "restless")

spent just more than two years sitting as a Green in the Bundestag. But she says the Greens used her to attract pensioners' votes without rewarding the Greys with promised constituencies.

Equipped with a cloth cap and megaphone, she is ready to take on the established political parties in next year's general election. She will campaign for a guaranteed minimum state pension of up to DM1,500 a month (£500), and pledges to put an end to "old people being totally at the mercy of the system and the welfare mafia."

As far as possible, the Greys want to do without homes for the old, care institutions or psychiatric establishments. Old people should have a free choice of residence, where their freedom would be maintained and the necessary level of care provided.

"We want to lead autonomous lives, and move away from the concept that old people must be manageable," she said at the party's spacious headquarters in Wuppertal, which is also a "cultural centre" for pensioners.

B Work in pairs. Here is the last part of the same article, printed here with no paragraphs. Decide with your partner where you would break it into paragraphs. (The original text consisted of eight paragraphs.)

"We need cooperation and not polarisation," Professor Lehr said. Both the economy and society had to face the enormous challenge of adjusting to the demographic changes caused by a drastic fall in birth-rates, she said. But she added that a minimum pension would not solve the problems linked to aging. "The Greys have opted for the wrong path." At present, some 90 per cent of the two million West Germans who need care are looked after by their families, and 600,000 people live in homes. But staffing problems in hospitals and in the care sector have reached alarming proportions, and reports of "scandalous conditions" in old people's homes make headlines almost every week. The anger of those involved in caring for the old has recently been fuelled by a decision of a Mannheim court which, in response to a complaint from residents in a small town in Baden-Wuerttemberg, ruled that old people's homes should not be situated in "high-quality residential areas." The plaintiffs argued that they were "disturbed at night by the sound of ambulances and occasional screams from home inmates." It was high time, Mrs Unruh said, that those in power in Bonn realised that West Germany was fast becoming a society hostile not only to children, but also to the aged. She said her proposals for greater integration of the old and reduced dependence on the state welfare system had exposed the serious gap between private care provided by the family and the official welfare system in hospitals, homes and other institutions.

9.5   A discursive essay   Creative writing

What will you live on when you retire?
Plan now to enjoy your retirement . . .

Properly planned, retirement should give you some of the best years of your life – with money to spend and the leisure to enjoy it. The Personal Pension Plan, from National Mutual Life, will give you just that.

With your own Personal Pension Plan you can retire with a pension for life, a substantial capital sum, and the opportunity to turn your dreams into reality!

It's your future. The sooner you start, the greater your pension. The later you leave it, the more you will have to pay for a similar benefit.

A   Work in groups and discuss these questions:
- What are your reactions to the advertisement above?
- How is life for retired people in your country different from the kind of life they lead in other countries?
- What can we learn from other cultures about attitudes to older people?
- How would you set about improving conditions for older people in your country and perhaps changing people's attitudes?

B Write an essay on one of these topics. Make notes first.

1 Put yourself in the shoes of a retired person you know (this could be a person you really know, one of your relatives or an imaginary old person). Describe how your life changed after you stopped working and the problems and pleasures of being retired.
OR

2 Explain how the position of older people in your country can be improved. What should the State and local communities do? What should younger people, relations and children do?

C Work in pairs. Show your completed work to a partner and ask for comments on your use of paragraphs, as well as on the ideas.

9.6 *Ages*

Idioms

A Work in pairs or do this as homework. Fill the gaps in these sentences, using the phrases below.

1 Columbus sailed from the .... to the ....
2 If you are .... you're not allowed to buy drinks in a pub.
3 In an attempt to bring .... into the department, they're only recruiting people under the age of 25.
4 She used to be in love with Terry – he's an .... of hers but she hasn't seen him ....
5 If you're a .... to the firm and you don't know the ropes, you can ask one of the .... for advice.
6 We are both .... of the same school and whenever we meet we reminisce about ....
7 The Great Lakes in America are .... not saltwater lakes.
8 She didn't enjoy her work, so she decided to make a .... by applying for a new job.
9 I prefer paintings by the .... to modern paintings.
10 People in Britain .... at 18, when they are officially 'adults'.
11 You can't catch a cold from getting wet – it's an .... However, plenty of .... can keep you healthy.
12 Grandfather's ideas are terribly out of date – he still seems to think he's living in the .... not the .... My grandmother, I'm happy to say, is still .... and she always says 'You're only ....'

> come of age   for ages   space age   Stone Age   under age
> fresh air   fresh start   freshwater   new blood   New World
> newcomer   old boy/old girl   old flame   old hand   old master
> old times   old wives' tale   Old World   as old as you feel
> young at heart

B [icon] Decide which are the most useful idioms in **A** that you don't already use. Highlight them to help you remember them. Then write your own example sentences using the idioms.

10 It takes all sorts . . .

10.1 What do they look like?

Functions and vocabulary

A 📼 You'll hear six of these people being described. Match the descriptions you hear to the photos below.

B On the next page you'll see some ideas for describing a person's appearance and some expressions you might use if someone asked you these questions:
- What's special or remarkable about him or her?
- How would someone else recognise him or her?

First impressions and personality:
He or she looks a bit like / reminds me of ... (*name of well-known person*)
He or she strikes me as / comes across as ...
   ambitious   glamorous   easy to get along with   insensitive   self-conscious

▶ See 10.3 for more vocabulary.

Age:
He or she is ...
   thirty-something   in her mid-twenties   middle-aged   in his teens
   over sixty   in her early/late thirties   fortyish

Face, hair, eyes and complexion:
He or she has ...
   an open face   curly/wavy/straight hair   a pale/dark complexion
   bushy eyebrows   a good tan   wrinkles   a double chin   laughter lines

Height and build or figure:
He or she is quite/very/fairly/rather ...
   athletic/well-built   slim/skinny   plump/chubby

Clothes:
He or she usually wears ...
   casual/smart/conventional clothes   a formal suit   a sweater/jumper/pullover
   cardigan   sports jacket
He or she takes ...
   a pride in his appearance   a lot of trouble with her appearance

Family background and past achievements:
He or she is ...
   an only child   the eldest child   single   a single parent
He or she ...
   has a pilot's licence   once spent a year in the States   has two kids

Job and interests:
He or she ...
   is a lawyer/solicitor/attorney   works in the city   used to be an engineer
He or she ...
   enjoys sailing   spends a lot of time reading   is quite sporty

C   Work in pairs. Now take it in turns to describe the people in the picture
on the previous page that the speakers *didn't* describe.
   Ask your partner to comment on the accuracy of your descriptions.

★ If you're talking about a person's less admirable or less attractive
features, you can reduce the negative or critical effect like this:

> She's a bit too ambitious.   He's sort of / kind of moody.
> He's a little bad-tempered.   She's slightly insensitive.

D Work in groups. Take a good look at each other and then take it in turns to describe one of the members of the group – but do this WITH YOUR EYES CLOSED, so that you have to do it from memory.

Even if you can quickly guess who is being described, get each speaker to continue by asking questions to test their memories and powers of description.

If there's time when everyone in the group has been described, describe some of the members of the other groups too.

E 🎭 Work in pairs. One of you should look at Activity 38, the other at 61. Describe the people in the photo you'll see to your partner.

10.2 Modal verbs   Grammar

A Work in pairs. Discuss the difference in meaning between these sentences and decide how each one might continue.

1 They might tell me but ...
   They may have told me but ...
   They might have told me but ...
   They may tell me but ...

2 We could have tea early because ...
   We were able to have tea early because ...

3 You mustn't tell her that ...
   You don't have to tell her that ...
   You needn't tell her that ...
   You oughtn't to tell her that ...

4 I should have trusted him but ...
   I had to trust him but ...
   I shouldn't have trusted him but ...
   I didn't have to trust him but ...
   I needn't have trusted him but ...

5 She can't have lunch because ...
   She can't be having lunch because ...
   She couldn't have lunch because ...
   She can't have had lunch because ...

6 He may not have seen her, so ...
   He can't have seen her, so ...
   He may not be seeing her, so ...
   He can't be seeing her, so ...
   He may not see her, so ...
   He can't see her so ...

B Match the modal auxiliaries underlined below to these meanings:

Certainty → Probability → Possibility → Impossibility
Ability + Capability
Permission
Prohibition
Offers + Requests + Suggestions
Advisability + Duty + Obligation + Necessity

1 I didn't know you <u>couldn't</u> swim.
2 The party <u>could</u> last all night.
3 You <u>can't have</u> lost it, surely?
4 He <u>must</u> be in a bad mood as usual.
5 I told him he <u>must</u> be more careful.
6 It <u>shouldn't</u> be too difficult.
7 What <u>can</u> we do when we've finished?
8 <u>Could</u> you give me a hand?
9 I <u>couldn't</u> help laughing.
10 She <u>might</u> well think it's funny.
11 I don't think you <u>should</u> see her again.
12 You <u>can't</u> smoke in this room.

⫸→

C Work in pairs. Each of these groups contains two or more pairs of sentences that share the same meaning.

Match the pairs of sentences that mean the same as each other. The first is done as an example.

1 You must be joking. ———————— You've got to tell a joke
You have to tell a joke. ———————— You can't be serious.

2 Can you speak English?   I'd like you to speak English.
Do you know how to speak English?   Can you speak English, please?

3 You probably won't take too long.   I advise you not to take too long.
You shouldn't take too long.   It shouldn't take you too long.

4 You'd better tell her sooner or later.   You have to tell her sooner or later.
You ought to tell her sooner or later.   You've got to tell her sooner or later.
You needn't tell her yet.   You can't tell her yet.
You don't have to tell her yet.   You mustn't tell her yet.

5 It wasn't a good idea to tell her.   I didn't have to tell her.
I shouldn't have told her.   It wasn't necessary to tell her.

6 You might have told me.   You may have told me.
I'm not sure whether you told me.   You should have told me.

7 We'll probably have lunch soon.   We might as well have lunch soon.
Maybe we'll have lunch soon.   We might well have lunch soon.
We've got nothing better to do so let's have lunch soon.

D Work in pairs. Find the thirteen mistakes in this letter and correct them.

Dear Jane,

As you can already know, we must start looking for a new receptionist in our office last month. Mr Brown, our boss, can have chosen someone who already worked in another department but he didn't able to find anyone suitable so he got to advertise in the local paper. There ought have been a lot of applicants but surprisingly only a couple of replies came in and only one of those was suitable. I told Mr Brown that he had better to get in touch with her at once. He decided we needn't to phone her as there was no hurry, and we must as well send her a card. Unfortunately we heard no more from her, so we've had to start advertising again — in vain so far.

For the time being, the job's being done by Mr Brown's son who hasn't to be working really because he's unhelpful and sometimes he should be quite rude to visitors. I haven't to tell you that we're all pretty fed up with the situation. Well, as I don't have to say any more, I'll stop there.

E Work in groups. Look at the 'rules for office staff' from a 19th century office noticeboard on the next page. Discuss these questions and the questions on the next page with your partners:

- What were clerks allowed/forbidden to do in that office in 1852?
- Why were the various rules applied?
- What might have happened if any rules had been broken?

> ## Office Staff Practices
>
> 1. Godliness, cleanliness and punctuality are the necessities of a good business.
> 2. This firm has reduced the hours of work, and the clerical staff will now only have to be present between the hours of 7 a.m. and 6 p.m.
> 3. Daily prayers will be held each morning in the main office. The clerical staff will be present.
> 4. Clothing must be of a sober nature. The clerical staff will not disport themselves in raiment of bright colour.
> 5. Overshoes and top coats may not be worn in the office but neck scarves and headwear may be worn in inclement weather.
> 6. A stove is provided for the benefit of the clerical staff. Coal and wood must be kept in the locker. It is recommended that each member of the clerical staff bring 4 pounds of coal each day during cold weather.
> 7. No member of the clerical staff may leave the room without permission from Mr Rogers. The calls of nature are permitted and clerical staff may use the garden beyond the second gate. This area must be kept in good order.
> 8. No talking is allowed during business hours.
> 9. The craving for tobacco, wines, or spirits is a human weakness and as such is forbidden to all members of the clerical staff.
> 10. Now that the hours of business have been drastically reduced the partaking of food is allowed between 11.30 a.m. and noon, but work will not on any account cease.
> 11. Members of the clerical staff will provide their own pens.
>
> The owners will expect a great rise in the output of work to compensate for these near Utopian conditions.

- What is allowed/forbidden NOW in an office (or classroom)? Why?
- What might happen if any of these rules are broken?
- Supposing you could change the rules in the place you work or study in, what changes would you make to the things people could / could not do and would have to / would not have to do?

10.3 Personalities

Word study

A Work in pairs. When describing someone we usually talk about their personality and behaviour. Some characteristics are more attractive or endearing than others.

Which of these characteristics do you and your partner consider to be more attractive and less attractive? Which unattractive characteristics can you tolerate in your friends and relations?

ambitious	enthusiastic	outspoken	self-confident
artistic	frivolous	passionate	sensitive
cautious	gregarious	reserved	serious
earnest	introverted	resourceful	shy
easy-going	outgoing	ruthless	spontaneous

87

B   Work in pairs. The adjectives on the left are the OPPOSITES of the ones on the right. Match them up.

clever	prejudiced	conceited	open-minded
generous	relaxed	cruel	self-confident
kind	shy	mean/stingy	silly/foolish
modest	sensible	naive	stupid
narrow-minded	sophisticated	nervous	tolerant

C   Decide which of the adjectives on the left have a SIMILAR MEANING to the ones on the right.

clever	jolly	absent-minded	insincere
cunning	level-headed	bright	kind
excitable	reliable	cheerful	miserable
fair	self-confident	crafty	self-assured
forgetful	snobbish	direct	sensible
frank	surly	even-handed	stuck-up
glum	two-faced	grumpy	trustworthy
good-natured		highly-strung	

D   Work in pairs. Use a suitable prefix or suffix to form the OPPOSITE of each of the adjectives below. Here are some examples:

un-	unhappy	unpleasant	**in-**	insincere	incredible
dis-	dishonest	dissatisfied	**im-**	impolite	impossible
-less	careless	harmless	**il-**	illegible	illegal

agreeable	discreet	kind	predictable
approachable	efficient	likeable	reasonable
articulate	enthusiastic	logical	reliable
biased	flexible	loyal	respectful
competent	friendly	mature	sensitive
considerate	helpful	obedient	sociable
contented	hospitable	organised	tactful
decisive	imaginative	patient	thoughtful
dependable	intelligent	practical	tolerant

E   Work in groups. Discuss these questions with your partners:

- Which are your 'Top Ten' personality traits? Which qualities do you find most admirable or endearing? Explain why.
- What qualities do you think are:
  needed in a good friend?   hoped for in a parent?
  required in a dangerous situation?
- Which traits do you find most objectionable or annoying? Why?
- Are there any characteristics you would like to add to the lists above?
- Which FIVE adjectives can you use to describe (only) the admirable or likeable side of each person in one of the other groups.

F   Work in pairs. Make a list of some members of your family (OR some people you work or have worked or studied with). Describe each of them to your partner and explain what you like or admire about them.

10.4 Your lucky stars

Work in groups.

1 Referring to the information below and on the next page, discuss to what extent the ideas are true about you and the others in your group.
2 Apply this to other people you know well (friends, relations, etc.).
3 Try to guess what sign your teacher(s) and the other members of the class might be. Later, find out what sign they really are.

 Highlight any useful new vocabulary that you find in the text.

Capricorn
22 December – 20 January

Their basic impulses are to organise, systematise, formulate and structure. They are patient and persevering and they can put up with hardship and frustrations. They like to plan carefully and coolly so that their ambitions can be achieved and they don't expect success to come quickly. They're cool and calculating and they can be too severe and demanding. They tend to worry unnecessarily and be pessimistic. They're suspicious of new ideas and inventions. They're faithful, serious and resourceful. They like the security of a fixed routine, can be somewhat shy and enjoy solitude.

Aquarius
21 January – 19 February

Their basic impulses are to reform, to create and to understand. They are thinkers and full of unusual, even eccentric ideas to change the world. They put intense energy into their cause but they can be dogmatic and even fanatical. They can be rudely tactless and touchy but they're broad-minded and inventive. They're friendly but people never know what's going to happen next when they're around and they sometimes find it difficult to get close to people. They tend to be impractical and are tremendously likeable, but they resent criticism.

Pisces
20 February – 20 March

Their basic impulses are to submerge themselves for the sake of others. They are compassionate and sympathetic. They cry easily and can't bear to see suffering. They are sensitive and emotional. They're sometimes indecisive and they can be temperamental and careless. They tend to get confused easily. They're artistic and rather impractical. They're escapists and lack ambition and are not competitive. They are good in jobs that require imagination and they don't like hurting other people. They can be absent-minded. They are lovable and adoring.

Aries
21 March – 20 April

Their basic impulses are to assert themselves and to initiate events. They are impulsive and impatient. They're pioneers and they want quick results. They think quickly and they're quick-witted but they're not rational or philosophical. They like to plan ahead but they tend to overlook details and don't foresee problems. They're perfect leaders but they can be bullies and tend to be thoughtless and inconsiderate. They're not very thorough. They're fearless and always ready to accept a challenge. They are punctual, walk fast and don't like being told what to do. They don't brood over their failures.

Taurus
21 April – 21 May

Their basic impulses are to make things clear, to be comfortable and to construct. They're practical, reliable and steadfast. They love good food and comfort. They have strong feelings and tend to be self-centred. They need security and possessions. They're patient, methodical and stable but they can be stubborn and resent being contradicted. They only work hard if they're enjoying what they're doing and they hate change. They are musical and good at gardening. They are slow to anger but can be bitter enemies. They have great warmth and this makes them loved.

Gemini

22 May – 21 June

Their basic impulses are to communicate, to make connections and satisfy their curiosity. They're adaptable, versatile and communicative. They're always on the go, talking and finding things out. They're good at languages and mentally agile. They're light-hearted and don't take things seriously. Their moods can swing suddenly and sometimes they can be inconsistent and people may think they're two-faced. They don't like hard monotonous work. They love variety and change. They are witty and can't stand waiting.

Cancer

22 June – 23 July

Their basic impulses are to provide security, to protect and to bring out the best in people. They need to feel safe and secure. They like to stay in one place and they're not keen travellers. Their moods change quickly and they sometimes appear to be aggressive, but under the surface they're sentimental. They have long memories, like to live in the past and hate to throw anything away. They're artistic, imaginative and sensitive. They tend to take things to heart and get upset easily. They're protective and like to look after people. They're untidy and good cooks.

Leo

24 June – 23 August

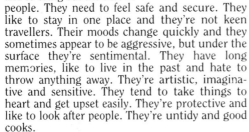

Their basic impulses are to shine as individuals and as leaders. They're stylish and they like to be the centre of attraction. They love power. They're generous and creative and good at encouraging other people to be happy and do their best. They're good organisers but sometimes they're too pompous and even conceited. No one could call them shy: they're gregarious and they like nothing better than enjoying themselves. Sometimes their ambition and their need to be a success may lead them into underhand dealings, but they can be loyal and faithful too. They are playful and like the sound of their own voices. They are poor judges of character.

Virgo

24 August – 23 September

Their basic impulses are to be of service, to analyse, criticise and to discriminate.

They're terribly fussy and like things to be perfect and places to be tidy. As perfectionists themselves, they don't suffer fools gladly, but they're modest and conscientious. They tend to suppress their emotions and worry about things. Sometimes they can be a bit hypocritical. They are practical people and good at remembering details. They're good learners and good teachers. They are calm and practical and find it hard to relax.

Libra

24 September – 23 October

Their basic impulses are to seek harmony, balance and justice. They like to be liked and they're sociable and very charming. Although they are ambitious, they try to get what they want with a smile rather than threats. They're good at persuading people and they're diplomatic. They are sometimes indecisive and over-sensitive, even remote and cold, but people like their unselfishness and considerateness and think they're charming. They find it easy to make friends. They love nice smells and they're very romantic. They're idealists. They find friends everywhere and are great entertainers.

Scorpio

24 October – 22 November

Their basic impulses are to bring about change, to investigate and transform. Their feelings are intense and they have a magnetic quality. They tend to be jealous and stubborn. They're not prepared to trust people and they can be cruel and vindictive. They have a strong sense of purpose and they can be subtle and secretive. They're strong, silent types. They can be courageous but they can be dangerous too. They have good self-control. They enjoy solving problems and can be difficult to live with.

Sagittarius

23 November – 21 December

Their basic impulses are to extend horizons through speculation, travel and widespread interests. They're deep thinkers, open-minded and love sport and outdoor activities. They have a sense of adventure and like exploring. They tend to be outspoken and can be tactless and inconsiderate. Their restlessness means that they don't like to be committed or tied down. They can be extravagant and boastful but they are kind to other people and optimistic. They are unpredictable and impatient, but generous and always good-humoured.

10.5   *Give* and *take*

A   Fill the gaps in these sentences with *after, back, in, out* or *up*.

1 As it was so difficult he gave .... trying.
2 Please give me .... my book.
3 I've given .... eating meat.
4 She takes .... her mother.
5 Have you given .... your homework?
6 You should take the empty bottles ....
7 She was giving .... leaflets.
8 He's decided to take .... golf.

B   Rewrite the sentences, replacing the phrases in italics with a suitable phrasal verb or idiom from the list below.

1 There was so much information that we couldn't *absorb* it all, though we tried to *make notes on* as much as we could.
2 Looking after the family *occupies* all their time.
3 This job carries a lot of responsibility – are you willing to *undertake* it?
4 *Considering* her inexperience it's amazing they *gave her the job*.
5 We *assumed* that you'd want to *participate in* the game.
6 She did a brilliant *impression* of the boss's voice over the phone but we weren't *deceived* when she said we could all *have a day's holiday*.
7 Everyone enjoyed the show, *except perhaps* a few people.
8 To reach a decision there has to be some *willingness to compromise* and there'll be deadlock if no one is prepared to *yield*.
9 She gets very upset when people *don't appreciate her*.
10 It's not my fault, so you shouldn't *get angry with* me.
11 As I'd never tried skiing before, I didn't think I'd *develop a liking for* it.
12 Don't *dismantle* something unless you know how to reassemble it.
13 He puts our backs up by not *giving consideration to* our feelings.
14 *Revealing* the secret *led to* some rather unexpected consequences.
15 I'm sorry I was rude to you – I *admit I was wrong in* everything I said.

> give away   give or take   give rise to   give way   give-and-take
> given   take account of   take apart/take to pieces   take back
> take down   take in   take in   take it for granted/take it as read
> take it out on   take on   take on   take part in
> take someone for granted   take the day off   take to   take up
> take-off

'Well, first of all, you're very naive.'

11 Fame and fortune

11.1 Who do you admire?

Listening and vocabulary

A 🔲 You'll hear four speakers talking about people they admire. Note down the names of the people and the MAIN reason they admire them.
Compare your notes with a partner.

B Fill the gaps in these sentences with suitable words from the list below. In most cases, SEVERAL of the words can be used.

1 Marie Curie, one of the world's .... scientists, was awarded two Nobel prizes. Her success can be attributed to three factors: ...., ... and .... Her most .... achievement was her work on radioactivity.

2 A(n) .... murderer may get more .... than a scientist, but his .... is likely to be relatively ....

3 Although there are .... many reasons for her success in politics, I certainly don't .... her and I am far from being one of her ....s. There's no denying that, like many leaders, she has great ....

4 The success of a sportsman like Pelé is a classic .... story, where a poor boy became a(n) .... for young soccer players all over the world.

> admire   admirer   charisma   clearly   effort   ephemeral
> evidently   fan   foremost   hard work   hero   idol   infamous
> inspiration   leading   look up to   lucky chance   most eminent
> notorious   outstanding   plainly   publicity   rags to riches
> reputation   respect   role model   serendipity   short-lived
> significant   undoubtedly

C Work in groups. Ask your partners:
– which living woman they most admire
– which living man they most admire
– which figure from the past (or historical figure) they most admire
Ask them to explain why the people are famous and why they admire them.

▶ Of all the people mentioned by your partners, which ONE do you admire most of all, and why?

11.2 Remarkable Charlie

A Before you read this magazine article, write down FIVE questions that you would like to find the answers to in the article.
(If possible, read the article before the lesson.)

Remarkable Charlie

ALEXANDER WALKER looks at his life and times

HE WAS BORN in the slums of south London. He wore his mother's old red tights cut down for ankle socks. He was sent to a workhouse when she was temporarily sent to the madhouse. Dickens might have created Charlie Chaplin's childhood. But only Charlie Chaplin could have created the great comic character of "The Tramp", whose ragged dignity, subversive mischievousness, hard-grained resilience and soft-hearted sentimentality gave his creator the dimensions of an immortal.

This month, that immortality will have the official seal that only a centenary celebration can put on it. Sir Charles Spencer Chaplin was born 100 years ago on April 16, 1889, and you will not be allowed to forget it. Already, Chaplinmania has broken out in Britain. Ironical, in a way, since Britain did not altogether venerate the Little Fellow on the screen when Chaplin was alive. Thames TV has mounted a mini-series, *Young Charlie Chaplin*. Last month, the new Museum of the Moving Image on London's South Bank opened a nine-part exhibition.

This month, *City Lights* will be shown in London with Chaplin's original – but lost – musical score reconstructed from his notes by Carl Davis. And to come is Sir Richard Attenborough's projected film of Chaplin's life.

If it all sounds too much, too suddenly, that is only the way time has of remedying its curious neglect of Chaplin as far as Britain was concerned. Mo Rothman, the shrewd film distributor who handles the world-wide sales of Chaplin's films in association with the family's holding company, admits that other countries – France, Italy, Spain, even Japan and Korea – show more surpassing love (and profit) where Chaplin is concerned than the land of his birth. It's not just that Chaplin quit Britain for good in 1913 when he journeyed to America with the Fred Karno vaudeville troupe to perform his mime, juggling and comedy acts on the stage where Mack Sennett's talent scouts recruited him for the Hollywood slapstick king.

Sad to say, many English filmgoers between the wars thought Chaplin's Tramp a bit, well, "vulgar". Certainly the middle-class filmgoers did: the working-class audiences were warmer towards a character who defied authority, using his wicked little cane to trip it up, or aiming a well-placed kick on its broad backside with the flat of his down-at-heel boot. All the same, Chaplin's comic persona didn't seem all that English or even working class. English tramps didn't sport tiny moustaches, baggy pants or tail coats: European dictators, Italian waiters and American *maître d's* wore things like that. Then again, the Tramp's ever-roving eye for a pretty girl had a promiscuousness about it that was considered, well, not quite nice by English audiences – that's how foreigners behaved, wasn't it? And for over half of his screen career, Chaplin had no screen voice to confirm his British nationality.

Indeed, it was a headache for Chaplin when he could no longer resist the talkies and had to find "the right voice" for his Tramp. He postponed that day as long as possible: in *Modern Times* in 1936, the first film in which he was heard as a singing waiter, he made up a "nonsense language" which sounded like no known nationality. He later said he imagined the Tramp to be an Oxford-educated gent who'd come down in the world. But if he'd been able to speak with an Oxford accent in those early slapstick shorts, it's doubtful if he'd have achieved world fame – and the English would have been sure to find it "odd".

Yet all this ambiguity Chaplin found very sympathetic. The Nazis once denounced him as a Jew and banned his films. Although, as David Robinson proved in his official biography in 1985, the Chaplin family had no Jewish ancestry, Charlie never denied it. He later said that if he had, he would have seemed to be distancing himself from the huge historical suffering of that race. He was an immensely complex man, self-willed to a degree unusual even in the ranks of Hollywood egotists. The suddenness of his huge fame gave him the freedom – and, more importantly, the money – to be his own master. He already had the urge to explore and extend a talent he discovered in himself as he went along. "It cawn't be me. Is that possible? How extr'ordinary," is how he greeted the first sight of himself as the Tramp on the screen.

But that shock set his imagination racing. Unlike Buster Keaton, Chaplin didn't work out his gags conceptually in advance. He was the kind of comic who used his physical senses to invent his art as he went along. Inanimate objects especially helped Chaplin make "contact" with himself as an artist. He turned them into other kinds of objects. Thus, a bust alarm clock in *The Pawnbroker* became a "sick" patient undergoing an appendectomy; boots were stewed in *The Gold Rush* and their soles eaten like prime plaice (the nails being removed like fish bones); and his café waiter slinging chairs over his back at closing time turned himself into an immense human porcupine. This physical transformation, plus the adroitness with which he managed it again and again, are surely the secrets of Chaplin's great comedy. It may be a legacy from working alongside jugglers and acrobats on the English music-hall stage in his youth and developing something of their sensory proficiency. But Chaplin not only charged things with energy, he altered their personalities – and, in so doing, extended his knowledge of his own.

He also had a deep need to be loved – and a corresponding fear of being betrayed. The two were hard to reconcile and sometimes – as in his early marriages – the results were disastrous. Yet even this painfully-bought self-knowledge found its way into his comic creations. The Tramp never loses his faith in the flower girl who'll be waiting to walk into the sunset with him; while the other side of Chaplin, the man who's bought his cynicism dearly in the divorce courts, makes *Monsieur Verdoux*, the French wife killer, into a symbol of man's misogyny.

It's nice to know that life eventually gave Charlie Chaplin the stable happiness it had earlier denied him. In Oona O'Neill Chaplin, he found a partner whose stability and affection effaced the 37 years age difference between them that had seemed so ominous when the Santa Barbara registrar, who was marrying them in 1942, turned to the luminous girl of 17 who'd given notice of their wedding date and said, "And where is the young man?" – Chaplin, then 54, had prudently waited outside. As Oona herself was the child of a large family with its own turbulent centre, she was well-prepared for the battlefield that Chaplin's life became as unfounded charges of Communist sympathies engulfed them both – and, later on, she was the fulcrum of rest in the quarrels that Chaplin's act of stern fatherhood sometimes sparked off in their own large brood of talented children.

Chaplin died on Christmas Day, 1977. A

few months later, a couple of almost comic body-snatchers stole his coffin from the family vault and held it for ransom: the Swiss police recovered it with more efficiency than the Keystone Cops would have done. But one can't help feeling Chaplin would have regarded this macabre incident as his way of having the last laugh on a world to which he had bequeathed so many.

B Find the answers to your own questions in the article. Then decide which of these statements are true or false according to the article.

1 Chaplin's childhood was very poor but happy.
2 More people appreciate Chaplin abroad than in the country of his birth.
3 In the USA, Chaplin was a stage performer before he got into films.
4 To British audiences Chaplin's Tramp was unmistakably English in origin.
5 The Little Tramp never appeared in a talking picture.
6 Chaplin would probably not have become famous if his early films had been talkies.
7 Chaplin's comic scenes were carefully planned and scripted.
8 Chaplin seemed to bring objects and things to life in his films.
9 His last wife was half his age when they got married.
10 After their wedding Chaplin's professional and family life were tranquil.

C Highlight the following words and phrases in the article – if any are unfamiliar, try to work out their meanings from the context.

*subversive   resilience   self-willed   gags   inanimate   bust
adroitness   charged   corresponding   reconcile   effaced
ominous   prudently   turbulent   unfounded   charges   macabre*

Match these definitions to the words you highlighted in the article:

ability to recover from setbacks   allegations   broken   erased
filled   harmonise and resolve   horrifying   jokes   matching
not living   skill   stubborn   threatening
undermining authority   unsubstantiated   violent   wisely

D Work in groups. Discuss these questions with your partners:
- What were Chaplin's most admirable qualities – and what were his less admirable attributes?
- What were his greatest achievements?
- What brought him the greatest disappointment and the greatest happiness, according to the article?
- Why was he (and is he still) so famous and well-loved? How can you account for his success?
- What does the image of the Little Tramp signify for us today?

E Work in pairs. Select the information in the article that you would use in a 250-word article on 'The life and times of Charlie Chaplin', and decide which you would omit. Make notes.
   Compare your notes with another pair and justify your own decisions.

11.3 Walt Disney

A ▭ You'll hear part of a broadcast about the life of Walt Disney. Complete the unfinished sentences below.

1 Walt Disney first studied cartooning by doing a ....

2 The first character that Walt Disney and Ub Iwerks invented was ....

3 Mickey first appeared in *Steamboat Willie*, which was the first ....

4 Mickey's voice was provided by ....

5 Mickey Mouse was nearly called ....

6 Roy Disney was the .... of Disney Studios and Walt was the ....

7 Walt was not a good artist but he was an amazing ....

8 Many of the famous Disney characters were first drawn by ....

9 *Snow White and the Seven Dwarfs* (19............) was the first .... – it required .... drawings and .... years' work.

10 Then came *Pinocchio* (19............), *Fantasia* (19............) and *Dumbo* (19............).

11 Disney's image of kindly 'Uncle Walt' was tarnished when ....

12 In Disney's 'True Life Adventures' wildlife photography was accompanied by a jokey .... and tricky ....

13 Disney was one of the first film producers to see the .... of TV.

14 Disneyland in Los Angeles opened in 19............ at a cost of $................

15 When he died in 19............ he was working on the plans for .... (opened in 19............) and the EPCOT Center ('E............ P............ C............ O............ T............').

16 Disney's films are sometimes criticised for lack of .... and .... but they still appeal to ....

B Work in groups. Find out from your partners:
- why it's hard to imagine a world without Mickey Mouse
- which Disney films they have seen and which they enjoyed most
- what they enjoy and dislike about Disney films
- why they think cartoon films are so popular
- who their favourite cartoon characters are – ask them to explain why they like them
- why they would like / not like to visit Disneyland or Disney World

11.4   If they'd lived . . . Communication activity

A   Work in pairs. Find out from your partner:
- what he or she already knows about these two people
- who he or she considers to be the most attractive man and the most attractive woman of all time

B   [icon] One of you should look at Activity 25, the other at 47, where you will see some more information about James Dean and Marilyn Monroe.
   Share the information and ideas with each other, using some of these expressions:

> *As you probably know ...*   *One thing I didn't realise ...*
> *Did you know that ... ?*   *It's hard to believe that ...*
> *If he/she were still alive ...*   *It's tragic/amazing to think that ...*

C   Work in groups. Look at this chart of people who died before their time. Discuss with your partners:
- what each person achieved during their life
- if their characters matched the supposed characteristics of their star signs (see 10.4)
- how old they would be today if they hadn't died (except the first four)
- what they might have achieved if they had lived longer

	Born	Star sign	Died	Age
Wolfgang Amadeus Mozart	1756	Aquarius	1791	35
Vincent Van Gogh	1853	Aries	1890	37
Rosa Luxemburg	1871	Aries	1919	47
John F. Kennedy	1917	Gemini	1963	46
Marilyn Monroe	1926	Gemini	1962	36
Martin Luther King Jr	1929	Sagittarius	1968	39
Elvis Presley	1931	Capricorn	1977	42
James Dean	1931	Aquarius	1955	24
Buddy Holly	1936	Virgo	1959	22
John Lennon	1940	Libra	1980	40

11.5 Style, tone and content

A   Work in groups. Look at these opening paragraphs from magazine articles about James Dean. Decide what features of each paragraph you prefer and why.

Look at the STYLE of writing, the writer's attitude as shown in the TONE of the article and the CONTENT or information that is given.

Highlight the stylistic features you think are most effective.

James Dean was born on 8 February 1931 and died in a car crash on 30 September 1955 at the age of 24. For his generation he symbolised the torment and rebellion of the teenager. Even today his moody good looks, vulnerable eyes and that unmistakable glance from beneath his hair strike a chord with young people everywhere. His charismatic screen performances are all that we know of him. He died so young that he remains a mystery: the man, the actor and the characters he played are all the same to us.

James Dean was a young screen actor who was killed in a car crash at the age of 24. He made three films: *East of Eden*, *Rebel Without a Cause* and *Giant*, of which only the first had been released before his death. Young people of his generation admired his good looks and identified with his charismatic screen performances. The parts he played matched the image of the man: moody, rebellious and angry – yet vulnerable, arousing our protective instincts and perhaps making us want to defend him and comfort him.

Go into any poster shop in the world and there are two people whose images you will find there: one is Marilyn Monroe, the other is James Dean – a young man who had made only three films when he died at the age of 24 and who scarcely had time to make his mark on the world. So how can we explain the reasons for his continued appeal? Is it his moody good looks and his vulnerable eyes? Or is it that he symbolises for every generation the rebellious feelings and torment of being young, awakening a protective instinct in his fans? His screen performances were undoubtedly charismatic, but it is his image that lives on, not his acting.

B   Work in groups.

1 Make notes for a similar opening paragraph for a magazine article about Marilyn Monroe – decide what information from Activity 47 you will include.
2 Working alone, write a first draft, using the stylistic features that you thought were most effective in **A**.
3 Show your completed draft to your partners and ask for their comments and criticisms.
4 Then rewrite your paragraph, incorporating any improvements that have been suggested.

11.6 Household names Creative writing

A Work in groups. Make a list of twelve people who are 'household names' in YOUR COUNTRY – famous people from your country who everyone has heard of. Try to include both women and men in your list.

2 historical figures   2 national or local politicians
2 singers or entertainers   2 actors or film stars
2 industrialists or business people   2 sports personalities

B People who are famous in your country may not be so well known in other parts of the world. What would you need to tell a foreign visitor about the people you discussed in **A**, to explain why they're famous?

Work in pairs. Take it in turns to role play a conversation between yourself and a foreign visitor. For example, most British people know who this person is. If a foreigner wanted to know who it was, I might reply:

'That's Anita Roddick. She's the woman who founded the Body Shop – one of the best-known chains of shops in Britain. They sell shampoos, perfumes and many other beauty products, and they're all made from natural ingredients like plants and natural oils. She spends a lot of time travelling round the world on the lookout for new products. She was born in 1944 and she opened her first shop in 1976. It was a big success and now there are over 300 Body Shops in 33 countries – there's one in every High Street in Britain.'

C Work in pairs. Make notes on THREE of the people you discussed in **A** and **B** in preparation for writing about their lives and achievements. (You may need to gather more information before you begin writing.)

Imagine that you're writing for a reader who may have heard of the people, but who knows nothing about their lives or achievements. Look at the model paragraph below.

Show your completed work to a partner and ask for comments.

```
Anita Roddick, the woman who founded the Body Shop and built
it up into one of Britain's best-known chains, was born in
1944. Her shops sell shampoos, perfumes and many other beauty
products, all of which are made from natural ingredients such
as plants and natural oils. Anita Roddick spends much of the
year travelling round the world searching for new products to
sell. Her first shop, which opened in 1976, was a great
success and since then over 300 more Body Shops have opened
in 33 countries, with one in every High Street in Britain.
```

11.7 *For, on* and *off* Idioms

A Fill the gaps with the phrases below. The first is done as an example.

1 Trains leave every hour *on the hour*.
2 She claimed it wasn't her fault and that she hadn't done it ....
3 I should like to thank you .... the whole department.
4 He promised to help me .... I returned the favour another time.
5 Would you like to come .... with us on Sunday?
6 She was .... for several days with flu.
7 It was a long drive so we stopped .... to have a meal.
8 How much does a worker earn .... in your country?
9 In 1941 Walt Disney's artists went ....
10 Did you see the news .... last night?
11 I won't have a second helping because I'm ....
12 It takes much longer to get there .... than by bus.
13 If you need any advice, someone will be .... to help you.
14 No, I don't dislike Chaplin at all: ...., I admire him greatly.
15 We've done a lot of this recently, so let's do something else ....

> for a change   for a walk   off work   on a diet   on average
> on behalf of   on condition that   on foot   on hand
> on purpose   on strike   on television   on the contrary
> on the hour ✓   on the way

B Rewrite each sentence, replacing the words in italics with a suitable
form of the word on the right and adding FOR or ON. The first is done as an
example.

1 *Everyone knows her name because* she broke the world record.   famous
   She is famous for breaking the world record.
2 What are you *trying to find*?   search
3 What shoes *was she wearing*?   have
4 Would you like to *give me your opinion of* my work?   comment
5 We admire her *because of* her intelligence.   account
6 I think you can *trust* her.   rely / count
7 I *am sorry that I was* rude to you.   apologise
8 I don't want you to *sympathise with* me.   feel sorry
9 The price they charge *varies according to* the quantity you order.   depend
10 Some music sounds awful at first but *you develop a liking for it*.   grow
11 He stopped to look in a shop window and then *continued walking*.   walk
12 She *knows all about* cars.   an expert
13 To hear the next track you should *make* the tape *go forward*.   wind
14 It was a tall story but he is so gullible that he *believed* it.   fall
15 I told the visitor you'd be late but she *was determined to* wait.   insist

C [icon] Decide which are the most useful idioms in **A** and **B** that you
don't already use. Highlight them to help you remember them. Then write
your own example sentences using the idioms.

12 Rich and poor

12.1 Millionaires

A   Work in groups. Before you
listen to the recording, discuss these
questions with your partners:

- Who is the richest person in your
  country?
- Is it relatively easy to become a
  'millionaire' in your country's
  currency – how much is 'a
  million' worth in dollars or
  sterling?
- What do you know about the
  person in the picture? What
  would you like to know about
  him? Write down FIVE questions
  about him that you would like to
  know the answers to.

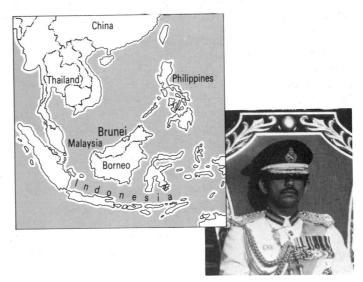

B   🔲   Listen to the recording and find the answers to your own
questions. Then fill the gaps in this summary.

1 Brunei is .... the size of Belgium, with a population of under ....
    Its wealth comes from its natural resources of .... and ....
2 The Sultan's annual income is $..................... and his total wealth is $.....................
3 The Sultan is a .... man who avoids .... He has ....
    wives, each of whom has her own .... His second wife used to be
    ....
4 The larger palace overlooks the .... It cost $..................... to build and it has
    .... rooms. There are .... toilets, ... chandeliers and
    .... lifts.
5 The smaller palace, built in the ...., has five ...., one of which is
    .... size.
6 He loves playing .... and he has 200 ...., which are kept in
    ....
7 He likes acquiring possessions, such as .... and ...., and the
    members of his family enjoy .... shopping.
8 The people of Brunei have free ...., free .... and pay no
    ....

C   ❏   Work in pairs. One of you should look at Activity 58, the other at
64. You'll each find out more about some of the world's richest people.

101

12.2 Around the world

A Fill the gaps in these sentences with suitable words from the list below.

1 Nowadays £1 billion usually means £.............. million. (In older British English texts £1 billion meant £1 million million.) In the USA, $1 .... has always meant $1,000 million.

2 Members of rich families .... money when their parents die. A lot of their income is .... , coming from .... and property the family owns. A .... , on the other hand, has worked hard for his or her success.

3 People in .... probably think that the .... of people in richer countries is strange and unnecessary.

4 When .... are high, people repaying a mortgage are less ....

5 In most .... countries, the .... is much higher than in Europe.

6 Japan is the world's wealthiest nation even though it lacks .... and there is a .... of agricultural land.

> 1,000   billion   conspicuous consumption   developing nations
> inflation rate   inherit   interest rates   investments
> raw materials   self-made man/woman   shortage   Third World
> unearned   well-off

B Work in groups. Look at this information about average incomes in various parts of the world and discuss these questions:
● What other countries have incomes above $10,000, do you think?
● What other countries have per capita incomes below $1,000?

Per capita income

Country	Income	Population million	Country	Income	Population million
Brazil	$1,900	150	Mozambique	$270	13
Brunei	$20,500	0.25	Spain	$4,800	40
China	$300	1,000	Switzerland	$15,000	6
Ecuador	$1,400	10	Taiwan	$6,000	20
Ethiopia	$120	45	Tanzania	$240	21
France	$10,500	55	UK	$9,200	55
Greece	$4,000	10	United Arab Emirates	$24,000	1.6
India	$260	750	USA	$14,000	240
Indonesia	$560	160	USSR	$4,500	280
Japan	$16,000	120	Vietnam	$160	60
Kampuchea	$70	7	W. Germany	$11,500	60

C Work in groups. Consider the situation of your own country (or countries). What are the ADVANTAGES and DISADVANTAGES of its/their:
> location   climate   natural resources   human resources
> culture and traditions   history   + other factors
● What problems does your country face?

D Work in groups. Each group should consider a different country, not represented in the class, and discuss these questions:
● What problems does the country face?
● How might these problems be solved?

12.3 Conditional sentences Grammar

A Work in pairs. Discuss the differences in meaning between these sentences:

1 When it rains our roof leaks.   If it rains our roof will leak.
  If it rains our roof leaks.   If it rained our roof would leak.
  When it rained our roof would leak.

2 I'd go first class if I could afford to.   I go first class when I can afford it.
  I'll go first class if I can afford to.   I'll go first class when I can afford it.
  I'd have gone first class if I could have afforded it.

3 She could get a rise if she asked her boss.   She should get a rise if she asks her boss.
  She might get a rise if she asked her boss.   She might get a rise if she asks her boss.
  She would get a rise if she asked her boss.   She will get a rise if she asks her boss.

4 I couldn't have gone there on holiday – unless I'd saved up all year.
  I couldn't have gone there on holiday if I hadn't saved up all year.

5 You should save your money in case you want to go on holiday.
  You should save your money if you want to go on holiday.
  You should save your money otherwise you'll want to go on holiday.

6 If you should / If you happen to see him, give him my love.
  If you see him, give him my love.

7 If you won't lend me the money, I'll have to ask someone else.
  If you don't lend me the money, I'll have to ask someone else.

8 If only I hadn't spent all my money and had saved some!
  If I hadn't spent all my money and had saved some . . .

B You'll hear a conversation in which different conjunctions are used instead of IF. Before you listen, use a pencil to fill as many of the gaps in this summary as you can.

🔲 Listen to the conversation and fill the gaps with the words used by the speakers.

Andrew: I'm wondering whether to buy a new hi-fi system to replace my old stereo. If I .... one, I .... one that plays compact discs. What do you think?

Bill: .... if I .... to, I .... a CD player. I think the quality of cassettes is perfectly adequate.

Claire: .... you're sure you .... to, I think you .... and buy a CD player.

Dave: Well, ... you really .... one, I .... there .... why you shouldn't buy one.

Emma: I think it .... a good idea, ... you .... you really need one.

Frank: .... you .... a system that .... both CDs and cassettes, you .... cassettes, which are much cheaper.

⟫→

103

C Work in groups. Take it in turns to begin similar conversations to the one in **B**, asking your friends' advice on these topics:
– buying a new bike *or* car
– whether to go on holiday to the USA next summer
– whether to invite everyone in the class out for a meal on your birthday
– if you should take up an energetic sport like squash or volley-ball.

D Correct the errors in these sentences – one sentence contains no errors.

1 If you would have bought it last week, the price didn't have go up.

2 If you have been feeling unwell you should go to see the doctor.

3 She says that if it weren't for the tax system she'll be much better off.

4 There wouldn't be so much poverty when less money is spent on arms.

5 If you shouldn't arrive in time they won't let you into the concert.

6 If I were born rich I hadn't needed to work.

7 If you'd let me know if you arrived I'd meet you at the airport.

8 I'll be surprised unless prices go up next year.

E Work in groups. Find out your partners' reactions to these photos by asking questions, beginning:

    What if you . . .?   *Supposing that you . . .?*   *Suppose that you . . .?*

F Particularly in FORMAL style, these structures are sometimes used without IF. Look at the examples and then fill the gaps below:

Were it not for his oil revenues, the Sultan would not be so rich.
Had it not been for his oil revenues, he could not have built two palaces.
Should you see her tonight, please remind her to get in touch with me.

1 Had they .... that the exam .... so difficult, they .... more time revising for it.
2 Should .... enough space, continue your work on a separate sheet.
3 .... the weather .... more favourable, we .... our holiday more.
4 .... us to send you a sample, please enclose a cheque for £2.
5 I .... have plenty of money now, ... for having to save up.

12.4   Sharing opinions

Functions

A   You'll hear some people giving their opinions. Imagine that they are friends of yours. How would you reply to each person, using the expressions below?

I agree + *reason*

> *That's right, because ...*   *Yes, absolutely!*
> *Right!*   *Quite right.*
> *That's true, because ...*   *Quite!*
> *I couldn't agree more ...*   *Sure, because ...*
> *That's just what I think.*   *You've got a point there.*
> *– especially when ...*   *– for example when ...*

I don't agree *or* I partly agree + *reason*

> *That's not true.*   *I think you're wrong.*
> *I don't agree at all.*   *Oh, surely not?*
> *Oh no, I can't agree with you there ...*   *What makes you say that?*
> *With all due respect, I'd say that ...*   *I'm not sure I agree.*
> *That's not quite the way I see it.*   *Do you really think so?*
> *I'm not sure I quite agree ... Are you sure?*   *I see what you mean, but ...*
> *I see what you're getting at, but ...*   *I couldn't agree more but ...*
> *There's a lot in what you say, but ...*

Avoiding giving an opinion

> *Do you think so?*   *It's difficult to say.*
> *I suppose it depends on your point of view.*   *I think it all depends.*
> *I really don't know, I'm afraid.*   *That's interesting.*
> *I'm not really sure.*

▶ Which of the expressions above might sound aggressive or dogmatic in a conversation with a superior or a stranger?

⫸→

B ▭ You'll hear ten short conversations, in which the second speaker reacts to the first one's opinion. Listen carefully to the tone of voice used. Decide whether the second person agrees with the first one or not.

C ▣ Work in groups of three or four. Student A should look at Activity 2, student B at 39, C at 73 (and D at 67). You will be taking it in turns to introduce and chair discussions about various topics. Before you begin, decide whose turn it will be to start the first discussion.

12.5 Using synonyms and opposites – 1

Word study

Improving your active vocabulary involves not only learning new words but also learning to use synonyms for common words you might otherwise use too frequently (e.g. *good, small, large, beautiful, hot, cold,* etc.).

The emphasis in these exercises is on USE and experimentation, not just on understanding and there are, unfortunately, no easy short cuts.

A Look at these expressions and decide which of them mean VERY RICH, RICH, POOR or VERY POOR. The first are done as examples.

affluent = rich   broke = poor   comfortably off
desperately poor   down on one's luck   down to one's last penny
feeling the pinch   in dire straits   in the red
living from hand to mouth   loaded   low-paid   on the breadline
penniless   prosperous   rolling in money   stinking rich
unable to make ends meet   well-to-do

B Work in pairs.

a) Decide which of these words mean:

VERY LARGE, LARGE, SMALL or VERY SMALL

big   broad   colossal   extensive   gigantic   immense   little
majestic   miniature   miniscule   minute   not worth mentioning
roomy   spacious   tiny · tremendous   vast   wide

b) Use a dictionary to check the pronunciation of any you're not sure about.

c) Which of them would you use to describe each of the following:

> a city   a mountain   a lake   a fortune   a crowd
> a hotel room   a ballroom   a palace   a luxury car   a car park
> a toy gun   a mistake   an avenue   a city square

C Work in pairs. Now do the same with the words opposite:
a) Discuss the meaning of the words. (In some cases you may feel that some of the words fall between the categories, or even exceed them.)
b) Make sure you can pronounce them.
c) Decide which can be used to describe the things listed.

1 Very beautiful → beautiful → ugly → very ugly
   attractive   enchanting   good-looking   glamorous   graceful
   grotesque   handsome   hideous   lovely   plain   pretty
   unpleasant
   a city   James Dean   Marilyn Monroe   Frankenstein's monster
   Sylvester Stallone   a cathedral   a ballet dancer   a building
   a friend's husband or boyfriend   a friend's wife or girlfriend
   a young child   a palace

2 Very clean → clean → dirty → very dirty
   disgusting   filthy   grubby   immaculate   messy   neat
   neglected   obscene   polluted   rude   smoky   spotless
   squalid   stained   tidy
   a city   a tablecloth   an old building   a joke   an acquaintance
   someone's hands   a cup or glass   a lounge   a carpet
   a back street   a garden   some written work

3 Very hot → hot → cold → very cold
   biting   bitterly cold   boiling   chilly   cool   draughty
   freezing   frosty   lukewarm   scorching   spicy   sweltering
   tropical   unemotional   unsociable   wintry
   a country   a wind   a friend   a rival   the sun   an afternoon
   an evening   a curry   a cup of tea   an office

4 Very expensive → expensive → cheap → very cheap
   a bargain   costly   cut-price   economical   exorbitant
   inferior   invaluable   priceless   reasonable   reduced   shoddy
   tacky   unreasonable   valuable   valueless   vulgar   worthless
   a souvenir   a necklace   a pair of jeans   a hotel   a meal
   a car   an action   a service   a piece of work   a fur coat
   a prize   a painting

5 Very important → important → unimportant → very unimportant
   insignificant   leading   major   minor   modest   prominent
   remarkable   secondary   significant   urgent   unpretentious
   a city   a painting   a politician   a poet   a phone call
   a film star   some work

6 Very famous → famous → unknown → completely unknown
   anonymous   distinguished   exclusive   celebrated   infamous
   mysterious   notorious   obscure   on the map   popular
   private   prominent   renowned   secret   well-known
   a city   a night club   a tourist resort   a mountain village
   a criminal   a singer   a writer   a politician   a millionaire

★ NOTE: Expressions that consist of a phrase, rather than a single adjective, can normally only be used like this: *The mistake was not worth mentioning* and NOT like this: *It was a not worth mentioning mistake.* ✗

▶ There is more on synonyms and opposites in 16.5.

12.6 *Look* and *see* Verbs and idioms

A   Fill the gaps in these sentences with a suitable particle or preposition:

1 I'm looking .... my keys.
2 She came to see me .... at the station.
3 Look ....! There's a car coming.
4 We all saw .... his lies.
5 She looked .... the word in a dictionary

6 The pupils look .... their teacher.
7 The police are looking .... the crime.
8 If you're leaving I'll see you ....

B   Rewrite the sentences, replacing the phrases in italics with the expressions below.

1 If you're travelling in the rush hour, *beware of* pickpockets.
2 If you're ever in London, don't forget to *call in to see me*.
3 If we're both at the show, let's *keep watching for* each other in the interval.
4 Can I *see* the photos? Oh, you and your sister do *have a similar appearance*, don't you?
5 He *regards* people who are less intelligent than himself *as inferior*.
6 When I said that I looked up to her, she *glanced at me strangely*.
7 In this case, as you have such a good excuse, I *won't take account of* what you have done wrong.
8 They have a lovely room, it *has a view of* the sea.
9 '*Listen to me*, if you don't give me back my money I'll call the police,' I shouted. Soon a crowd of *curious people* had gathered around us.
10 She's due to retire soon, but she says she's not leaving the firm until she has *completed* her current project.
11 Even the best of friends don't always *agree* on everything.
12 A group of *tourists* were waiting outside the palace, hoping to catch a glimpse of the Queen.
13 Leave all the arrangements to me: I'll *attend* to everything.
14 His story was obviously a pack of lies and we all *disbelieved* it.
15 When she called him stupid he *became very angry*.
16 Old people like to *remember* their younger days with nostalgia.

    onlookers   overlook   overlook   give someone a funny look
    have a look at   look alike   look back on   look here
    look down on/look down one's nose at   look out for
    look out for   look someone up
    see eye to eye   see red   see something through
    see through something   see to something   sightseers

C   Match these beginnings to the endings below:

1 She glanced at ...   3 He gazed at ...   5 She noticed ...
2 She stared at ...   4 She peered at ...   6 He watched ...

    ... two men having a fight   ... a programme on television
    ... the painting   ... her lovingly
    ... the person sitting opposite on the bus
    ... the small print in the brochure   ... the view of the mountains
    ... someone arriving late

13 Communication

13.1 Get the message?   Vocabulary

A Work in groups. Discuss these questions with your partners:
- In which countries is your language spoken and by how many people?
- Which languages have you studied? Why?
- What are some of the reasons why people learn foreign languages?

B Fill the gaps in these sentences with suitable words.

1 Words like 'the telly', 'the tube' or 'the box' are c................. words which are more common in i................. conversation than in f................. writing.
2 Although she said she was fine, her e................. conveyed her real feelings.
3 A smile or a frown are examples of non-v................. communication.
4 We can often find out about people's feelings by listening to their i................. and t................. of voice, and watching their g.................s and b................. language.
5 'It's a small world' is a s................. or ex................. we might use when we are surprised at meeting someone in an unexpected place.
6 'Many hands make light work' and 'Too many cooks spoil the broth' are contradictory p.................s.
7 In writing we can u................. a word or *print it in i*................. to emphasise it, whilst in conversation we would s................. the word more strongly.
8 Most people in Britain speak with some kind of r................. accent.
9 A variety of a language which has its own non-standard vocabulary and grammar is known as a d.................
10 When he said my work was 'brilliant' I realised he was being s.................
11 Every profession has its own j................. that is only used within that trade.
12 The accent of British English used by educated middle-class speakers from the South-East of England is known as R.P. (R................. P.................).
13 She was brought up in Singapore and is b................. in English and Chinese.
14 Learners are often advised to avoid using s................. words in a foreign language, in case they sound out of date or aren't used a.................ly.

C Work in groups. Discuss these questions with your partners:
- How many different national or regional accents of your own language can you recognise?
- How many different or regional accents of English can you recognise?
- Are there any differences in writing in the spelling, vocabulary or grammar of different varieties of your own language?

13.2 A 'typical' English conversation

A Before you listen to the recording, look at the flowchart below and see if you can think of some examples to fill the gaps.

🔲 Listen to the recording and fill the gaps with some of the examples given by the speaker.

A typical one-to-one conversation begins with this Opening Phase:

1   Participants make eye contact.
            ↓

2   They assume conventional facial expressions: e.g. ....
       ↓

3   They reach a position of comfortable proximity: e.g. ....
       ↓

4   They adopt an appropriate posture: e.g. ....
       ↓

5   They exchange ritual gestures: e.g. ....
          and greetings: e.g. ....
       ↓

6   They exchange channel-opening remarks: e.g. ....
       ↓

7   The main business phase can begin . . .

And the conversation ends with this Parting Phase:

1   One or both of the participants decides it's time to stop.
       ↓

2   They exchange appropriate cordial facial expressions: e.g. ....
       ↓

3   They exchange ritual gestures: e.g. ....
      and phrases to signal parting: e.g. ....
       ↓

4   They increase the distance between them: e.g. ....
       ↓

5 Eye contact is broken, the participants turn away and the conversation has ended.

B 🔲 You'll hear part of the interview you heard in **A** again. Fill the gaps in this transcript of the extract.

Sarah: ... encouragingly or something like that.
Presenter: Oh, I see, yes.
Sarah: Then they reach a...a 'position of comfortable proximity'.
Presenter: W...what is...what .... ?
Sarah: Well, er...basically we're .... Er...for ....
        or...or...or .... 50 to 60 centimetres apart i...is usual.
        But for .... 20 to 30 centimetres.
Presenter: Wow! What happens when .... ?

Sarah: Well, that actually ....
Presenter: Yeah?
Sarah: ...because of course what usually happens is that...that the...the...
             um...North American will .... to try and make
             .... between them.
Presenter: Because the Latin American ....
Sarah: ....!
Presenter: I know it.
Sarah: Er...then of course what they do is ...

C   Work in groups. Discuss these questions with your partners:
* How does a 'typical conversation' begin and end differently if the
  participants are, for example:
      complete strangers   very close friends or relations
      boss and employee
* How is a 'typical conversation' different in your country and in other
  countries you know? Make a similar flowchart.
* How is a telephone conversation different? Make a similar flowchart.
* How does a 'typical English lesson' begin and end?

D   Work in groups of three (or four). Student A should look at
Activity 46, B at 68 and the other(s) at 74. In this role play, you will be
taking part in a typical conversation that might happen at an airport.

Try to behave and speak just as you really would in this situation without
pretending to be someone else.

13.3   Gestures

A   Here are two extracts from a chapter in a book. Read them both and
then answer the questions on the next page.

GESTURES

A gesture is any action that sends a visual
signal to an onlooker. To become a gesture, an
act has to be seen by someone else and has to
communicate some piece of information to
them. It can do this either because the gesturer
deliberately sets out to send a signal – as when
he waves his hand – or it can do it only
incidentally – as when he sneezes. The hand-
wave is a Primary Gesture, because it has no
other existence or function. It is a piece of
communication from start to finish. The
sneeze, by contrast, is a secondary, or Incidental Gesture. Its primary function is mechanical
and is concerned with the sneezer's personal
breathing problem. In its secondary role, however, it cannot help but transmit a message to

his companions, warning them that he may
have caught a cold.

Most people tend to limit their use of the
term 'gesture' to the primary form – the
hand-wave type – but this misses an important
point. What matters with gesturing is not what
signals we think we are sending out, but what
signals are being received. The observers of
our acts will make no distinction between our
intentional Primary Gestures and our uninten-
tional, incidental ones. In some ways, our
Incidental Gestures are the more illuminating
of the two, if only for the very fact that we do
not think of them as gestures, and therefore do
not censor and manipulate them so strictly.
This is why it is preferable to use the term
'gesture' in its wider meaning as an 'observed
action'.

A convenient way to distinguish between

Incidental and Primary Gestures is to ask the question: Would I do it if I were completely alone? If the answer is No, then it is a Primary Gesture. We do not wave, wink or point when we are by ourselves; not, that is, unless we have reached the unusual condition of talking animatedly to ourselves.

SYMBOLIC GESTURES

A Symbolic Gesture indicates an abstract quality that has no simple equivalent in the world of objects and movements.

How, for instance, would you make a silent sign for stupidity? You might launch into a full-blooded Theatrical Mime of a drooling village idiot. But total idiocy is not a precise way of indicating the momentary stupidity of a healthy adult. Instead, you might tap your forefinger against your temple, but this also lacks accuracy, since you might do precisely the same thing when indicating that someone is brainy. All the tap does is to point to the brain. To make the meaning more clear, you might instead twist your forefinger against your temple, indicating 'a screw loose'. Alternatively, you might rotate your forefinger close to your temple, signalling that the brain is going round and round and is not stable.

Many people would understand these temple-forefinger actions, but others would not. They would have their own local, stupidity gestures, which we in our turn would find confusing, such as tapping the elbow of the raised forearm, flapping the hand up and down in front of half-closed eyes, rotating a raised hand, or laying one forefinger flat across the forehead.

The situation is further complicated by the fact that some stupidity signals mean totally different things in different countries. To take one example, in Saudi Arabia stupidity can be signalled by touching the lower eyelid with the tip of the forefinger. But this same action, in various other countries, can mean disbelief, approval, agreement, mistrust, scepticism, alertness, secrecy, craftiness, danger or criminality. The reason for this apparent chaos of meanings is simple enough. By pointing to the eye, the gesturer is doing no more than stress the symbolic importance of the eye as a seeing organ. Beyond that, the action says nothing, so that the message can become either: 'Yes, I see', or 'I can't believe my eyes', or 'Keep a sharp look-out', or 'I like what I see', or almost any other seeing signal you care to imagine. In such a case it is essential to know the precise 'seeing' property being represented by the symbolism of the gesture in any particular culture.

So we are faced with two basic problems where Symbolic Gestures are concerned: either one meaning may be signalled by different actions, or several meanings may be signalled by the same action, as we move from culture to culture. The only solution is to approach each culture with an open mind and learn their Symbolic Gestures as one would their vocabulary.

(from *Manwatching* by Desmond Morris)

1 What do a sneeze and a wave of the hand have in common?
2 What kind of gesture is a yawn?
3 What kind of gesture is a raised fist?
4 Write down three more examples of incidental gestures.
5 Write down three more examples of primary gestures.
6 Why is the phrase *unusual condition* used at the end of the first section?
7 How many different signs does the writer describe for stupidity?
8 What is the 'local gesture' for stupidity in your country?
9 How many different meanings does the writer describe for the gesture of touching the lower eyelid with the tip of the forefinger?
10 What is the meaning of touching the lower eyelid in your country?
11 How does the writer suggest one should learn the gestures of different cultures?

B 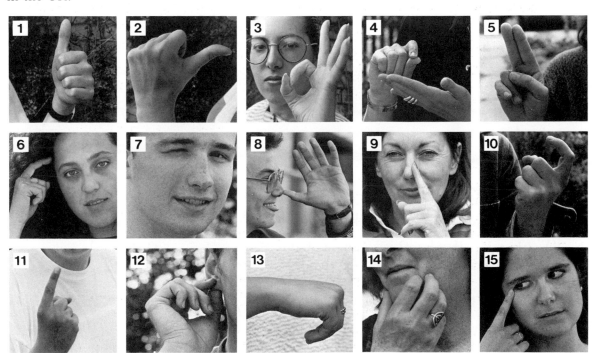 Highlight the following words in the first section of the text:

*onlookers   primary   incidental   role   distinction between
illuminating   censor   manipulate   distinguish between   animatedly*

Now fill these gaps with a suitable form of the words above:

1 People occasionally underestimate the .... of marketing in business.
2 After the accident a crowd of .... gathered around.
3 Someone who is colour-blind usually cannot .... red and green.
4 In most sports there is a .... amateurs and professionals.
5 A skilful politician is good at .... people.
6 The film was .... because it contained scenes that might have upset people.
7 I learnt a lot from your report – it was very ....
8 They discussed the idea .... for half an hour.
9 Apart from the basic costs of accommodation and food, everyone has .... expenses, such as snacks and reading matter.
10 The .... purpose of advertising is to persuade people to buy goods.

C According to the writer, a sneeze and a yawn are involuntary, incidental gestures. Working in pairs, decide what these gestures mean when they are done deliberately:

blinking   clearing your throat   clenching your fist   folding your arms
licking your lips   scratching your head   sighing   sniffing
tapping your fingers on a table   grabbing someone's wrist

D Work in groups. Look at these pictures and decide (or guess) what each of the gestures might mean to a British person AND to someone from your own country. One or two of them would be considered 'incidental gestures' in the UK.

A   One way of putting extra information into a single sentence is to use
RELATIVE CLAUSES, as in these examples:

1 A gesture is any action **that** sends a visual signal to an onlooker.
2 A Symbolic Gesture indicates an abstract quality **that** has no simple equivalent in the world of objects and movement.
3 Tracy, **who** used to go out with David, has just got engaged to Paul, **who** is his best friend.
4 Many people have their own local stupidity gestures, **which** we would find confusing.
5 The office **in which** she works has fluorescent lighting, **which** gives her headaches.
6 Paul has just got engaged to Tracy, **who** is the daughter of Claire and Frank, **who** are the owners of Acme Bookshops Ltd, **which** has just opened a branch in the new shopping centre, **which** we went to last weekend with David, **who** used to go out with Tracy and **whose** best friend is Paul – **which** goes to show that it's a small world!

▶ Work in pairs. Decide which of the relative pronouns **in bold print** can be replaced with a different one (*which* instead of *that*, *that* instead of *who*, etc.).

▶ Too many relative clauses in a single long sentence can be confusing for the reader. Rewrite the last example above in shorter sentences.

B   Another technique for adding extra information is to use PRESENT or PAST PARTICIPLES – look again at 7.1 C. Rewrite these sentences using *-ing* forms or past participles.

1 You might rotate your forefinger against your temple, which indicates 'a screw loose'.
2 You might rotate your finger close to your temple, which signals that the brain is going round and round.
3 As soon as she realised what had happened she called the police.
4 The first island which was discovered by Columbus was one of the Bahamas.
5 Albert Sukoff wrote a long article, which he did without the use of a single full stop.

C   Find the errors in these sentences and correct them.

1 The person, which phone number you gave me, was not very helpful.

2 The most important point what he made was that we should approach each culture with an open mind.

3 The person, whom I spoke to, was rather rude that upset me.

4 I'd like to thank Pat without help the work would have been impossible.

5 Considered that you're so clever and you're the one, that usually know the answers I'm surprised you got it wrong.

D Rewrite these notes as complete sentences, using *-ing* forms, past participles or relative clauses. Change the form of the verbs as necessary, bearing in mind that the events happened in the PAST. The first is done as an example.

1 While – David stays with us – finds out about Paul and Tracy's plans
   While staying with us, David found out about Paul and Tracy's plans.
2 After – hears about their plans – is upset and angry
3 Feels absolutely furious – pushes over the table – knocks our best glasses to the floor
4 While – picks up the broken glass – cuts his finger – starts bleeding
5 Takes his handkerchief from his pocket – wraps it round the cut
6 After – gathers up most of the broken pieces – the pieces are on the floor – apologises profusely
7 Realises how stupid he is – offers to replace the broken glasses
8 Intends to buy us a new set of glasses – knows they are good quality ones – goes to a store in town – the store has a good stock of glassware
9 Looks round the store – discovers the glasses are very expensive – this gives him quite a shock
10 Since – breaks those glasses – is careful to keep his temper!

13.5 I ♥ sign language   Discussion activity

In this section we'll be looking at the meaning of slogans, symbols, signs and logos.

A Work in groups. Here are some well-known slogans. What does each one signify and what ideas do you and your partners associate with it?

I ♥ New York   *Feed the world*
Small is beautiful   *Power to the people*
Make love not war   *Nuclear power – no thanks*
Survival of the fittest   *All you need is love*
The world's favourite airline   *Unity is strength*
Liberty, fraternity, equality   *One man, one vote*
The customer is always right   *Workers of the world, unite*
Man was born free and everywhere he is in chains

▶ Can you think of some more political or advertising slogans?

B What do these symbols signify for you? Can you think of some more?

1

2

3

4

5

6

115

C Work in pairs. Can you explain what these signs mean?

D Work in pairs. Which of these logos can you draw from memory? Here are some examples:

Kelloggs   Kodak   Ford   Adidas   Esso   Fiat   VW

(You'll find the correct logos in Activity 12.)

13.6 What happened?

Creative writing

A Work in pairs. Make up an imaginary story about yourself, including all of these pictograms. Make notes on the main events.

B Write a narrative with yourself as the main character:
EITHER in the style of a short story in a magazine,
OR as if you're writing a letter to a friend abroad.

13.7 Colours

A   What do the phrases printed in italics below mean? Don't use a
dictionary – the context will help you to guess.

1 The whole class passed the exam *with flying colours*.
2 She didn't go to work because she was feeling a little *off colour*.
3 The detailed descriptions in the story gave *local colour* to the book.
4 Far more men are *colour-blind* than women.
5 All the documents in this office are *colour-coded*.
6 What do you think of the *colour scheme* in this room?
7 It was only when he had won the match and started jeering at his opponent that we saw
 him *in his true colours*.
8 Don't allow your personal interest to *colour* your judgement.

B   Replace each phrase in italics with one of the idioms below:

1 Most *manual* workers receive wages and are paid weekly.
2 He phoned me *completely unexpectedly* to tell me he was back in town.
3 Right-wing politicians often label their opponents as *communists*.
4 We read more and more about *environmental* issues in the press.
5 They were *very jealous* when they saw my new Porsche.
6 She *became very angry* when I told her she had made a mistake.
7 The police caught her *in the act of committing the crime*.
8 I'm ready to start when you *tell me to go ahead*.
9 Our new clerk makes so many mistakes because he's still *inexperienced*.
10 A lucky coincidence like this happens *very rarely*.
11 I can't afford to buy anything because I'm still *in debt* after my holiday.
12 Dealings with government offices usually involve *bureaucratic delays*.

RED	in the red	red-handed	see red	red tape	reds
BLUE	once in a blue moon	out of the blue	blue-collar		
GREEN	green	green	green with envy	give the green light	

C   Fill the gaps in these sentences with one of the idioms below:

1 She showed her disapproval by giving me a ....
2 Send me a letter about this – I need to have all the details ....
3 During the war, most things could be bought on the ....
4 It's a hilarious .... about an unsuccessful murderer.
5 He must have been in a fight – he's got a ....
6 They're not getting married in a registry office: they're having a ....
7 I told a .... because I didn't want her to get into trouble.
8 Most .... workers receive a salary and are paid monthly.
9 She had a .... and didn't regain consciousness for several minutes.
10 No one uses the new conference centre – it is a ....

BLACK AND WHITE   black comedy   black eye   black look
black market   blackout   in black and white
white-collar   white elephant   white lie   white wedding

14 The English-speaking world

14.1 English in the world

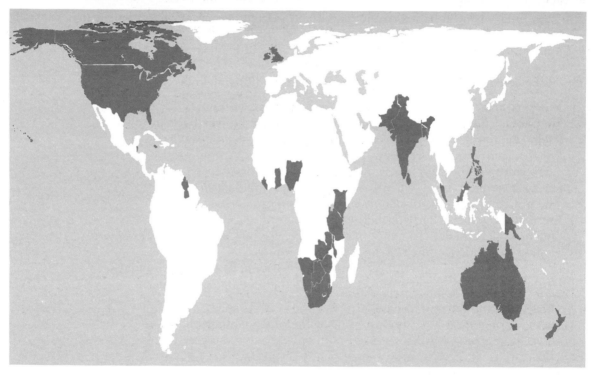

A 🖍️ Read this passage and highlight any unfamiliar words you find.

World English

In the minds of many people, there is no longer an issue. They argue that English has already become a world language, by virtue of the political and economic progress made by English-speaking nations in the past 200 years, and is likely to remain so, gradually consolidating its position.

An impressive variety of facts about usage support this view. According to conservative estimates, mother-tongue speakers have now reached around 300 million; a further 300 million use English as a second language; and a further 100 million use it fluently as a foreign language. This is an increase of around 40% since the 1950s. More radical estimates, which include speakers with a lower level of language fluency and awareness, have suggested that the overall total is these days well in excess of 1,000 million. The variation results largely from a lack of precise data about English language use in such areas as the Indian sub-continent, where the historical impact of the language exercises a continuing influence on many of its 900 million people, and China, where there has been a burst of enthusiasm for English language studies in recent years, with over 100 million people watching the BBC television English series *Follow Me*. Even if only 10% of these learners become fluent, the effect on totals is dramatic: the number of foreign learners is immediately doubled.

Surveys of range of use carried out by UNESCO and other world organizations reinforce the general statistical impression. English is used as an official or semi-official language in over 60 countries, and has a prominent place in a further 20. It is either dominant or well established in all six continents. It is the main language of books, newspapers, airports and air-traffic control, international business and academic conferences, science, technology, medicine, diplomacy, sports, international competitions, pop music, and advertising. Over two-thirds of the world's scientists write in English. Three-quarters of the world's mail is written in English. Of all the information in the world's electronic retrieval systems, 80% is stored in English. English radio programmes are received by over 50 million in 120 countries. Over 50 million children study English as an additional language at primary level; over 80 million study it at secondary level (these figures exclude China). In any one year, the British Council helps a quarter of a million foreign students to learn English, in various parts of the world.

(from *The Cambridge Encyclopedia of Language* by David Crystal)

B   Work in groups. Discuss these questions with your partners:

- Which statistic or piece of information given in the passage surprised you most?
- In which countries is English spoken as a first language?
- In which other countries is English used as a second language or *lingua franca* between people who speak different local languages?
- English can help you to communicate with people from other non-English-speaking countries: how many different nationalities have you communicated with in English yourself?
- Which variety of English have you chosen to learn: the British, the American or another? Why?

14.2   Indirect speech   Grammar

Although direct speech is often used like this in novels and stories:

"Shh! Be quiet!" she whispered urgently, "My husband's in the other room and he mustn't know you're here . . ."

– it's not used so much like this in everyday conversation or writing. It's generally easier to remember the GIST of a conversation than to remember the exact words. Moreover, the actual words may not always be terribly interesting:

"Hello," he said. "Hello," I said, "How are you?" I asked. "I'm fine," he said. "Good," I said, "and . . . er . . . how's your wife?" I asked. "Oh, very well," he said . . .

A Work in pairs. Discuss the differences in meaning (if any) between these sentences:

1 He told us that he had visited Australia in the summer.
   He told us that he visited Australia in the summer.
   He told us that he would be visiting Australia in the summer.

2 She asked me if I had been to New Zealand.
   She asked me when I had been to New Zealand.
   She asked me whether I had been to New Zealand.

3 David says he wants to visit his relations in Canada.
   David said he wanted to visit his relations in Canada.
   David said he wants to visit his relations in Canada.
   David said, 'He wanted to visit his relations in Canada.'

4 Ruth phoned to say that she would be flying to India the next day.
   Ruth phoned to say that she would be flying to India tomorrow.
   Ruth phoned to say that she was flying to India the next day.

5 I didn't find out when the show starts.
   I didn't find out when the show started.
   I didn't find out when the show will start.
   I didn't find out when the show would start.

B  Work in groups of four or five – two of you should look at Activity 9, the others at 44. You will each have two passages to rewrite into direct and reported speech. Look at this example first:

He told me he didn't like that book he was reading then.

I don't like this book I'm reading now.

C Reported speech may not show the TONE of direct speech – but an appropriately chosen verb can reflect the tone that was used.

How many of the following verbs can you use to fill each of the gaps in these sentences:

1 She .... that she came from Australia.
2 They .... us/me that they were feeling tired.
3 He .... me to lend him some money.

admit	allow	announce	ask	assure	beg	call out
claim	convince	cry out	deny	encourage	explain	imply
inform	insist	instruct	invite	mention	mumble	mutter
notify	order	permit	persuade	reiterate	repeat	reply
scream	shout	suggest	tell	urge	warn	whisper	yell

⟦ht⟧ Work in pairs. Highlight the ten most useful verbs in **C** that you don't already use. Then compose five sentences, each including one of the verbs you have chosen.
Compare your sentences with another pair.

D ⟦cassette⟧ You'll hear seven people talking about the places where they were brought up.
Make notes as you listen and then write a short report (a couple of lines only) giving the GIST of what each person said. The first speaker is Blain, and what he said is done as an example:

1 *Blain said he was brought up in Northern Canada, where he lived in very tiny isolated settlements. He remembered that the summers were very hot and the winters extremely cold with a great deal of snow.*

The other speakers are:
Rupert, Gay, Enzo, Nick, Ken and Karen.

E Each of these sentences gives a report of what various people said. Rewrite each report, using direct speech, giving the exact words you think each person might have used. The first is done as an example.

1 I tried to find out what part of America Kate came from.
"Could you tell me what part of America you come from, Kate?"
2 Kate wanted me to guess, but in the end she revealed that she came from Toronto – in Canada!
3 Jane complimented me on my handwriting.
4 Jerry suggested that I should enrol for a course in Japanese.
5 Pippa insisted on paying for the whole meal, including the drinks.
6 Stephen encouraged me to go in for the exam and reassured me that I had a good chance of passing.
7 I warned Stephen not to be too confident as it was a long time since I'd last taken an exam.
8 Although they were strangers I asked the people in the corridor to stop talking so loudly as it was after midnight.

F ⟦cassette⟧ You'll hear two passages read aloud – one about Australia and the other about New York.

1 Work in pairs. One of you should make notes on the first passage and the other on the second one. Note down the main points made in the passage.
2 Rewrite your notes as a short report, giving the GIST of what the speakers said. As much of the information is presumably still true, use present tenses where appropriate. Begin like this:

The first speaker talked about Australia/New York. He/She said that...

3 Show your report to your partner. Compare your reports with the original texts in Activity 66.

14.3   Spelling and pronunciation 1 – Consonants

This section deals with the main problem areas of spelling and pronouncing consonants.

There is a pronunciation key on the cassette for exercises **A**, **B** and **C**.

★ In the various accents of English, it is the intonation and vowel sounds that tend to be different. The CONSONANT sounds don't differ very much – apart from these sounds:

    r at the end and in the middle of words: far   farmer   harder   charge
and t in the middle of words: forgotten   butter   better

A   Decide which of the words below are pronounced /tʃ/ as in **ch**eer, /ʃ/ as in fi**sh**, /ʒ/ as in u**s**ual or /dʒ/ as in **j**ump:

average   badge   beige   cabbage   courage   damage
decision   future   injury   insurance   literature   machine
march   vision   moustache   opposition   partial   picture
prestige   question

B   Arrange these words into four groups, according to the pronunciation of the letters *gh* or *g*. The first four are done as examples.

1 /g/   *ghost*   3 /f/   *enough*
2 /dʒ/   *giant*   4 [silent]   *high*

enough   high   giant   ghost   nought (∅)   gesture   sign
signature   margarine   guilty   draught   gypsy   thorough
sigh   naughty   borough   gymnasium   gherkin   generation
laughter   ginger   George   giggle   genuine   drought
engineer   genius

C   Here are some groups of words, each containing the letter on the left. <u>Underline</u> the words in which the letter on the left is pronounced (i.e. not silent). The first group have been done as an example.

k   knowledge   <u>acknowledge</u>   knot   kneel   knife   <u>nickname</u>
b   climbing   subtle   symbol   numb   dumb   debt   bribed
g   campaign   hungry   champagne   ignorance   foreign
h   honour   exhibition   rehearsal   behalf   exhausted   ghost
     vehicle   honorary   inherit
l   behalf   salmon   chalk   yolk   yield   failure   palm
p   psychology   psychiatry   couple   cupboard   receipt
     raspberry   hypnotise   pseudonym
t   castle   attitude   Christmas   whistle   postpone   soften   bright
d   sandwich   sadness   Wednesday   handkerchief   second-hand

D   Everyone has difficulties with English spelling – even educated native speakers sometimes have to think twice about some words. Correct the spelling mistakes in these words – but be careful because three of them are correctly spelt. The first is done as an example.

~~adress~~ *address* acomodation advertisement arguement
agressive comittee developing embarassed foriegner
four o'clock independant medecine pronounciation
recieve reliable replaceing responsability sieze
skillfull therefor untill

To remind yourself of the words *you* spell wrongly, look at your own previous written work and highlight the spelling mistakes you made.

E In British English and American English some words may be spelt (British) / spelled (American) differently.

The following words are printed in the usual American English way. Work in pairs and decide how they would usually be written in British English. Look at the examples first.

catalog *catalogue* center *centre* color *colour* defense *defence*
draft beer favor honor humor jewelry kidnaper labor
pajamas quarreling skillful specialty theater
traveler's check traveling TV program woolen

▶ Can you think of any more words that are written differently in British and American English?

★ These words can be spelt either **-ize** or **-ise** in British English:
realize/realise modernize/modernise apologize/apologise etc.
but normally with **-ize** in American English (except *advertise*).

★ Although you may see spellings like *gotta* and *wanna* in the lyrics of songs, for example, they aren't used in normal American English writing.

14.4   British and American English

A few words are sometimes used differently on either side of the Atlantic. However, most of the vocabulary is identical, so British and American people do understand each other perfectly well most of the time!

A   Look at the words in the first list, which are often used in American English. Match them to the common British English terms below.

> **AmE**   apartment*   attorney   to call someone*   checkmark
> closet   couch*   downtown   drugstore/pharmacy*   the fall
> faucet   garbage/trash   movie*   movie theater   potato chips
> schedule*   sidewalk   zero*   zipper

> **BrE**   autumn*   chemist's   cinema   city/town centre*
> cupboard/wardrobe*   film*   flat*   rubbish*   nought(∅)
> pavement   potato crisps   to ring someone up   solicitor/barrister
> tap*   tick(✓)   timetable*   zip   🔈

B   Work in pairs. Fill the gaps in these sentences with suitable words from the lists below – one of you using the British English words, the other the American ones. The first is done as an example.

1 Turn left at the next... *crossroads* (BrE) / *intersection* (AmE).
2 When you arrive, report to the reception desk on the .... floor and then take the .... or walk up the stairs to the .... floor.
3 Every man was wearing a three-piece suit: jacket, ... and ....
4 Does the .... go all the way to the airport or do I have to take a bus?
5 There was a long .... for tickets at the .... station.
6 We had to drive off the .... to fill up with ....
7 If there's a power cut you may need to use a .... to see in the dark.
8 Do you need to go to the .... before we leave?

> **BrE**   *crossroads*   *first floor*   *ground floor*   *lift*   *motorway*
> *petrol*   *queue*   *railway*   *toilet*   *torch*   *trousers*
> *underground*   *waistcoat*

> **AmE**   *bathroom*   *elevator*   *first floor*   *flashlight*
> *freeway/highway*   *gas*   *intersection*   *line*   *pants*   *railroad*
> *second floor*   *subway*   *vest*

▶ Can you think of any more words with different meanings in British and American English?

★ In different regions of Britain there are some variations in vocabulary. In Scotland, for example, these words are sometimes used:
> *wee*(=small)   *aye*(=yes)   *infirmary*(=hospital)   *bairn*(=child)
> *carry-out*(=take-away meal)   *pinkie*(=little finger)

* These words are also sometimes used in the other dialect, with similar meanings.

A   Fill the gaps in the sentences with suitable forms of the verbs below.

1 I should know the answer tomorrow, can you .... me .... then?
2 I can't make up my mind right away, I'll need to .... it ....
3 I know she doesn't want to do it, but I'll try to .... her .... helping us.
4 It's very annoying when experts .... you because they think you know nothing about their subject.
5 I'm afraid I can't hear you very well, could you ...., please.
6 We'll .... it .... tonight and then let you know tomorrow.
7 We'll have to .... the lecture .... because the speaker is ill.
8 In many countries all young men are .... at the age of eighteen and stay in the armed forces for a year or more.
9 He was afraid to .... at the meeting in case he made a fool of himself.
10 I always .... my aunt .... on her birthday.

> call off   call up   call up   call back   speak up   speak out
> talk down to   talk someone into   talk over   think over

B   Replace each phrase in italics with a suitable form of the expressions below.

1 I'll start pouring out your wine – please *tell me when to stop pouring*.
2 When two business people meet, they often *discuss work or business*.
3 They had an argument and now they are *not on friendly terms*.
4 *It's obvious* that it takes time to get used to an unfamiliar accent.
5 'It's terribly hot, isn't it?' '*I agree with you entirely*.'
6 'Can you turn on the air conditioning?' 'That's *more difficult than you might expect* because the switch is broken.'
7 'Could you open the window, please.' 'Yes, *that can be done quickly*.'
8 She always *expresses her views frankly*.
9 I knew it was an empty threat, so I *challenged him to carry it out*.
10 The voters *have a low opinion of* the present government's record.
11 I haven't made up my mind yet, I was just *saying my thoughts out loud*.
12 We were going to go by car, but then we *decided it wasn't a good idea*.
13 The influence of the USA in the world is a favourite *discussion topic*.
14 It sounded a good idea, but I believe you should *reconsider*.

> call someone's bluff   say when   easier said than done
> it goes without saying   no sooner said than done
> You can say that again!   not on speaking terms
> speak one's mind   talk shop   talking point   think again
> think aloud   think better of it   don't think much of

C   [icon] Work in pairs. Decide together which are the TEN most useful idioms in **A** and **B** that you don't already use. Highlight them to help you to remember them. Then compose five sentences, each including one of the idioms you have chosen.
    Compare your sentences with another pair.

15 How strange!

15.1 Into the unknown . . .   Vocabulary and listening

A   Work in groups. Ask your partners these questions – and encourage them to expand on their answers:

- Do you believe in ghosts?
- Have you (or has anyone you know) ever had your fortune told?
- Have you ever had a dream that predicted the future?
- Are any of the following believed to be lucky or unlucky in your country:
    a black cat crossing the road in front of you
    walking under a ladder   spilling salt   keeping your fingers crossed

B   Fill the gaps in these sentences with suitable words from the list below.

1 Some people enjoy reading .... stories about ghosts and the ....
2 She told us her plane had crashed in the jungle and it was a .... she had survived. But her story sounded so .... that we were very ....
3 I had a sense of .... as if I was in a situation I had experienced before.
4 The magician sawed his assistant in half, but we knew it was a(n) ....
5 She was .... when her door flew open in the middle of the night.
6 It may be a .... that some people are accident-prone.
7 He always avoids walking under ladders because he is very ....
8 We hadn't seen each other for years but we were both sitting on the same bus in Cairo – it was an amazing ....!

    coincidence   creepy   déjà vu   fallacy   far-fetched   illusion
    miracle   scared stiff   scary   sceptical   supernatural
    superstitious   terror-struck

C   Work in groups. Ask your partners these questions:

- Can some people communicate thoughts to each other by telepathy?
- Are you superstitious? If the only vacant rooms in a hotel were numbers 7 and 13, which would you choose and why?
- What was the last coincidence that happened to you?
- Do you know anyone who seems to be accident-prone?

D   🖭   You'll hear a story. Discuss your reactions to it with a partner.

A   Read this passage and find the following information in the text:

1 What do modern legends reflect?
2 Apart from being retold by people, how are modern legends and tales disseminated widely?
3 Find an example of an ancient legend and a modern legend.

New Legends for Old

We are not aware of our own folklore any more than we are of the grammatical rules of our language. When we follow the ancient practice of informally transmitting "lore" – wisdom, knowledge, or accepted modes of behavior – by word of mouth and customary example from person to person, we do not concentrate on the form or content of our folklore; instead, we simply listen to information that others tell us and then pass it on – more or less accurately – to other listeners. In this stream of unselfconscious oral tradition the information that acquires a clear story line is called *narrative folklore*, and those stories alleged to be true are *legends*. This, in broad summary, is the typical process of legend formation and transmission as it has existed from time immemorial and continues to operate today. It works about the same way whether the legendary plot concerns a dragon in a cave or a mouse in a Coke bottle.

It might seem unlikely that legends – *urban* legends at that – would continue to be created in an age of widespread literacy, rapid mass communications, and restless travel. While our pioneer ancestors may have had to rely heavily on oral traditions to pass the news along about changing events and frontier dangers, surely we no longer need mere "folk" reports of what's happening, with all their tendencies to distort the facts. A moment's reflection, however, reminds us of the many weird, fascinating, but unverified rumors and tales that so frequently come to our ears – killers and madmen on the loose, shocking or funny personal experiences, unsafe manufactured products, and many other unexplained mysteries of daily life. Sometimes we encounter different oral versions of such stories, and on occasion we may read about similar events in newspapers or magazines; but seldom do we find, or even seek after, reliable documentation. The lack of verification in no way diminishes the appeal urban legends have for us. We enjoy them merely as stories, and we tend at least to half-believe them as possibly accurate reports. And the legends we tell, as with any folklore, reflect many of the hopes, fears, and anxieties of our time. In short, legends are definitely part of our modern folklore – legends which are as traditional, variable, and functional as those of the past.

Whatever the origins of urban legends, their dissemination is no mystery. The tales have traveled far and wide, and have been told and retold from person to person in the same manner that myths, fairy tales, or ballads spread in earlier cultures, with the important difference that today's legends are also disseminated by the mass media. Groups of age-mates, especially adolescents, are one important American legend channel, but other paths of transmission are among office workers and club members, as well as among religious, recreational, and regional groups. Some individuals make a point of learning every recent rumor or tale, and they can enliven any coffee break, party, or trip with the latest supposed "news." The telling of one story inspires other people to share what they have read or heard, and in a short time a lively exchange of details occurs and perhaps new variants are created.

(from *The Vanishing Hitchhiker* by Jan Harold Brunvand)

B   Now referring back to the text, answer these questions.

According to the writer,
1 Why are we not aware of our own folklore?
2 When do legends acquire a clear story line?
3 What kinds of rumours and tales are current nowadays?
4 Why do legends still play an important part in our lives today?
5 Why are urban legends never documented?
6 Why do we accept such stories even though they cannot be verified?
7 Where in the USA are you most likely to hear a modern legend?
8 What generally happens when people in a group have heard a legend?

C   Work in groups. What examples can you think of from your own country of both ancient and modern legends?

D   Highlight the following words in the text:
*aware   ancient   unselfconscious   acquire   alleged
widespread   rumour/US rumor   documentation   merely   anxiety*

Fill the gaps in these sentences with the words you have highlighted.

1 As we get older most of us tend to .... more and more possessions.
2 After the thunderstorm, there was .... flooding.
3 The police .... that he had committed the crime.
4 Are you .... of the difference between a religion and a sect?
5 According to a .... I have heard, our firm will soon be bankrupt.
6 All the .... is filed in this cabinet.
7 Children are often more .... than adults.
8 I didn't mean to upset you. I .... wanted to know what you thought.
9 Most people suffer from .... before an important event.
10 Western civilisation originates in .... Greece.

E   Work in pairs. One of you should look at Activity 8, the other at 49. You'll each have another urban legend to retell to your partner.

15.3 Sequencing ideas

A Work in pairs. Study the picture for a few minutes and discuss it with
your partner.
  Make notes on what seems to be happening in it.

('Relativity' by M.C. Escher, 1953, © 1990 M.C. Escher Heirs/Cordon Art – Baarn – Holland)

B   Which of these paragraphs do you prefer? What features make each one more or less effective?

We can look at this enigmatic picture from three sides but not from above. The artist is playing with our sense of direction and creating illusions: as we turn the page different people come into view with the staircases apparently connecting each scene. In all, there are sixteen people, with featureless heads like tailors' dummies, going about their business in or near the same house.

The picture is an enigma, playing with our sense of direction and creating illusions. We can see sixteen people in the picture, but as we look at it from the left, from the right or from below (but not from above), different ones come into view on or near each interconnected staircase. The heads of the people going about their business are like tailors' dummies: their heads and clothes have no features.

The artist is forcing us to question what is 'true', creating the illusion that the staircases are interconnected. We can look at the picture from three sides but not from above. As we turn it round sixteen different people come into view, going about their business in or near a house. But they aren't really people: they are just tailors' dummies with featureless heads.

C   Complete each of these paragraphs describing the picture. Pay attention to the way in which your ideas in each paragraph are sequenced.

Looking at the picture from below we can see...
Looking at the picture from the right-hand side we can see...
Looking at the picture from the left-hand side we can see...

D   The class is divided into an even number of pairs. Half the pairs should look at Activity 34, the others at 45. Each pair has a different picture to describe.

Write a description of it which you will later show to another pair. Try to cover some of these aspects:

What has happened?   Are there any people? Who are they?
What is happening now?   What is going to happen next?

E   When you have finished, show your paragraphs to another pair and ask for comments. They should compare your paragraphs with the picture you were looking at in 34 or 45.

15.4   That's magic!   Communication activity

The class is divided into an even number of pairs. Half the pairs should look at Activity 17, the others at 70. You will have a magic trick to learn, which you can then perform to another pair, as your 'audience'.

15.5 Evangelists

A Work in groups. Read this extract and then discuss the questions below.

For richer and poorer: evangelism still thrives in the USA
David Blundy

WITH a flash of diamond and gold from finger, wrist and chest, the Rev Jim Whittington was doing what he does best, talking about imminent death.

"The Death Angel is tapping on your door — tap, tap, tap," said Mr Whittington, tapping his pulpit. "Death is only a heartbeat away. Where will you go if you die in the next two minutes?"

His audience, a mixture of black and white, young and old, in a large circus tent pitched opposite the Walmart supermarket in Augusta, Georgia, last week was riveted and a little disturbed. People batted away mosquitoes in the fetid air, with fans provided free by the local Williams' Funeral Parlour.

"Tap, tap, tap," shouted Mr Whittington. "Hamdillah, Bakdollah," he said, talking momentarily in tongues. "My own body will lie in the cold clay of North Carolina, like a dog," he said.

But release for the audience was on its way. Mr Whittington also offers everlasting life in *de luxe* conditions. "That Queen of England lives in Buckingham Palace. That ain't nothing compared to the house waiting for you in heaven," said Mr Whittington. "It ain't nothing. You have all just won a trip to heaven, the greatest vacation of them all."

And if his audience does not wish to pass away yet, he offers prosperity, health and happiness on earth with a menu of cures and miracles. They can be bought with a contribution to the Whittington Ministry.

For many Americans it is a potent appeal which has made Mr Whittington a millionaire and a rising star in the tough, vicious, competitive world of America's evangelical move-ment. He has a TV ministry, 500,000 followers and is constantly on tour.

Unlike many evangelists who are tight-lipped about their personal wealth, Brother Jim is boastfully prosperous. His cross is encrusted with diamonds, his ring has an enormous diamond, flashing like a laser beam, and he has another which belonged to the entertainer Liberace.

Nor does he pretend to give much help to the poor or the infirm. "I don't have hospitals, schools and all that. I concentrate on eternal life," he said.

He sent some money to Haiti but was vague about how much. He sent food to Jamaica after the hurricane, although he feels the hurricane was God's way of making the Jamaicans less arrogant.

As Mr Whittington pitches his tent in Georgia, the multi-evangelist

- What are your reactions to what you have read?
- What do you think attracts people to the Reverend Jim Whittington?
- What seems to be the writer's attitude to Mr Whittington? How is this shown? How fair is he being, do you think?

B Work in pairs. One of you should look at Activity 20, the other at 40. You'll each have a different half of a newspaper article to read which appeared under this headline:

Mental twist to TV preacher's tale

Ask your partner to tell you what he or she has found out about Jim Bakker, an American TV evangelist and founder of the PTL Ministry.

15.6 Transcendental meditation

A Work in groups. Discuss these questions with your partners:

- Have you ever practised meditation or yoga?
- How do most people cope with stress and with depression?
- What do you already know about Transcendental Meditation?

B 📖 Read the brochure and highlight any unfamiliar words. Then answer the questions in **C** on the next page.

WHAT IS TM?

TM – Transcendental Meditation – is a simple, natural technique which is easy to learn and is profoundly refreshing for the mind and body.

After the practice of TM the mind is calmer and more alert, thinking is clearer and energy is increased.

Coordination between mind and body is greatly enhanced, and people find they can achieve more with less effort. Work, recreation and relationships are all more rewarding.

The benefits from regular practice of TM are cumulative.

TM is practised for twenty minutes twice a day sitting comfortably with the eyes closed.

It is effortless and pleasant, and is suitable for anyone regardless of age, religion, or educational background.

TM works naturally, regardless of expectations or attitude. It can be practised virtually anywhere – even on a noisy bus or train.

HOW DOES IT WORK?

During TM we experience progressively quieter levels of thinking, leading to a refreshing state of *restful alertness*.

At the quieter levels of the mind, we are able to draw on the energy, intelligence, and creativity that are natural to the mind in its most settled state.

As a result, after the practice, we find the mind works more clearly, effectively, and creatively – whatever we are doing.

As the mind settles down to quieter levels of thought, the body also settles down to a deep state of physical rest – twice as deep as during deep sleep.

This rest dissolves accumulated tension and stress, the root cause of a high proportion of illnesses, and allows the body's natural healing mechanisms to function fully.

SCIENCE SAYS YES!

Over 350 scientific research studies on the effects of TM have been conducted at universities and research institutes around the world since 1970. These studies have found TM to be safe, effective and reliable, benefiting many areas of life.

These benefits include:
- Increased happiness and fulfilment
- More stamina and greater efficiency
- Improved job performance and job satisfaction
- Improved academic performance
- Reduction of high blood pressure
- Increased inner calm and contentment
- Decreased anxiety
- Relief from insomnia
- Decreased use of cigarettes and alcohol

- Improvements in angina, bronchial asthma, diabetes, chronic headache, allergies, and other disorders
- Decreased need for tranquillizers, sleeping pills, anti-depressants, and non-prescribed drugs
- Increased emotional stability and maturity
- Greater confidence and self-esteem

"More than 600 doctors in Great Britain practise TM and recommend it to their patients.

TM is something that people can do by themselves, for themselves, and leads to all round improvements in health."

Dr Elizabeth Young

TM has been taught for the past 27 years under the guidance of Maharishi Mahesh Yogi. More than 3 million people have learnt TM in 140 countries worldwide, over 130,000 in the United Kingdom. In Great Britain TM is taught under the auspices of a registered educational charity through 60 local teaching centres.

C According to the brochure,
1 How long does TM take per day?
2 Does TM involve any religious beliefs?
3 What kind of people can benefit from taking up TM?
4 What happens after practising TM?
5 Who introduced the world to the benefits of TM?
6 Where can one learn TM in Britain?

D Work in groups. Find out your partners' reactions to what they have read in the brochure.
  What do they think might be some of the drawbacks of taking up TM?

15.7   My advice is . . .   Creative writing

A Work in pairs. Thinking back to what you found out about TM, what advice would you give to a friend or colleague who you think might benefit from taking it up?

B Here is part of a letter you have received from a friend of yours called Jo. Write a suitable reply to it.

> Anyway, I've been feeling pretty fed up since Alex and I decided to split up. The trouble is that I've been under a lot of pressure at work lately, which has made matters worse and I'm finding it quite hard to get a good night's sleep, too.
> Someone at work suggested that something called, I think, 'transcendental meditation' might help — do you know anything about it?

C Show your letter to a partner and find out whether your partner would have found your advice helpful, if he or she were your friend Jo.

15.8 *Day* and *time*

A   Replace the expressions in italics with a synonym from below. The first is done as an example.

1 I wasn't paying attention because I was *daydreaming* about my holiday.
   thinking pleasant thoughts
2 OK that's enough, I think we'd better *call it a day*.
3 'Do you think you'll be boss soon?' 'Haha, *that'll be the day*!'
4 Today's a *red-letter day*: I take delivery of my new car this afternoon.
5 He hates having to do the same boring chores *day in and day out*.
6 It'll *make his day* if she agrees to go out with him.
7 *One of these days* I'm going to go into my boss's office and tell her what I really think of her.
8 Today has been *one of those days* I'm afraid.
9 Watching that horror film on video *scared the living daylights out of* him.
10 I'm sorry I've made another mistake – *it's not my day* today.
11 Remember when we were at school together? *Those were the days*!

> a bad day   being unlucky   decide to stop   every single day
> make someone happy   thinking pleasant thoughts   eventually
> special day   terrify   that's very unlikely
> that was a wonderful period

B   Fill the gaps in these sentences with one of the expressions below. The first is done as an example.

1 Legends have been told ..*from time immemorial*.. and they are still being told today. Folk stories often begin with the words: '.................'
2 I haven't received a reply from my friend, ... she wrote back.
3 You only have to do two writing tasks in the exam but there's a two-hour ....
4 You can borrow the book, I don't need it ....
5 There's no quick and easy way to learn idioms, it's a .... process.
6 I've warned her .... that she should be more careful but .... she just doesn't seem to take any notice. You know, ... I feel that I'm .... talking to her.
7 A good actor or comedian has to have .... when on stage.
8 There's no hurry, so you can .... and do the work ....
9 If you go to Disneyland I'm sure you'll have ....
10 We didn't manage to get there .... for the start of the meeting – it had already begun. Next time we'll try to be there ....

> at times   for the time being   from time immemorial
> good timing   half the time   in time   in your own time
> it's about time / it's high time   on time   once upon a time
> take your time   the time of your life   time and time again
> time-consuming   time limit   wasting my time

C   Decide which are the most useful idioms in **A** and **B** that you don't already use. Highlight them to help you remember them.

16 Travellers

16.1 Other places

Vocabulary

A Work in groups. Find out from your partners:
- which foreign countries they haven't visited but would like to visit
- which parts of their own country they would like to visit one day
- what they enjoy and don't enjoy about travelling

B Work in pairs. Fill each gap in these sentences with a suitable word from the list below.

1 If, on first acquaintance, people seem a little shy or even unfriendly they may simply be .... of strangers.
2 In very .... regions, outside the main tourist areas, the only people you meet are the locals, who are very ....
3 In some parts of the countryside the local people still wear their traditional .... and the local .... and .... are still kept alive.
4 Ten years ago this little village was delightfully .... but now it has been discovered by the tourists and has become quite ....
5 A long-distance footpath takes hikers along the .... where there is a wonderful .... from the cliffs down to the beach below.
6 People travel to the mountains because of the spectacular ....
7 People love spending time in the countryside because it is so ....
8 Great cities are fascinating places, even though they're too ....
9 However much I travel I still get nervous when I cross a ....
10 The first leg of our .... went smoothly and we arrived at the .... in good time to catch the ferry. Unfortunately, the sea was very rough, so we had a terrible .... and we were all seasick.

> border   coast   commercialised   costume   crossing   crowded
> customs   folklore   frontier   hospitable   inaccessible
> isolated   journey   landscape   peaceful   port   remote
> scenery   suspicious   unspoilt   view   wary

C Now look at the words you DIDN'T choose from the list – where could they be used? What other words (not in the list) can you think of that would fit equally well in the gaps in **B**?

D Work in groups. Ask your partners these questions:
- Why do people travel? Why do YOU travel?
- Can you think of five good and/or bad reasons for wanting to travel?
- What is the difference between a 'traveller' and a 'tourist'?

16.2   The travel writer

A   Work in groups. Find out from your partners if they:
– use a guide book when visiting an unknown place. Why/Why not?
– sometimes read stories about other people's travels. Why/Why not?

B   Read this passage by the English travel writer, Jonathan Raban, and then note down your answers to the questions opposite.

Yet actual journeys aren't like stories at all. At the time, they seem to be mere strings of haps and mishaps, without point or pattern. You get stuck. You meet someone you like. You get lost. You get lonely. You get interested in architecture. You get diarrhoea. You get invited to a party. You get frightened. A stretch of country takes you by surprise. You get 5 homesick. You are, by rapid turns, engrossed, bored, alert, dull, happy, miserable, well and ill. Every day tends to seem out of connection with every other day, until living from moment to moment turns into a habit and travelling itself into a form of ordinary life. You can't remember when it wasn't like this. There is a great deal of liberating pleasure to be had 10 from being abroad in the world, continuously on the move, like a lost balloon, but a journey, at least as long as it is actually taking place, is the exact opposite of a story. It is a shapeless, unsifted, endlessly shifting accumulation of experience.

For travelling is inherently a plotless, disordered, chaotic affair, where 15 writing insists on connection, order, plot, signification. It may take a year or more to see that there was any point to the thing at all, and more years still to make it yield an articulate story. Memory, not the notebook, holds the key. I try to keep a notebook when I'm on the move (largely because writing in it makes one feel that one's at work, despite all appearances to 20 the contrary) but hardly ever find anything in the notebook that's worth using later. Trifles are described at inordinate length. Events that now seem important aren't mentioned at all. The keeper of the notebook sounds stupid and confused. He grouses too much about tides and timetables, and all the forgettable mechanics of the journey; he fails to 25 notice what I remember observing in near-photographic detail. When I'm writing the book, I get precious little help from him . . . the odd proper name, a date, an ascertainable fact here and there, but little or nothing in the way of intelligent comprehension of what he was doing at the time. Why was he so blind? Because he was travelling and I am writing, and the 30 two activities are chalk and cheese.

Memory, though, is always telling stories to itself, filing experience in narrative form. It feeds irrelevancies to the shredder, enlarges on crucial details, makes links and patterns, finds symbols, constructs plots. In memory, the journey takes shape and grows; in the notebook it merely 35 languishes, with the notes themselves like a pile of cigarette butts confronted the morning after a party.

In 1982, I took six months to sail slowly round the British Isles, stopping at every place I'd known as a child and adolescent. A year later, I was still trying to begin the book that was based on the journey. I had 30,000 40 words, but they seemed forced and wrong. There was writing, but as yet no story worth the telling. There was a title *Foreign Land*, but it didn't fit the writing.

(from *For Love and Money* by Jonathan Raban)

1 How is a real journey different from a story?
2 Are journeys a happy experience for the writer?
3 Why doesn't he write his books straight after his return from a journey?
4 How is a travel writer 'two people'?
5 Why does he always make notes during a journey?
6 Why are his memories of a journey more productive than the notes he made at the time?
7 What useful information can he get from his notebook?
8 How did the writer travel round Britain in 1982?

C Highlight these words in the text and try to deduce their meanings without using a dictionary. Then choose the word on the right that is closest in meaning. The first is done as an example.

1 *haps* (line 2)   misfortunes   pleasant happenings √   disasters
2 *accumulation* (line 14) collection   lack   selection
3 *inherently* (line 15)   by the way   by no means   by nature
4 *articulate* (line 18)   long   amusing   clear
5 *trifles* (line 22)   meetings   unimportant things   exciting events
6 *inordinate* (line 22)   fascinating   excessive   insufficient
7 *grouses* (line 24)   writes   celebrates   grumbles
8 *languishes* (line 36)   loses vitality   becomes interesting   improves

D Work in groups. Ask your partners these questions:
• How do your own experiences of travelling compare with Jonathan Raban's?
• Have you ever written a diary or used a notebook during a holiday?
• Do you take photos during a holiday? Why / Why not?
• Which travel book would you recommend to someone who was visiting your own region for the first time?

E Work in groups. Tell your partners about a long journey or holiday that you remember well.

16.3   A rendezvous   Reading

The American travel writer, Paul Theroux, also travelled round the coast of the British Isles in 1982 – but he was on foot.

Paul and Jonathan arranged to meet in Brighton on the South Coast of England, where their journeys coincided.

Work in pairs. One of you should look at Activity 11, the other at 27. One of you will read Paul's account of the meeting, the other Jonathan's.

When you've read your passage discuss these questions:
• How were they both feeling in anticipation of the meeting?
• What lies did they tell?
• What does each writer say about the other's behaviour?
• Whose book would you like to read more of: Paul's or Jonathan's?

16.4 Comparing and contrasting Grammar

The Solar System: statistics

	Distance from Sun (million km)	Length of one year	Diameter at equator (km)	Length of one day
THE SUN	—	—	1,322,900	—
Mercury	58	88 days	4,880	59 days
Venus	108	223 days	12,104	243 days
Earth	150	365¼ days	12,756	24 hours
Mars	229	687 days	6,787	24½ hours
Jupiter	780	12 years	142,800	9¾ hours
Saturn	1,427	29½ years	120,000	10¼ hours
Uranus	2,871	84 years	51,800	11 hours
Neptune	4,496	165 years	49,500	16 hours
Pluto	5,913	248 years	6,000	6⅓ days

(The Moon is ⅓ million km from the Earth and 3,473 km in diameter.)

A   The examples below (about space travel!) show the use of comparatives and superlatives. Fill the gaps with suitable words, using the information given in the table.

1 The Earth is closer to the Sun than Mars.
2 Venus is .... from the Sun .... Mercury.
3 Pluto is the most distant planet from the Sun.
4 Mercury is .... the Sun.
5 Jupiter is not as close to the Sun as Mars.
6 Jupiter is further from the Sun than Mars.
7 Venus is much closer to the Sun than Saturn.
8 Neptune .... the Earth.
9 Pluto's year is nothing like as short as Mercury's.
10 A Martian year is about twice as long as an Earth year.
11 A year on Jupiter is about half the length of a year on Saturn.
12 A day on Uranus is .... Earth.
13 A year on Venus .... a year on Mercury.
14 Venus is about the same size as Earth.
15 A day on Mars is slightly longer than a day on Earth.
16 A day on Jupiter is .... Saturn.
17 A day on Neptune is eight hours shorter than a day on Earth.
18 A day on Venus is .... a year!

B   Work in pairs or alone. Write nine more sentences, comparing the planets. Each sentence should be about a different planet.

▶ Compare your sentences with another pair's (or with a partner's).

C Work in groups. Discuss the pros and cons of space travel and exploration. Would you like to travel to another planet yourself one day?

▶ Report the main points of your discussion to the rest of the class.

D Work in pairs. Fill the gaps in these sentences with suitable words.

1 The .... I travel, the less ....
2 Winter holidays are .... than summer holidays.
3 Travelling by bus isn't .... as travelling by train.
4 To get from Paris to London it takes .... to go through the Channel Tunnel .... go by plane.
5 China is the third .... in the world.
6 China has .... in the world.
7 Liechtenstein is one .... in Europe.
8 The older I get, the more ....
9 The .... a journey is, the more ....
10 Rather than travel abroad, I'd prefer to ....
11 The higher the mountain, the ....
12 The longer I am away from home, the harder it is ....

E Look at these phrases which can be used when comparing things. Decide which you'd find more useful in writing than in conversation.

Describing similarities
   ... (A) ...   is very like   is similar to   is identical to
is much the same as   is comparable to   is equivalent to
reminds me of   resembles   seems like   corresponds to
has a lot in common with   ... (B) ...

   Similarly, ...   In the same way, ...   By the same token, ...

Describing differences
   ... (B) ...   is very unlike   is quite different from   isn't the same as
differs from   bears no resemblance to   stands out as
has very little in common with   ... (C) ...

   On the other hand, ...   In contrast, ...   Conversely, ...

F Work in pairs. Choose any of the topics below that take your fancy and MAKE NOTES on both the similarities AND the differences. Then write a couple of paragraphs, using some of the phrases given above. When you've finished, show your paragraphs to another pair and ask them to comment.

Living in the country	↔	Living in a large city
Staying in a hotel	↔	Camping or self-catering
Life in your country	↔	Life in Britain
Tourism nowadays	↔	Tourism ten years ago
The climate in your country	↔	The climate in Britain
Working in an office	↔	Working in a factory
Learning English	↔	Learning your language
The British sense of humour	↔	Your country's sense of humour
Travelling today	↔	Travelling in the future

16.5   Using synonyms and opposites – 2

▶ Before you start these exercises, look again at 12.5.

A   Work in pairs. Rearrange these adjectives according to their meaning:

Very friendly → friendly → → unfriendly → very unfriendly
   *affable   approachable   courteous   hospitable   hostile
   inhospitable   insulting   malicious   reserved   sarcastic
   sociable   sullen   surly   suspicious of strangers
   wary of strangers   welcoming*

Thinking of some places you know or have visited, how would you describe
your FIRST IMPRESSION of the people or atmosphere in each place?

B   Work in pairs. Look together at the words in italics in this section:
a) Discuss the meaning of the words. (In some cases you may feel that some
   of the words fall between the categories, or even exceed them.)
b) Make sure you can pronounce them – use a dictionary if necessary.
c) Decide which can be used to describe the things listed below.

1 Very pleasant → pleasant → → unpleasant → very unpleasant
   *agreeable   annoying   appalling   atrocious   awful   charming
   delicious   delightful   disgusting   dreadful   enchanting
   frightful   horrible   picturesque   spectacular   splendid
   wonderful*
   a person   a cocktail   a glass of home-made wine   a village
   a beach   a flight   a holiday   a meal   a view

2 Very old → old → → new → very new
   *all the rage   ancient   childish   dilapidated   disused
   historical   just out   the latest   obsolete   run-down
   traditional   ultra-modern   unfashionable   up-to-date
   worn-out   youthful*
   a city   a video   a game   an evening dress   a dinner jacket
   a carpet   an airport   a district   a hairstyle   a record or cassette
   a church   my flat or house

3 Very safe → safe → → dangerous → very dangerous
   *exposed   guarded   harmful   harmless   hazardous   insecure
   precarious   protected   reliable   risky   secure   unsafe
   vulnerable*
   a city   a castle   a friend   a method   a pile of crockery   a job
   a drug   an apartment block   a flight in an airliner
   a flight in a hot-air balloon   New York   the district I live in

4 Very far → far → → near → very near
   *a long way away   accessible   adjacent   close   convenient
   distant   faraway   handy   isolated   nearby   neighbouring
   next door   opposite   out-of-the-way   remote*
   a city   a grocer's shop   a friend's flat   a village   Australia
   my hometown   my flat   a café

140

5 Very quiet → quiet → → noisy → very noisy
   calm   deafening   earsplitting   hushed   loud
   loud enough to wake the dead   peaceful   restful   restrained
   silent   sleepy   unobtrusive   uproarious
   a city street   a park   a hotel room   wallpaper   a check shirt
   a tie   an explosion   a party   the sea   a group of people

C   Work in pairs. One of you should note down the POSITIVE aspects, the other
the NEGATIVE aspects of a place you both know. Then compare your ideas.

16.6   Describing a place   Functions

A   You'll hear a description of these places:
   Rome   New York   Amsterdam   Austin, Texas

1 Before you listen, find out what your partner knows about each city.

2 [cassette] Listen to the recording and make notes on the main points.

3 Discuss with a partner which of the places sounded most attractive.

B   Work in groups and discuss how you would answer these questions
about YOUR OWN CITY OR TOWN (or perhaps the district you live in).
   Try to imagine what it might seem like to a stranger. If you're very
familiar with a place it's hard not to assume that 'it's obvious what it's like'
– so you may have to try to distance yourself.

First impressions   Imagine you're returning there after being away – as
   you arrive there, what strikes you about the place? What kind of
   atmosphere is there? What is special about the place?
Basic facts   How big is it and where is it? (population of
   metropolitan area, distance from other cities, distance from coast, etc.)
Transport   How do people get about within the city and how do
   they get into it or out of it? (amount of traffic, public transport, commuter
   travel, rail connections, airport, etc.)
Districts   What are the various areas of the city and what are
   they like? (old town, commercial areas, industrial zones, shopping centre,
   residential districts, suburbs, slums and shanty towns, etc.)
Buildings   What is the style of the architecture? Where do
   people live? (public and commercial buildings, blocks of flats, etc.)
Open spaces   Where do people gather together out of doors
   (squares, parks, open-air cafés, etc.)? When is the weather suitable for this?
Roads and streets   What kinds of roads are characteristic of the place?
   (main thoroughfares, back streets, avenues, boulevards, alleyways, etc.)
Entertainment   What do members of the community do in their
   leisure time? (sports, cinemas, theatre or opera, museums and galleries,
   night clubs, restaurants, bars and cafés, etc.)
Employment   How do people earn their living? (main industries,
   commerce, public sector, etc.) What is the unemployment situation?

⟫→

Education   What facilities are there for secondary and tertiary
education? (schools, colleges, university, evening classes, etc.)

Visitors   Would you recommend the city as a place to visit as
a tourist? What are the sights that tourists visit? What might a newcomer
from abroad find strange or difficult about living there?

YOU   How do you fit in to all this? What do you like
about the place? What do you dislike about it?

▶ What other important information is NOT covered by the questions?

C   Now split up and find someone from another group who does NOT
know the place you've been discussing very well. Find out about your new
partner's city and tell him or her about yours.

D   Write a description of your own city or town, introducing it to British
or American people who have not been there before. Explain the essential
differences between your city or town and places in the UK or USA.

OR

Make notes for a presentation to the rest of the class about your city, town
or district. Give a short talk to the class about it, using your notes.

16.7   *Come, go* and *run*   Verbs and idioms

A   Fill the gaps with suitable forms of the phrasal verbs below:

1 A button has .... my shirt
2 Is Ann .... John?
3 Oh dear, the milk has ....
4 She .... unexpected difficulties.
5 Don't wait for me, ...

6 I'm thinking of .... the competition.
7 I've .... stamps: I need some more.
8 A bomb .... outside the embassy.
9 Call an ambulance, someone's been ....!
10 If you didn't understand I'll .... it again.

    come off   come up against   go ahead   go in for   go off
    go off   go out with   go over/through   run out of   run over

B   Replace the phrases in italics with suitable forms of the expressions
below.

1 We'll need one for every person so can you *photocopy* twenty copies?
2 I don't trust that dog, it looks as if it might *attack* me.
3 If I was given a choice where I could live, I'd *choose* living in a city.
4 He was the last person we expected to *produce* the answer.
5 I used to love travelling alone, but now I've *stopped enjoying* it.
6 I can't go abroad because my passport has *expired*.
7 A holiday doesn't always *match* your expectations.
8 At the beginning of her holiday she *caught* flu.
9 I *agree with* you on the first point but not on the second.
10 I'll *discuss* this with you later, when I've *examined* the figures again.

    come up to   come up with   go along with   go down with
    go for   go for   go off   go over   go through/over   run off
    run out

142

17 Love stories

17.1 Talking about love – and stories
Vocabulary

A   Work in groups. Ask your partners these questions:

● What were the titles of the last two books you read? What were they about and who were they written by?
● How much time do you spend reading – during the week, at weekends and on holiday?

B   In these sentences tick the expressions given that will fit in the gaps and <u>underline</u> or highlight the ones that you think DON'T fit. The first is begun as an example.

1 It's such a(n) .... book you won't be able to put it down.
   amusing ✔   <u>best-selling</u>   entertaining ✔   gripping ✔   literary   poetic   popular   predictable   thought-provoking   well-written
2 Her characters are so lifelike and attractive that it's easy to .... them.
   empathise with   **feel sorry for**   follow   identify with   laugh at
3 I enjoy her books because her style of writing is very ....
   clear   complex   hard to understand   lucid   readable   simple
4 Have a look at this .... in the book – it's really amusing.
   appendix   bibliography   blurb   chapter   character   district   dustjacket   extract   footnote   foreword   index   page   paragraph   passage   preface   quotation   section   unit
5 There are many genres of literature, but as bedtime reading I prefer ....
   autobiographies   best-sellers   biographies   classic novels   comic novels   crime stories   drama   historical novels   mysteries   non-fiction   poetry   propaganda   romances   science-fiction   thrillers   Westerns   whodunits

▶ Now look again at the words that didn't fit in the sentences above – decide when you would use them.

C   Fill the gaps with suitable words.

1 If a story is told in the ...., the narrator is a character in the story.
2 The story concerns the .... between two young people.
3 If you don't want to refer to someone as your boyfriend/girlfriend or husband/wife you can call them your ....
4 How long had they been .... before they got engaged?
5 At a wedding the most important people are the .... and ....
6 To me, a book or film with no love interest in it tends to be ....

》》→

D   Rearrange these expressions, grading them according to their meanings:

love → like → → dislike → hate

HE/SHE . . .

is madly in love with	*can't bear*	*is attracted to*
fancies	*can't live without*	*is crazy about*
is devoted to	*is fond of*	*doesn't think much of*
is indifferent to	*is infatuated with*	*is keen on*
thinks the world of	*admires*	*detests*
doesn't get on with	*is incompatible with*	*gets on really well with*
can't stand the sight of	*loathes*	*has gone off*
has fallen out with	*adores*	*puts up with*

. . . HER/HIM

E   Work in groups. Ask your partners:
– how many stories and films they can think of that *don't* involve any
  aspect of love or relationships between people
– what kinds of books they enjoy reading and why
– what kinds of books they never read and why

17.2   Small World   Reading

A   Read the passage carefully (preferably at home) *before* you look at the
questions on the next page.

THE job of check-in clerk at Heathrow, or any other airport,
is not a glamorous or particularly satisfying one. The work is
mechanical and repetitive: inspect the ticket, check it against
the passenger list on the computer terminal, tear out the
ticket from its folder, check the baggage weight, tag the   5
baggage, ask Smoking or Non-smoking, allocate a seat, issue
a boarding pass. The only variation in this routine occurs
when things go wrong – when flights are delayed or can-
celled because of bad weather or strikes or technical hitches.
Then the checker bears the full brunt of the customers' fury   10
without being able to do anything to alleviate it. For the most
part the job is a dull and monotonous one, processing people
who are impatient to conclude their brief business with you,
and whom you will probably never see again.
    Cheryl Summerbee, a checker for British Airways in   15
Terminal One at Heathrow, did not, however, complain of
boredom. Though the passengers who passed through her
hands took little notice of her, she took a lot of notice of
them. She injected interest into her job by making quick
assessments of their characters and treating them accord-   20
ingly. Those who were rude or arrogant or otherwise
unpleasant she put in uncomfortable or inconvenient seats,
next to the toilets, or beside mothers with crying babies.

Those who made a favourable impression she rewarded with the best seats, and whenever possible placed them next to some attractive member of the opposite sex. In Cheryl Summerbee's hands, seat allocation was a fine art, as delicate and complex an operation as arranging blind dates between clients of a lonely hearts agency. It gave her a glow of satisfaction, a pleasant sense of doing good by stealth, to reflect on how many love affairs, and even marriages, she must have instigated between people who imagined they had met by pure chance.

Cheryl Summerbee was very much in favour of love. She firmly believed that it made the world go round, and did her bit to keep the globe spinning on its axis by her discreet management of the seating on British Airways Tridents. On the shelf under her counter she kept a Bills and Moon romance to read in those slack periods when there were no passengers to deal with. The one she was reading at the moment was called *Love Scene*. It was about a girl called Sandra who went to work as a nanny for a film director whose wife had died tragically in a car accident, leaving him with two young children to look after. Of course Sandra fell in love with the film director, though unfortunately he was in love with the actress taking the leading role in the film he was making – or was he just pretending to be in love with her to keep her sweet? Of course he was! Cheryl Summerbee had read enough Bills and Moon romances to know that – indeed she hardly needed to read any further to predict exactly how the story would end. With half her mind she despised these love stories, but she devoured them with greedy haste, like cheap sweets. Her own life was, so far, devoid of romance – not for lack of propositions, but because she was a girl of old-fashioned moral principle. So she was still waiting for Mr Right to appear. She had no very clear image of what he would look like except that he would have a hard chest and firm thighs. All the heroes of Bills and Moon romances seemed to have hard chests and firm thighs.

(From *Small World* by David Lodge)

B Work in pairs. Ask your partner these questions about the text:

1 Is this the kind of book you'd like to read more of? Why (not)?
2 What is the equivalent to 'Bills and Moon' type romances in your country? How popular are photo romances? Do you read them?
3 How do you predict the story that Cheryl was reading will end?
4 How do you predict Cheryl's own story will end?
5 Do you think Cheryl's job sounds 'dull and monotonous'? In what way?
6 What kind of person do you imagine Cheryl to be?
7 Give some examples of jobs generally regarded as 'glamorous' or 'satisfying'.
8 What is the difference between a *proposition* (line 54) and a *proposal*?
9 What did you enjoy most in this passage?

C ht Highlight these words and phrases in the text and see if you can deduce their meanings from the context. Underline the words or phrases that help you to deduce the meanings.

a technical hitch (line 9)   *made the world go round* (line 35)
the full brunt (line 10)   *did her bit* (line 35–6)
to alleviate (line 11)   *slack periods* (line 39)
accordingly (line 20–1)   *a nanny* (line 42)
a blind date (line 28)   *keep her sweet* (line 48)
a lonely hearts agency (line 29)   *devoid of* (line 53)
by stealth (line 30)   *not for lack of* (line 54)
instigated (line 32)

▶ Use a dictionary to look up any phrases you couldn't deduce the meanings of.

D Find an example in the text of each of the following:

1 HUMOUR – something that made you smile
2 INFORMATION – something you didn't realise or know before
3 OPINION – a point of view expressed by the writer
4 SOCIAL COMMENT – a comment on the way people behave
5 EMPATHY – something that made you share the writer's or Cheryl's feelings

E This is the cover of a genuine Mills and Boon romance:

Work in pairs. What happens if the roles are reversed (i.e. male journalist and female lighthouse keeper)?

Draft a blurb for the back cover of another M&B paperback romance.

17.3   How romantic are you?   Listening

A   We asked some people this question: 'Do you believe in love?'
Work in groups. Listen to the recording and then find out your partners'
reactions by asking them these questions:

- To what extent do you share the views of each speaker?
- Which speakers do you agree with and disagree with? Why?
- Which speaker would you most (and least) like to meet in person?

- What is *your* definition of 'love'?
- What is the difference between 'being in love' with someone and 'loving' someone?
- Are you a romantic person? What are your reactions to this magazine cover?

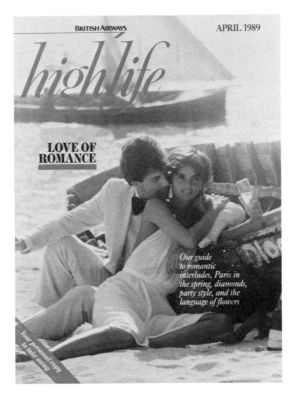

B   Find a cassette of a favourite modern British or American song – a song
about love or, if you prefer, about something else. Write down the words or
run off a copy, so that the others in your group can see them.

Present your song to the others in your group and explain why you like it –
what makes it special? Show them the words and point out your favourite lines.

17.4   First meetings   Storytelling and listening

A   Work in groups. Discuss these questions with your partners:
- How easy is it in your country/city for young men and women to meet
  and spend time alone together?
- At what age is it customary for people to get married and how long do
  engagements last?
- How much have 'boy-meets-girl' customs changed since your parents were
  young?

>>>→

B   We asked some people to describe their first meeting with their present partner. This is how their replies began:

'I was on my way home from junior high school ...'
'I'd arranged to have a drink with a friend of mine ...'
'We met at a fancy-dress party ...'
'I'd arranged to go to the cinema with a group of friends ...'
'I first met him when he was on a boat and I was on the river bank ...'

Work in pairs. Use your imagination to work out how TWO of the stories might have continued.
   Then tell your stories to another pair.

C   🔲   Now listen to the stories – how close were your ideas to what really happened?

17.5   Expressing feelings   Effective writing

A   In a conversation we often show our attitude or feelings through smiles, frowns, sympathetic expressions, etc. In writing we have to express these feelings in words.
   Add three more words that express each of these feelings. The first is begun as an example.

'How marvellous!'	→ I am/was delighted	_pleased_	_thrilled_	
'Oh dear!'	→ I am/was dismayed			
'What a surprise!'	→ I am/was amazed			
'How annoying!'	→ I am/was annoyed			
'How strange!'	→ I am/was puzzled			

▶ Look again at 2.5 and 2.6 to remind yourself of some of the vocabulary used to express feelings.

B   Imagine that you have just received this card from Pam and Max, two former classmates of yours. It's quite a surprise because you didn't even know Pam and Max were seeing each other.

> *Sandra and Rupert Dupont*
> *are pleased to announce the engagement*
> *of their daughter*
> **Pamela**
> *to*
> **Max Steiner**
> *eldest son of Maria and Richard Steiner*
> *of Geneva, Switzerland*

Write a letter to Pam and Max. Imagine that you haven't been in touch with either of them for ages.

Here are some phrases that can be used when you're sending someone greetings or congratulations:

```
Dear ...  ,

Congratulations to you (both) on your ... engagement / exam
success / new job / wedding, etc.
I was ... to hear that ...

I really must apologise for not having kept in touch with you.
Since we were last in touch, a lot of things have happened: ...
You'll never believe what has happened to me ...

Please give my love / regards / best wishes to ...
My very best wishes for the future.

                        All my love,
                My very best wishes,
                All the very best,
```

17.6 A wedding . . .   Listening and creative writing

A You'll hear six people describing weddings they have attended. Make notes on the aspects of each wedding that are DIFFERENT from your own experiences of weddings in your country.
   Which of the weddings sounded the most fun?

B Work in groups. Find out if your partners have ever attended a wedding and get them to describe it to you. Find out how the various guests at the wedding felt – was everyone happy?

C Write a description of a traditional (or unconventional) wedding in your own country, preferably one that you have attended.
OR
Write a description of another family event that you have participated in: a birthday celebration, an anniversary party, a christening, etc.

A These are the opening paragraphs of six well-known books. First of all just read them through and work out what kind of book each one is.

1 EMMA WOODHOUSE, handsome, clever, and rich, with a comfortable home and happy disposition, seemed to unite some of the best blessings of existence; and had lived nearly twenty-one years in the world with very little to distress or vex her.
   She was the youngest of the two daughters of a most

2 IT was the best of times, it was the worst of times, it was the age of wisdom, it was the age of foolishness, it was the epoch of belief, it was the epoch of incredulity, it was the season of Light, it was the season of Darkness, it was the spring of hope, it was the winter of despair, we had everything before us, we had nothing before us, we were all going direct to Heaven, we were all going direct the other way – in short, the period was so far like the present period, that some of its noisiest authorities insisted on its being received, for good or for evil, in the superlative degree of comparison only.
   There were a king with a large jaw and a queen with a plain face,

3 THERE were four of us – George, and William Samuel Harris, and myself, and Montmorency. We were sitting in my room, smoking, and talking about how bad we were – bad from a medical point of view I mean, of course.
   We were all feeling seedy, and we were getting quite

4 Last night I dreamt I went to Manderley again. It seemed to me I stood by the iron gate leading to the drive, and for a while I could not enter, for the way was barred to me. There was a padlock and chain upon the gate. I called in my dream to the lodge-keeper, and had no answer, and peering closer through the rusted spokes of the gate I saw the lodge was uninhabited.
   No smoke came from the chimney, and the little lattice

5 IT was a bright cold day in April, and the clocks were striking thirteen. Winston Smith, his chin nuzzled into his breast in an attempt to escape the vile wind, slipped quickly through the glass doors of Victory Mansions, though not quickly enough to prevent a swirl of gritty dust from entering with him.
   The hallway smelt of boiled cabbage and old rag mats

6 I was three or perhaps four years old when I realized that I had been born into the wrong body, and should really be a girl. I remember the moment well, and it is the earliest memory of my life.
   I was sitting beneath my mother's piano, and her music was falling around me like cataract

B  Work in pairs. Highlight TWO phrases or ideas in each extract that intrigue you, as readers, and encourage you to read on.

C Work in groups of three. Student A should look at Activity 5, student B at 19 and C at 75. You'll each have more information about the books to share with your partners.

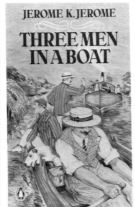

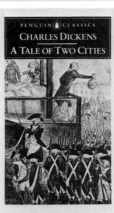

D Make notes on a favourite book of yours. Explain why you liked the book, what it is about and why you recommended it to other readers.

- Style – how well-written and readable is it
- About the writer – his or her background and other books
- The characters – what kind of people they are
- Plot – what happens in the story
- Setting – where the action takes place
- Why you enjoyed it
- Why other people would enjoy it

Prepare a short talk about it to the other members of your group or the whole class.

Give a presentation about the book and answer questions about it.

E Write a description of the book persuading someone else to read it.

Show your written work to two or three other people and read their work too.

17.8 Head over heels . . .

The idioms in this section are all connected in some way with the head – 18.7 looks at idioms connected with other parts of the body.

A Fill the gaps in these sentences with *head*, *brain* or *mind*. The first is done as an example.

1 The driver of the car that overtook us needs his ___head___ examined.
2 If there's an emergency, don't panic – try to keep your ___
3 They were in two ___s whether to get married.
4 We couldn't solve the problem, but suddenly I had a ___wave.
5 I'll spin a coin to see – do you want to call ___s or tails?
6 That's too difficult for me to follow – it's over my ___
7 I couldn't make up my ___ whether to phone or write.
8 They were ___ over heels in love.
9 She can't climb a ladder because she has no ___ for heights.
10 She's very good at maths – she has a good ___ for figures.
11 A good book can help to take your ___ off your troubles.
12 When it comes to politics, I try to keep an open ___
13 He's been behaving very strangely – he seems to be off his ___
14 I'm sorry I didn't make that phone call, it slipped my ___
15 If there's a problem to solve, two ___s are better than one.

B Fill these gaps with *hair*, *face*, *eye*, *nose*, *ear* or *mouth*.

1 I can't tell you exactly what to do – you'll have to play it by ___
2 I tried to catch the waiter's ___ but he didn't look my way.
3 I have to go away for a while, can you keep an ___ on them for me?
4 They normally see ___ to ___ but in this case they disagreed.
5 I was just going to say that – you took the words out of my ___
6 During the wedding someone started giggling and I couldn't keep a straight ___
7 Windsurfing looks ever so easy – I could do it with my ___s shut.
8 When they said they'd got engaged I couldn't believe my ___s.
9 She's such a snob – she looks down her ___ at everyone.
10 Don't bother to tell me how to get there – I'll follow my ___
11 You can't support both sides at once – don't be so two-___d.
12 If you admit making such a serious mistake you may lose ___
13 He knew the risks and went into it with his ___s open.
14 There's no real difference – you're just splitting ___s.
15 Anything you say to them goes in one ___ and out the other.

C Work in pairs. Decide together which are the TEN most useful idioms in **A** and **B** that you don't already use.

Highlight them to help you to remember them. Then compose five sentences, each including one of the idioms you have chosen.
  Compare your sentences with another pair.

18 Body and mind

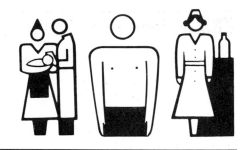

18.1 How are you?

A Work in groups. Ask your partners these questions:
- How are you?
- If you ask people in your country 'How are you?', do they usually tell you about their health – or do they always say they are well?
- What are the most common causes of people taking days off work or school due to illness in your country?

B You'll need to use a dictionary to answer some of the following questions. If possible, prepare this section at home before the lesson. In each case, one answer is given as an example.

1 How many ways can you think of for someone to keep fit?
   e.g. *Playing football...*
2 How do the various people you know stay slim (or try to get slim)?
   e.g. *By eating less...*
3 How many different illnesses or diseases can you think of? e.g. *Measles*
4 How do people tend to feel if they ...?
   don't take enough exercise – *unfit*   have drunk too much   have overslept
   have just run a marathon   eat only junk food   have had a bad night
   have had a bad day   have had a busy day
5 Who do you see if you ...?
   have toothache – *a dentist*   have sore feet   need an injection
   are having a baby   need an operation   have a sore throat
   are having a nervous breakdown
6 What would be the symptoms of each of these medical problems?
   Measles – *spots or a rash*   hayfever   flu   migraine   food poisoning
   sprained ankle   schizophrenia   a cut finger   a broken arm
7 What would be the normal treatment for each of these ailments?
   a cut finger – *put a plaster on it*   hayfever   a cold   bruise   scratch
   dog bite   headache   toothache   graze   bee sting   mosquito bite
   aching back   sprained wrist   a bad cough
8 Which of these people work in a hospital?
   anaesthetist ✓   consultant   convalescent   matron   midwife   outpatient
   porter   sister   specialist   surgeon   vet   victim

C Work in groups. Ask your partners these questions:
- What do you do if someone has hiccups?
- Imagine you have a friend who takes no exercise at all, what advice would you give him or her?
- Do you trust or mistrust doctors, nurses and dentists? Why?

153

18.2 Emphasis Grammar and pronunciation

A Work in pairs. Decide what is the difference in emphasis (if any) between these sentences:

1 Tim spends too much time eating and drinking.
Tim does spend too much time eating and drinking.
Tim spends far too much time eating and drinking.
Tim really spends too much time eating and drinking.

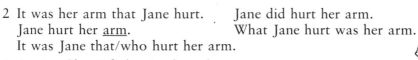

2 It was her arm that Jane hurt. Jane did hurt her arm.
Jane hurt her <u>arm</u>. What Jane hurt was her arm.
It was Jane that/who hurt her arm.

3 Ann's self-satisfied attitude makes me angry.
What makes me really angry is Ann's self-satisfied attitude.
It's Ann's self-satisfied attitude that makes me really angry.
Ann's self-satisfied attitude does make me really angry.
I'm angry because of Ann's self-satisfied attitude.
I <u>am</u> angry because of Ann's self-satisfied attitude.

4 <u>Chris</u> needs to take more exercise. Chris <u>needs</u> to take more exercise.
Chris needs to take <u>more</u> exercise. Chris needs to take more <u>exercise</u>.

B 🔲 You'll hear some short extracts from a conversation. Choose the phrase below that shows the IMPLICATION of each statement, putting the number(s) beside the phrases. The first three are done as examples.

1 to 7: 'Terry had a stomachache because the plums he ate were unripe.'

not the <u>apples</u> ..**1**...**3**.... not a <u>head</u>ache ....
not <u>over</u>ripe .... not <u>Sally</u> ...**2**....
it <u>is</u> really true .... not the one <u>you</u> ate ....

8 to 12: 'I need more time if I'm going to take up a new sport.'

not <u>money</u> .... not <u>less</u> time ....
not a new <u>hobby</u> .... not if <u>you</u> are going to ....

13 to 18: 'Most people like Helen because she has a friendly personality.'

not <u>everyone</u> .... they don't <u>dis</u>like her ....
not an <u>unfriendly</u> one .... not a friendly <u>smile</u> ....
they don't like <u>another person</u> ....

19 to 24: 'Ted has a cough because he smokes 30 cigarettes a day.'

not <u>Helen</u> .... not a <u>sore throat</u> ....
not <u>thirteen</u> .... not <u>cigars</u> ....
not per <u>week</u> ....

C Study these examples and then do the exercise in D below.

It is/was . . . that . . . can be used to emphasise almost any part of the sentence, apart from the verb.

Dr K. gave an injection to the wrong patient yesterday.

It was *Dr K.* who gave an injection to the wrong patient yesterday.

It was *the wrong patient* that Dr K. gave an injection to yesterday.

It was *yesterday* that Dr K. gave an injection to the wrong patient.

It was *an injection* that Dr K. gave to the wrong patient.

BUT NOT: **X** It was give an injection that ... **X**

To emphasise the whole sentence we can use **What . . . is/was . . .**

What Dr K. did was *give an injection to the wrong patient*!

What happened was that *Dr K. gave an injection to the wrong patient*!

What Dr K. did the day before was *operate on the wrong patient*!!

★ Note that **What . . . is/was . . .** can be used to emphasise the subject, object or verb:

What Dr K. gave to the wrong patient was *an injection.*

What the wrong patient was given by Dr K. was *an injection.*

What caused the mistake was *carelessness.*

What Dr K. did was *resign.*

But we use **The person / The one who . . . is/was . . .** if the subject or object is a person:

The person who gave the injection was *Dr K.*

The patient who Dr K. gave the injection to was *Mrs V.*

BUT NOT: **X** Who gave the injection was Dr K. **X**

     X Who was given the injection was the wrong patient. **X**

D Rewrite the sentences, changing the emphasis in the ways shown. The first is done as an example.

1 Terry had a stomachache after eating unripe plums.

It was Terry ... *who had a stomachache after eating unripe plums.*

It was eating ...

It was the unripe ... .   Terry was the one ...

2 I need more time if I'm going to take up a sport.

What I ...

It's ...   More time is ...

3 People like Helen because she has a friendly personality.

What people ...

What Helen has ...   Helen does ...

4 Ted has a cough because he smokes too many cigarettes.

It's because ... .   It's Ted ...

What Ted ...   The person who ...

5 Katy worried about her health all the time and this made her ill.

What Katy did was ...   What Katy worried ...

What happened was ...   What made Katy ill ...

E  Work in pairs. One of you should look at Activity 15, the other at 76. You'll each see some information that MAY be true and some information that you KNOW to be true about some friends of yours who have been away from work or class recently.

This is how your conversation might begin:

> I think Adrian was away because he had a cold.

> No, it's Claire who had a cold. Adrian was the one who had to go to hospital for an X-ray.

> Oh really, I thought it was Flora who had to have an X-ray.

18.3 What is The Body Shop?

Read and discuss

 Work in groups of three. Student A should look at Activity 7, student B at 22 and C at 33.

You will each have some information to read about the history of The Body Shop and its philosophy.

When you're ready, ask your partners these questions:

- What did you find out about The Body Shop?
- Which particular pieces of information impressed you most?
- What makes The Body Shop and its philosophy different from the mainstream cosmetics industry?

18.4 Using prefixes

Word study

A Work in pairs. Use one of these negative prefixes to form the OPPOSITE of each of the adjectives below. Here are some examples:

un	stable satisfactory helpful
dis	agreeable satisfied
in	accurate accessible adequate
im	mature moral patient perfect
il	legal legitimate

acceptable   approachable   appropriate   bearable   compatible
complete   conscious   contented   convenient   credible
decisive   desirable   discreet   excusable   experienced   faithful
flexible   foreseen   frequent   grateful   healthy   hospitable
legible   literate   logical   mortal   natural   obedient
organised   passive   personal   polite   probable   readable
respectful   sane   sociable   sufficient   variable   visible   willing

B Look at these examples of prefixes that alter the meaning of verbs. Then use the prefixes to alter the meaning of the verbs listed below. (Some can be used more than once.)

mis   calculate   understand   spell
      = wrongly: *'Accommodation' is a word that is frequently misspelt.*
out   grow   live   number
      = beyond, exceeding: *The girls outnumbered the boys at the party.*
re   write   build   decorate
      = again: *I've rewritten the letter but I'm still dissatisfied with it.*
un   tie   do   button
      = reversal of action· *This knot is so tight that I can't undo it.*

   bid   consider   count   do   dress   last   load   lock   name
   open   pack   play   print   quote   read   record   release
   report   roll   run   screw   sit an exam   tell   think   unite
   use   wind   wit   zip

C Look at these examples of prefixes that alter the meaning of nouns, adjectives and verbs. Then use the prefixes with the words listed below.

mid-   July   winter   way
      = in the middle: *It's warmer in mid-July than in mid-February.*
over   ripe   cook   polite   act   sensitive
      = excessively: *Overripe fruit doesn't taste good and may not keep well.*
under   powered   staffed   charge
      = inadequately: *The car is so underpowered that it won't go up hills.*
self-   control   interest   sufficient
      = to, for, by oneself or itself: *The country is self-sufficient in oil.*
ultra-   modern   sensitive
      = extremely: *I wouldn't like to live in an ultra-modern building.*

   air   assured   catering   cautious   compensate   confident
   contained   crowded   defence   discipline   dose   enthusiastic
   estimate   explanatory   exposed   fashionable   fifties   friendly
   governing   imaginative   life   loaded   point   polite
   privileged   qualified   react   respect   satisfied   simplify
   staffed   twenties   value   weight

D Fill the gaps with suitable words from sections **A**, **B** and **C**.

1 An .... new hospital is being built .... between the two towns to replace the old ones which have .... their usefulness.
2 She tends to get quite .... when people .... her.
3 I think he .... when he got so angry – I only suggested he should .... the last paragraph of the report because it was ....
4 Don't you think John and Mary are ....? He's so conceited and .... whilst she's so gentle and ....
5 It's ....! They've closed down the hospital because it's .... Apparently it won't be .... till they've recruited more nurses.
6 You need a lot of .... if you're working on your own, especially if you're a .... kind of person.

18.5 Bad feelings

Before you begin this section, look again at 2.5.

A 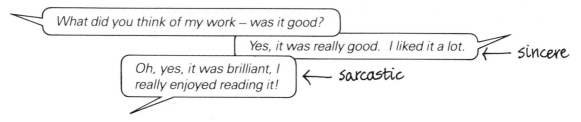 You'll hear twelve short clips from conversations – decide in each case whether the second speaker is being SINCERE or SARCASTIC. The first two are done as examples:

> *What did you think of my work – was it good?*

> *Yes, it was really good. I liked it a lot.* ← sincere

> *Oh, yes, it was brilliant, I really enjoyed reading it!* ← sarcastic

★ In most circumstances sarcasm is a dangerous weapon – it can easily upset or annoy people and may be misunderstood. But you do need to be aware if someone is being sarcastic to you.

B From time to time, especially when talking to friends, you may have to deal with people who are:
    unhappy or disappointed
    annoyed or angry
    bored or fed up

If someone is extremely unhappy, angry or bored, it may make matters worse if you say:

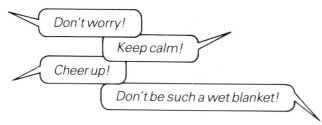

> *Don't worry!*

> *Keep calm!*

> *Cheer up!*

> *Don't be such a wet blanket!*

So, what should you say or do? It probably all depends on what exactly the matter is and how well you know each other.
    Work in pairs or groups. Ask your partners to suggest how they would deal with a friend who is:
– depressed because they have lost their job
– angry because their car has just been scratched while it was parked
– bored because they have broken their leg and can't leave the house

When you have decided how to deal with each friend, join another group and exchange ideas.

C Work in groups of three. Student A should look at Activity 29, student B at 54 and C at 71. In this role play you will be taking it in turns to play the role of someone with a problem and the others will have to try to cheer you up or calm you down.

18.6   First aid

A   Work in groups. Note down the things you would do and would NOT do if you were first on the scene in each of these cases:

Snake bite – in Britain the adder is the only poisonous snake and its bite is rarely fatal. (There may be other poisonous snakes in your country.)
Car accident – if you arrive at the scene and people have been injured.
Shock – all major injuries can bring about shock, a medical condition where the heart and circulation progressively lose power.

When you have done this, student A should look at Activity 13, B at 48 and C at 57, where you will find the medically approved versions.

B   Find out if any members of the class have had first-aid training. If so, find out from them how to treat:
● a patient with a suspected broken/fractured arm or leg
● a patient whose breathing has stopped
● a patient who is having an epileptic fit

18.7   *Hearts, hands, legs* and *feet*

Fill the gaps in these sentences with *heart, hand, leg, foot* or *feet*.

1 We had to learn the words by ....
2 You can trust her, I'm sure she has your interests at ....
3 If he's in hospital I'm sure he's in good ....s.
4 A lot of the staff are off sick, so we're rather short-............ed.
5 Ask someone who's been working here for years – one of the old ....s.
6 Even if it's hard to keep up your exercise programme, don't lose ....
7 You can do it by yourself I'm sure, you don't need me to hold your ....
8 My new job was hard at first, but I eventually found my ....
9 I used to really enjoy keeping fit but now my .... isn't in it.
10 The new manager was given a free .... to restructure the company.
11 You must decide – the decision is in your ....s.
12 I know you're upset but try not to take it to ....
13 They refused to help us, but in the end they had a change of ....
14 What he did was quite unjustified – he hasn't got a .... to stand on.
15 We decided not to enter for the competition because we had cold ....
16 Her behaviour was unfair and under............
17 I used to play a lot and I still play occasionally to keep my .... in.
18 If you need help, let me know and I'll give you a ....
19 Don't worry, leave it to me – I have the matter in ....
20 When she told him she was leaving him, it almost broke his ....
21 We all had to do as we were told when she put her .... down.
22 I shouldn't have mentioned his ex-wife – I think I put my .... in it.
23 Don't take it seriously, it was only a light-............ed remark.
24 When you've finished this work you'll be able to put your .... up.
25 I didn't mean what I said, I was only pulling your ....

19 On business

19.1   On the job

Vocabulary

A   Work in groups. Ask your partners:
– what jobs they have done, including holiday jobs
– what kind of work they're likely to be doing five years from now
– what kind of job they would least like to have

B   Fill the gaps in these sentences with suitable words.

1 If you're applying for a job you may need to fill in an .... form and send a copy of your .... (career history).
2 Blue-collar workers earn ...., while ....-collar employees earn a .... All workers make contributions to a p............... fund, so that they will continue to be paid when they retire.
3 If a firm is losing business to its c...............s and its sales are dropping, it may have to make some of its staff r...............
4 A large part of a firm's b............... is spent on marketing its p...............s and on maintaining a good sales f............... who meet c...............s personally.
5 A modern office uses w............... p...............s instead of typewriters.
6 Any piece of industrial equipment consists of a large number of c...............s – if the equipment breaks down the service engineer can supply s............... p...............s.
7 A formal meeting is controlled by a c............... who makes sure that the a............... is followed. Another person usually makes notes and keeps the m............... of the meeting.
8 People working in different departments of the same firm can get in touch on the i............... phone or send each other m...............s.
9 A business can communicate with its clients by letter or phone, by t............... or f..............., or even by e............... mail (from computer to computer).
10 Label the hardware in this illustration:

C Work in groups. Ask your partners which of these adjectives and phrases best describe the jobs or professions listed below:

strenuous   glamorous   challenging   repetitive   unpredictable
low-paid   highly-paid   unpleasant   undemanding
best done by women   best done by men

a ski-teacher   an airline pilot   a market trader
a merchant seaman   a fisherman   a nurse
a prime minister or president   a truck driver   a soldier
a receptionist   a telephonist   a managing director

Make a list of FIVE MORE jobs that match the adjectives and phrases above.
Compare your list with another group's list.

19.2   Great business deals?   Reading and listening

A Find the answers to these questions in the three reading texts:

1 How much was paid for the whole of Manhattan Island in 1626?
2 How much does an office block in New York cost now?
3 How much did Napoleon sell the entire Mississippi Valley for in 1803?
4 What was the price per hectare?   (2.5 acres ≃ hectare)
5 How big was the United States before this deal?
6 How big was the United States after this deal?
7 How much did the Tsar of Russia sell Alaska for in 1867?
8 What was the price per hectare?
9 How much gold has Alaska yielded?
10 How much coal is there in Alaska?

---

1. The best real estate deal in history

Even in the days when America was known as the New World, it was a country with a reputation for its spirit of enterprise and the ability of its people to make a good deal.

When the settlers started negotiating, the natives hardly knew what had hit them – and in the summer of 1626, probably the most spectacular real estate coup in history took place.

Governor Peter Minuit of the Dutch West India Company had the job of buying Manhattan Island from the Indians.

After some haggling with Chief Manhasset, the price was agreed at 24 dollars' worth of kettles, axes and cloth.

Today, $24 would not buy one square foot of office space in New York City, and an office block in central Manhattan changes hands for around $80 million. Even allowing for inflation, Minuit got himself a real bargain.

≫→

2. Not again, Josephine!

   You would think that the Manhattan deal would remain a one-off for ever. But less than two centuries later the loser was Napoleon, Emperor of France and (in his early years, at least) a brilliant military tactician.

   In 1803, Napoleon had his mind on European affairs (in particular, an invasion of Britain), so he decided to dispense with France's American possessions.

   He sold the entire Mississippi valley, an area of 828,000 square miles extending from Canada down to the Gulf of Mexico and westwards to the Rockies, for just over 27 million dollars.

   Through this deal, known as the Louisiana purchase, President Thomas Jefferson doubled the size of the United States for only around 5 cents per acre.

   The judgement of the Emperor, on the other hand, never seemed to be quite the same again.

3. Nice ice at a reasonable price

   Napoleon did just manage to reach Moscow in his ill-fated invasion of 1812 – but it would seem that news of his poor American deal did not.

   For, astonishingly, the Russians went on to become the *third* victims of major land deals with America.

   On March 30th 1867, the U.S. Secretary of State, William Seward, bought Alaska from Tsar Alexander II for a mere $7.2 million – thereby acquiring another 586,000 square miles of territory for less than 2 cents per acre.

   The Tsar presumably thought that this remote, frozen and virtually uninhabited piece of land had nothing at all to commend it – and at first, the American people agreed with him, for Alaska was known as 'Seward's folly' and 'Seward's ice box' for years.

   In 1896, however, gold was struck at Klondike in the Yukon, and since then, over 750 million dollars' worth has been mined.

   In 1968, black gold was discovered – and an estimated 100 billion tons of coal are also lying underground, just waiting to be dug up.

B   Now listen to the recording. You'll hear about three businessmen and some of the deals they made. Fill the gaps in the chart opposite with information given in the recordings.

1933   **Seller:** THE CANADIAN .... COMPANY

Place	Product	Price	Purchaser
Canada	Ten vessels	$ .... per ship	....

Outcome: Shipping began to boom when the .... ended and he became a
....

1923–5   **Seller:** ARTHUR FURGUSON

Place	Product	Price	Purchaser
London	Trafalgar Square	£	an American
London	....	£1,000	a tourist
London	Buckingham Palace	£ .... deposit	another tourist
Washington	The White House	$ .... per annum	a Texan
New York	....	$100,000	an ....

Outcome: Arthur Furguson was .... recognised, arrested and imprisoned
for five years. After his release he retired to .... and lived a life of luxury.

1925–34   **Seller:** 'COUNT' VICTOR LUSTIG

Place	Product	Price	Purchaser
Paris	Eiffel Tower: as 7,000 tons of	(not known)	André Poisson
USA	A machine to print	$	a millionaire
Chicago	A 'system' to double money on Wall Street	$5,000	....

Outcome: Victor Lustig was .... in 1934 but .... He was rearrested
in .... and found guilty of printing $ .... He died in prison in ....

19.3   Word order   Effective writing

A   Rearrange these words to make sensible sentences. There are several
possible arrangements for each group of words. The first is done as an
example.

1   a   business   find   hard   I   it   letter   to   usually   write

    I usually find it hard to write a business letter.

OR: *Usually I find it hard to write a business letter.*

OR, possibly: *I find it hard to write a business letter usually.*

2   get   in   should   as soon as possible   them   touch   We   with
3   a   fax   immediately   send   should   them   We
4   a   also   letter   send   ought   them   to   We
5   a   every day   send   shouldn't   telex   them   We
6   in   morning   never   phone   should   the   them   We
7   have   letter   long   really   to reply   shouldn't   so   taken   their   to   We
8   completely   finished   have   will   When   you?

163

B Rearrange these words to make complete sentences.

1 **They have a** ... block brand busy downtown heart in Manhattan new of office the
2 **She's got a** ... an company computer in job new software splendid up-and-coming well-paid
3 **The** ... early is taking member most of our permanent reliable retirement staff
4 **I** ... a a always beautiful beside family hotel in lake little lovely mountain stay traditional
5 **First I attended** ... a an and then business call committee I important long-winded made meeting monthly phone staff

C The beginnings and endings of these sentences are in the correct position, but the other words and phrases have been mixed up. Rearrange them to make a complete true story.

When you're ready, compare your sentences with another pair.

1 **In 1968,** ... a new one an American millionaire because found out London Bridge Robert McCulloch that was about to be demolished ... **was to be built.**
2 **He decided** ... and and beside Lake Havasu have them shipped in Arizona in the desert rebuilt the stones to America to buy ... **as a tourist attraction.**
3 **His offer of** ... an extra $1,000 $2.4 million for every one of his sixty years of age plus ... **was accepted.**
4 **It was** ... he had made he realised only later that ... **a slight mistake.**
5 **Apparently,** ... an ordinary and that that that he hadn't realised he had assumed he was buying it was just London Bridge Victorian stone Tower Bridge was ... **bridge!**

D Write a couple of paragraphs, retelling one of the 'Great business deals' stories you heard in 19.2, in your own words.

Show your story to your partner and ask for comments on the arrangement of words and ideas.

E Work in pairs. Look at the photo opposite and imagine that you were one of those people crossing London Bridge after a hard day's work in the City. Write a paragraph describing your day at work and your feelings.

Begin like this: *It was 5.30 on Friday afternoon and I was on my way home...*

- Make notes before you start writing.
- Show your completed paragraph to another pair and ask for comments.

19.4   On the phone

A   Work in groups. Ask your partners why:
– they like AND dislike using the phone
– using the phone is harder than talking to someone face to face
– talking to someone in another country on the phone is particularly hard

B   🖭 You'll hear Jane McCartney trying to get in touch with Larry
Allen on the phone. MAKE NOTES on the mistakes each person makes. What
SHOULDN'T each person have said or done and what should they have done
or said instead?
  Work in pairs or groups and discuss how YOU would have behaved
differently and what YOU would have said.
  Can you think of a friend or colleague who is particularly 'good on the
phone'? What special skills or techniques does he or she use, that you would
like to acquire?

C   ☎ 🎭 Work in groups of three. One of you should look at Activity
3, one at 21 and the other at 26. You will be role playing a series of phone
calls – but each time one of you will be 'OBSERVING' what the others are
doing by eavesdropping and giving feedback later.
  During each phone call the two callers should sit BACK-TO-BACK so that
they can only use their voices to communicate.

▶ Look at the next page for some phrases that are often used on the phone
and the questions that the 'observer' should consider.

165

> I'd like to speak to ......
> I'd like to leave a message for ......
> Is ...... available, please?
> Could you put me through to ......, please?

> I'm afraid he/she's still at lunch/in a meeting.
> Hold on, I'll just see if he/she's in.
> I think you may have the wrong number/extension.
> Could you say that again, please – it's a very bad line.
> Could you spell that for me, please?

> Could you ask her/him to call me back?
> We were cut off in the middle of the call.
> I tried calling earlier but I couldn't get through.
> It stopped ringing just as I was about to pick it up.

OBSERVER

While you are the 'OBSERVER', listen carefully to the two people on the phone and make notes on the following aspects:

● Are they speaking clearly?
● Do they sound friendly, sincere and polite?
● Is it the kind of call you'd like to receive yourself?

19.5 Could you take a message?

Listening

A 🖭 You'll hear three phone messages which have been left on the telephone answering machine. Imagine you are Jane Potter's assistant. Make notes so that you can pass the information on to Ms Potter when she gets back to the office.

The first part is done as an example:

> **MESSAGES**
> Karen White called from Chicago about your
> presentations on 14 + 15 July.

B ☎ 📳 Work in pairs. One of you should look at Activity 35, the other at 59. You'll each see some notes: these are the points you have to communicate to your partner. Imagine that you're on the phone, and sit BACK-TO-BACK. Note down the information your partner gives you.

At the end of the call, compare your notes with the notes your partner was referring to (in 35 or 59).

19.6   Carrying out a survey

The class is divided into two groups. Group A will carry out a survey based on questionnaire A and group B on questionnaire B below. Each group should follow this procedure:

1 Find out from the members of the other group how they rate the following aspects in your questionnaire. Note down their responses.
2 Return to your group and collate your findings to produce a table or chart summarising the results of your survey.
3 Prepare a presentation of your findings to present to the whole class.
4 Write a report of your findings.

A   JOB SATISFACTION

1 How important are the following to you in giving you job satisfaction?

   VERY IMPORTANT   IMPORTANT   NOT IMPORTANT   NOT RELEVANT

   being popular with colleagues   being praised by your
   being part of a team   superiors
   being promoted   being successful
   challenge   exercising power
   giving advice   helping others
   increased responsibility   influencing people
   learning new things   making money
   personal freedom   respect of colleagues
   security   seeing the results of
   setting up a new system   your actions
   starting a project   solving problems
   status   completing a project
   being asked for advice   working conditions

2 Which of the features exist in your present job (or the job you're planning to do one day)?

B   SUCCESS

1 How important are the following attributes in helping someone to be successful in their career?

   VERY IMPORTANT   IMPORTANT   NOT IMPORTANT   NOT RELEVANT

   a practical mind   ability to delegate
   ability to express yourself   ability to think on your feet
   ability to work fast   ability to write well
   being good at giving orders   being good at flattery
   accepting responsibility   ambition
   being good with figures   being good with people
   concentration   good 'connections'
   experience   popularity with colleagues
   good education   patience
   physical and mental toughness   ruthlessness
   good social background   willingness to take risks

2 Which of the attributes do you have yourself?

19.7 Applying for a job

A   Look at this outline CV and use it as a basis for your own.

▶ Discuss with a partner what information you should give before writing your own CV/resumé. It's not an application form, so you can devote as much space as necessary to the various sections.

Curriculum vitae

PERSONAL DETAILS

Full name

Address   ← *in block capitals*

Telephone number   (home)   (work)

Age   Date of birth   Place of birth

Nationality

EDUCATION AND QUALIFICATIONS

School / college / university

Examinations and qualifications

EXPERIENCE
                                          ← *work you have done*

OTHER INFORMATION
                                          ← *information about yourself*
                                            and your interests

REFEREES

1
                                          ← *names of two or three people*
                                            who know you and your work
2

B   Write a letter applying for one of these jobs:

Part-time hosts/guides

ACME Travel International arrange personalized world tours for small groups of people (up to ten), mainly from North America. We are looking for men and women who speak good English to act as local hosts and guides to accompany our clients during their time in your city.

We have vacancies for hosts who can only work weekends and evenings as well as weekdays.

Excellent hourly rates, plus a monthly retainer. Generous expenses.

Write me now: tell me about yourself, why you think you would be suitable and when you are available. Please enclose your résumé.

Elliot Western, ATI Inc, Suite 777, 454 Diamond St,
Philadelphia, PA 19107, USA

19.8 *Hard, soft, difficult* and *easy* Idioms

Fill the gaps in these sentences with *hard*, *soft*, *difficult* or *easy*. The first is done as an example.

1 Take it ..*easy*..! There's no need to get so worried just because you're .... up – it's payday tomorrow.
2 Computer equipment is known as ....ware and the programs are known as ....ware.
3 A printout from a computer provides the user with a .... copy.
4 A computer can save data on a floppy disk but much more can be stored on a .... disk.
5 This new fabric is so ....-wearing that it will last a lifetime!
6 You can buy tools, screws and nails at a ....ware store.
7 I realise that he makes people feel un................ when he's being .... , but deep down he's quite ....-hearted and ....-going – I must say I do have a .... spot for him.
8 It's sometimes .... to understand her because she's rather ....-spoken.
9 .... drugs like heroin are more dangerous than so-called .... drugs like marijuana.
10 We've been too .... on customers who don't settle their accounts on time. We should start to take a .... line.
11 These aren't guidelines, they are ....-and-fast rules.
12 A paperback is often half the price of a ....back.
13 A ....-hearted interviewer can give candidates a very .... time and make life .... for them.
14 I'm very thirsty, so I'd prefer a .... drink – is there any lemonade?
15 'When would you like to come?' 'I don't mind – I'm ....'
16 Some salespeople favour aggressive .... sell techniques, while others prefer gentle persuasion and go for the .... sell.
17 Dollars and Swiss francs (unlike the Albanian lek or Nicaraguan córdoba) are .... currencies.
18 After a hard day at the office, I like to take it ....

20 The natural world

20.1 Fauna and flora
Vocabulary

A   Work in groups. Ask your partners:
– what kinds of animals are popular as pets among their friends
– why they believe it's important to protect the environment

▶ Note down FIVE environmental issues that are in the news at the moment.

B   Work in pairs. Identify these animals and plants and make sure you can both spell and pronounce their names correctly.

1 Mammals

2 Birds

3 Insects and invertebrates

4 Reptiles and amphibians

5 Flowers

6 Trees and plants

7 Sea creatures

▶ Add two more species to each group.

C   [image] Work in pairs. One of you should look at Activity 55, the other at 63. When you have read the short passage there, tell your partner about it and then discuss these questions:

● Which would be worse: Eric or Gregor's situation? Why?
● What do you think might have happened next in each story?
● What kind of animal would you *most* like to be and why?

170

A   Work in pairs. Look at the two passages below: each of you should concentrate on a DIFFERENT passage.

Find out about your partner's passage. What are your reactions?

G R E E N P E A C E

Against all odds, Greenpeace has brought the plight of the natural world to the attention of caring people. Terrible abuses to the environment, often carried out in remote places or far out to sea have been headlined on television and in the press.

Greenpeace began with a pro-test voyage into a nuclear test zone. The test was disrupted. Today, the site at Amchitka in the Aleutian Islands is a bird sanctuary.

Then Greenpeace sent its tiny inflatable boats to protect the whales. They took up position between the harpoons and the fleeing whales. Today, commercial whaling is banned.

On the ice floes of Newfoundland, Greenpeace volunteers placed their bodies between the gaffs of the seal hunters and the helpless seal pups. The hunt was subsequently called off.

In the North Atlantic, Greenpeace drove its inflatables underneath falling barrels of radioactive waste. Now nuclear waste dumping at sea has been stopped.

In the North Sea, Greenpeace swimmers turned back dump ships carrying chemical wastes. New laws to protect the North Sea have been promised.

Peaceful direct action by Greenpeace has invoked the power of public opinion which in turn has forced changes in the law to protect wildlife and to stop the pollution of the natural world.

PLANET EARTH IS 4,600 MILLION YEARS OLD

If we condense this inconceivable time-span into an understandable concept, we can liken Earth to a person of 46 years of age.

Nothing is known about the first 7 years of this person's life, and whilst only scattered information exists about the middle span, we know that only at the age of 42 did the Earth begin to flower.

Dinosaurs and the great reptiles did not appear until one year ago, when the planet was 45. Mammals arrived only 8 months ago; in the middle of last week man-like apes evolved into ape-like men, and at the weekend the last ice age enveloped the Earth.

Modern man has been around for 4 hours. During the last hour Man discovered agriculture. The industrial revolution began a minute ago.

During those sixty seconds of biological time, Modern Man has made a rubbish tip of Paradise.

He has multiplied his numbers to plague proportions, caused the extinction of 500 species of animals, ransacked the planet for fuels and now stands like a brutish infant, gloating over this meteoric rise to ascendancy, on the brink of a war to end all wars and of effectively destroying this oasis of life in the solar system.

⟫→

B Before you listen to the recording, look at the summary below and see how many of the gaps you can already fill from your own knowledge of the subject. Use a pencil.

🔲 Listen to the recording and fill the gaps in this summary.

1 According to Sam Fuller, Europeans are becoming dissatisfied with the existing political parties and the Greens represent a ....

2 Helen Summerfield makes a distinction between the Green .... and the Green ....

3 The three main non-political environmental pressure groups in the UK are: .... , ... and ....

4 These organisations have been working to raise .... and raise .... of environmental issues.

5 One of their campaigns encourages people to use .... and persuades local governments to provide ....

6 According to Sam Fuller, the Greens don't only raise objections, they try to propose alternative .... , ... or .... These alternatives are less .... and often less ....

7 As it becomes more .... for people to care about the environment, the public will choose to buy .... products.

8 Governments will be expected to implement 'green' policies because, in the eyes of the voters, actions ....

C Work in groups. Ask your partners:
– what the equivalent pressure groups in their country/countries are
– what their views are on the Green Party and the Green Movement
– if they would vote for the Green Party – why/why not?
– if they think the Green Party could ever form a government

D 🔲 You'll hear ten clips recorded from conversations – but the last word or phrase of each one is not audible. Write down the missing word or phrase. Listen to the example first.

'... no, they live in Africa and they feed on leaves. I don't think they roar or make any noise. Oh, they've got these wonderful long necks. You've been to the zoo, haven't you? Now, when you were there did you see the *giraffes* .... ?'

E Work in groups. Find out your partners' views on the environmental issues raised by the speakers.

'Negotiate? What is there to negotiate?'

20.3   The future and degrees of certainty Grammar

A   Work in pairs. Discuss the difference in meaning between these
sentences:

1 I'll write to her tomorrow.
  I'm going to write to her tomorrow.
  I was going to write to her tomorrow.
  I'll be writing to her tomorrow.

  I <u>will</u> write to her tomorrow.
  I'm writing to her tomorrow.
  I'll have written to her tomorrow.
  I'll have to write to her tomorrow.

2 Are we going to make the first move?
  Shall we make the first move?

  Do we make the first move?
  Will we make the first move?

3 I'm just going to phone them now.
  I'm about to phone them now.
  I was just about to phone them now.

  I'm phoning them now.
  I've phoned them now.
  I'll phone them now.

4 Will you help us later?
  Are you going to help us later?
  Will you be helping us later?
  Won't you be helping us later?

  Are you helping us later?
  Were you going to help us later?
  Won't you help us later?
  Aren't you going to help us later?

B   Work in pairs. Spot the errors in these sentences – but be careful
because some contain NO errors.

1 I'm sure it doesn't rain tomorrow.
2 What time does the flight land?
3 I'll have a drink while I'm going to wait for her plane to land.
4 The meeting shan't begin until everyone will have arrived.
5 I probably won't have finished any work by the time you arrive.
6 Will I help you to carry the shopping?
7 I'll be glad when it will be time to go home.
8 I know you'll be angry when I tell you you've got to rewrite the letter.

C   Fill the gaps in these sentences, using the verbs below. All the sentences
refer to FUTURE events.

1 Fifty hectares of jungle .... during the next minute.
2 Next year another 250,000 square kilometres of tropical rainforest ....
3 By the end of the century most of the world's jungles ....
4 Toxic wastes .... in the oceans more and more in the future.
5 A complete, permanent ban on whaling .... eventually.
6 Many species of plants and animals .... extinct by the year 2000.
7 The use of pesticides .... to the evolution of chemical-resistant pests.
8 Pollution .... still .... damage to the environment in the 21st century.
9 Governments .... more notice of environmental pressure groups.
10 Energy conservation measures .... into effect at once.

   accumulate   become   cause   come   cut down   destroy
   devastate   impose   lead   take

173

D   Work in pairs. Match each sentence in the first column with one in the second column that means the same. The first is done as an example.

1 I don't think she'll be here on time.   She can't possibly arrive on time.
2 She's very unlikely to be on time.   I doubt if she'll be late.
3 I'm sure she'll be late.   She's not going to be late.
4 She'll probably get here on time.   I don't know if she's going to be late
5 She may get here on time.   I think she'll be late.
6 I know she'll get here on time.   There's a slim chance she'll be late.
7 I expect she'll be here on time.   I'm pretty sure she'll be late.
8 I'm almost certain she'll be on time.   She's unlikely to be late.

E   Work in pairs. This chart shows various people's predictions about the probable or possible effects of global warming. Decide where the sentences in italics below would fit into the chart, according to their meanings.

100% ↑	Temperatures will rise. I'm sure that temperatures will rise.	= **certain they will**
	Temperatures will probably rise.	= **probable**
↑ **50%** ↓	Temperatures may rise. I'm not sure whether temperatures will rise or not. Temperatures may not rise.	= **uncertain**
	Temperatures probably won't rise.	= **improbable**
↓ **0%**	I'm sure that temperatures won't rise. Temperatures won't rise.	= **certain they will not**

It looks as if it will get warmer.
I'm fairly sure it won't get warmer.
I doubt if it will get warmer.
It's going to get warmer.
In all probability it will get warmer.
I'm absolutely sure it will get warmer.
I wouldn't be surprised if it got warmer.
I suppose it might get warmer.
There's not much chance that it will get warmer.
There's a very good chance that it will get warmer.
There's no likelihood that it will get warmer.
In all probability it's going to get a great deal warmer.

I bet it will get warmer.
I guess it might get warmer.
I'd be surprised if it got warmer.
It's likely to get warmer.
Of course it won't get warmer.
It's sure to get warmer.
It's bound to get warmer.
I don't think it will get warmer.

F   Work in groups. Find out your partners' views on the 21st century and if they are optimistic or pessimistic:
● How much of the damage caused to the natural world is likely to be controlled or reversed during the 21st century?
● What scientific discoveries will be made? What political and cultural changes will there be? How will these events affect YOU?
● What will your OWN lives be like in the 21st century?

20.4   Compound words

A   Compound nouns

Work in pairs. Match each of the words in the first group with words in the second group to form compound nouns. The first four are done as examples:

acid rain   *chain reaction*   *coal mine*   *coffee break*

acid ✓   chain ✓   coal ✓   coffee ✓   charter   committee
computer   drinking   flight   food   holiday   language
meeting   ozone   palm   pet   post   pressure   progress
safety   steering   telephone   traffic   typing   video   waiting
washing   wastepaper   water   window   zoo

attendant   basket   break ✓   brochure   call   chain   cleaner
flight   food   group   keeper   layer   lights   machine
meeting   mine ✓   office   paper   point   precautions
pressure   rain ✓   reaction ✓   recorder   room   screen
teacher   test   tree   water   wheel

B   Compound adjectives

Work in pairs. Match each of the words in the first group with words in the second group to form compound adjectives. The first four are done as examples:

broad-minded   *duty-free*   *energy-efficient*   *environment-friendly*

broad ✓   duty ✓   energy ✓   environment ✓   good   green   hard
hard   heart   home   ill   loose   narrow   quick   record
self   short   time   under   user   well   well

behaved   breaking   broken   consuming   efficient ✓
employed   fingered   fitting   free ✓   friendly ✓   friendly ✓
hearted   informed   looking   made   meaning   minded ✓
minded   paid   staffed   witted   working

★ There are no hard-and-fast rules about whether the two elements of a compound NOUN are written as one or two words.
Look at these examples:

ONE WORD: *greenhouse   girlfriend   headache   railway*
            bookcase   sightseeing   breakdown   blackbird
            bookseller   raincoat   wildlife   classroom   rainforest
TWO WORDS: *station manager   headache tablets   railway station*
            power station   bus driver   bus stop   bus station
            greenhouse effect   sightseeing coach   wildlife reserve
            breakdown service

As a rule of thumb, the most common compound nouns tend to be written as single words. If you're unsure you should consult an up-to-date dictionary. If in doubt, write a compound NOUN as TWO WORDS, without a hyphen.

⟫→

★ Most compound ADJECTIVES are written with a hyphen:
    user-friendly   second-hand   self-satisfied   self-employed
but some are written as a single word:
    windproof   suntanned   breathtaking   homesick
and a few compound nouns are also written with a hyphen:
    make-up   follow-up   pick-up

20.5 The last frontier

A Did you know that Antarctica is as big as Australia and Europe combined, sunnier than California, drier than Arabia, higher than Switzerland and emptier than the Sahara? A hundred million birds breed there each year and the Southern Ocean contains the world's largest fish stocks. Beneath its surface are the world's largest coal deposits and probably the world's richest oil reserves ...

Find out more about Antarctica by reading this passage.

The Antarctic Environment

The Antarctic is the most remote continent and the last to be discovered, but it constitutes about a tenth of the world's land surface. It is also the only continent without an indigenous human population.

In the past it had a warm climate, supporting luxuriant vegetation and large animals, but the climate deteriorated over the last 30 million years, once the great continent Gondwana had drifted apart sufficiently for a southern circumpolar current to become established. This, the largest ocean current in the world, cut off Antarctica from the warmer oceans to the north and allowed the ice sheets, in places over four kilometres thick, to develop.

This region is the earth's major heat sink and contains ninety per cent of the world's ice and nearly three-quarters of its fresh water. Only two per cent of the continent is not covered by ice, and life retains a tenuous foothold there.

Nearly half of Antarctica's coastline is hidden by thick floating ice shelves or glaciers, and the rest is scoured by icebergs down to depths of 15 metres or more, which limits coastal life. But below this level, where water temperatures are stable, there is a colourful marine world containing a great diversity of life. The Southern Ocean makes up a tenth of the world ocean, and the expansion and contraction of the surrounding sea ice is the largest seasonal process on Earth. Recent work has shown that the pack ice provides a surprisingly productive Winter habitat for a number of small creatures, the most important of them being krill.

Krill

Krill, which looks like a small shrimp, probably has a total weight in excess of any other animal in the world, including the human race. It is the staple diet of the oceanic squids and of most Antarctic fishes, birds, seals and whales.

B Fill the gaps in these sentences with information from the passage.

1 Antarctica, which once had a .... climate, is separated from the warmer oceans by the ....
2 The Antarctic constitutes .... of the world's land surface.
3 Parts of the Antarctic ice cap are .... thick.
4 Antarctica contains .... of the world's ice and .... of the world's fresh water.
5 .... of Antarctica is buried beneath ice and snow.
6 The total weight of .... is greater than any other species of animal on earth. It is important in the Antarctic eco-system because ....

C Work in groups. Discuss the questions raised in the passage below with your partners.

The Last Frontier?

Today, Antarctica is about to enter a new age. After thirty years of unparalleled international co-operation under the aegis of the Antarctic Treaty, the continent is threatened by man's insatiable appetite for natural resources.

Antarctica is the last frontier – the last continent on earth to have escaped the worst of our destructive ingenuity. True, the great whales around Antarctica were hunted dangerously close to extinction, and species like the Blue – the largest creature ever to inhabit the planet – may never recover.

But Antarctica has remained until now a pristine environment, and a perfect natural laboratory for scientists to pursue knowledge for its own sake. Will things remain that way? A Minerals Convention may soon be ratified that will allow regulated mining in Antarctica for the first time, albeit within stringent environmental safeguards.

Should the exploiters be allowed in, to operate under tough protective controls? Or should Antarctica be declared a 'wilderness park', free from exploitation for ever? Perhaps the answer isn't as obvious as it appears. What is important, though, is that the questions should be asked by all of us, and not just by the tiny number of diplomats who administer Antarctica.

20.6 Spelling and pronunciation 2 – Vowels

A Although there are only five vowels in the alphabet, there are over 24 vowel and diphthong sounds in English.

Say these words aloud to remind yourself of the vowel sounds:

bad   end   calm   caught   bird   sleep
slip   pot   look   lunch   cool   fall

and diphthong sounds:

bite   now   toy   there   here   make   note
fuel   tired   tower   royal   player   lower

Work in pairs. Write down another word that RHYMES with each of the words above. The first two are done as examples.

bad – sad   end – friend

B Remember that the weak vowel sounds /ə/ and /ɪ/ occur in unstressed syllables. Look at these examples:

This kind of thing happens again and again.
/ðɪs kaɪnd əv θɪŋ hæpənz əgen ənd əgen/
All of us thought it was a pretty good party.
/ɔːl əv əs θɔːt ɪt wəz ə prɪti gʊd pɑːti/

Now highlight the unstressed weak vowels in these sentences – imagine they are spoken at normal conversational speed:

1 We all enjoyed your talk very much – the subject was very interesting.
2 The damage caused to the environment by industry is often overlooked.
3 Against all odds, Greenpeace has brought the plight of the natural world to the attention of caring people.

C Work in pairs. Look at these words that are pronounced the same but spelt differently.

Explain the difference in meaning between each pair (or group) of words. Take it in turns to give a definition or example, like this:

You: *A band is a group of musicians.*
Your partner: *If a film is banned it can't be shown.*
You: *'Damn!' is what you might say if you're annoyed.*
Your partner: *A dam holds back the water in a lake or reservoir.*

æ	**band/banned**	– damn/dam	
e	**weather/whether**	– bred/bread lent/leant red/read	
	scent/sent/cent sell/cell		
aɪ	**right/write**	– die/dye high/hi hire/higher	
	isle/I'll/aisle mind/mined sighed/side site/sight tire/tyre		
ɑː	**passed/past**	– draught/draft	
ɔː	**bored/board**	– cord/chord nor/gnaw or/awe/ore/oar	
	sword/sawed stalk/stork		
ɜː	**heard/herd**	– colonel/kernel fur/fir	
aʊ	**allowed/aloud**	– bough/bow flour/flower	
ɔɪ	**boy/buoy**		

eə	**there/their/they're** – air/heir	bear/bare	fair/fare

eə   **there/their/they're** – air/heir   bear/bare   fair/fare
       hair/hare   mayor/mare

ɪə   **here/hear**   – cereal/serial   deer/dear   peer/pier

eɪ   **break/brake**   vain/vein   wade/weighed   whale/wail

əʊ   **nose/knows**   – groan/grown   rode/road/rowed
       rose/rows   so/sew/sow   soul/sole   toes/tow

iː   **piece/peace**   – be/B/bee   he'll/heel/heal   key/quay
       read/reed   beetles/Beatles   steel/steal

ɪ   **mist/missed**   – which/witch

ɒ   **not/know**   – what/watt

uː   **root/route**   – dew/due   flew/flu   queue/cue

ʊ   **wood/would**

ʌ   **one/won**   – none/nun   some/sum   son/sun

▶ Think of some more pairs of words that are pronounced the same but spelt differently.

D   Put the words in each group into pairs, according to the way the stressed vowels are pronounced. The first two are done as examples.

i   mile   film   fright   firm   title   sir   island   kitchen
       mile – title   *film – kitchen*

a   watch   father   bald   share   ache   hand   says   castle
       yacht   scarce   factory   any   vague   yawn

ea   bear   team   break   threat   hearty   fear   search   weak
       jealous   earnest   pear   dreary   sweetheart   steak

au   sausage   naughty   laugh   daughter   draught   cauliflower
       (*note also:* gauge)

ei   receive   weight   leisure   their   foreign   height   perceive
       heir   ancient   either   neighbour   Leicester

ie   chief   fierce   friendship   die   pier   pliers   believe
       unfriendly

u   bury   bullet   butter   business   refuse   murder   flute
       butcher   burst   guess   busy   mustard

o   monkey   lose   folk   crowd   orange   boy   ordinary
       frontier   joyful   shower   glorious   soften   ghost
       movement

ou   enough   found   bought   cough   soul   through   should
       thorough   rough   although   could   trough   court
       plough   throughout   borough

oo   food   flood   floor   foot   book   loose   door   blood

E   Listen to the recording and write down each of the fifteen words you hear – you'll hear each one in a sentence to help you. The first one is:

1 handkerchief

F   Cross out the words below that are spelt incorrectly. The first is done as an example.

accross – across   advertisement – advertment
agressive – aggressive   campainging – campaigning

                                                    ⫸→

diphthong – dipthong   disruppted – disrupted
enthusiastically – enthusiasticly   extinction – extincsion
inconceivable – inconcievable   interrupted – interuppted
replaceable – replacable   sanctaury – sanctuary
seperate – separate   sieze – seize
underdeveloped – underdevelopped

G Look at your own previous written work and see which words you spelt incorrectly. How many of these are words that you know you often get wrong?

20.7 *Keep, hold, stand* and *turn* Verbs and idioms

A Fill the gaps with the appropriate form of *keep, hold, stand* or *turn*.

1 If you can't do it on Friday, the work can be .... over till next week.
2 They had to .... back before reaching the summit of the mountain.
3 The children were misbehaving, but their aunt .... a blind eye to it.
4 Make yourself at home – there's no need to .... on ceremony.
5 If you want to succeed in our office, you have to .... in with the boss.
6 Everyone else was against him, so we decided to .... for him.
7 The college .... a record of every student's attendance.
8 Concorde .... the record for the fastest round-the-world flight.
9 While on holiday I always .... a diary to help me to remember it later.
10 He's feeling lonely and upset, will you be able to .... him company?
11 The day he met Maria was a .... point in his life.
12 We were disappointed when they .... down our offer.
13 I've been trying to get .... of her on the phone, but there's no answer.
14 .... it! It's not time to start yet.
15 This new fabric can .... up to very heavy wear.
16 Bob is Mrs Reed's assistant: he .... in for her when she's on holiday. If he's away then someone else has to .... the fort.
17 In an emergency, try to .... your head – i.e. don't panic.
18 She can do a fantastic somersault and she can even .... on her head.
19 If you really want to do that, I won't .... in your way.
20 I knew the bad news would upset them, so I .... it back from them.

B  Decide which are the most useful idioms in **A** that you don't already use. Highlight them to help you remember them.
  Work in pairs. Write a mini-exercise consisting of six sentences with gaps (...............) using the idioms from **A**. Pass your exercise to another pair and get them to fill the gaps.

21 Here is the news

21.1   In the news

A   Work in groups. Ask your partners:
– to name one important event that happened last week
– to decide which is the most important event that has happened this year
– which newspaper they normally read and why – or why they don't
  normally read one
– which sections they normally read and if they ever read the editorial
– if they prefer a tabloid (e.g. *The Sun*) or a quality daily (e.g. *The
  Guardian*)

B   Fill the gaps in these sentences.

1 Candidates in the UK and USA are elected by a 'first past the post' system, where only
  the candidate who gets the most votes is elected in each c............., and politics is
  dominated by two major parties. Many other countries have a system of p............. r.............
  which gives other smaller parties more power.
2 After a general election, the party which has a m............. forms the government and the
  losing side becomes the o.............
3 The US Congress consists of the S............. and the House of R.............s.
4 The UK Parliament consists of the House of L............. and the House of C.............

▶ Describe the electoral and parliamentary system in your country.

C   Fill the gaps in this description of the English legal system:

The underlying p............. of English justice is that the defendant is i.............
until proved guilty.
    In England and Wales, if a person is s.............d of a serious crime, they are
a.............d and then q.............d by the police and c.............d with the crime.
Then they may be held in c............. or released on b............. until their case is
heard first at a Magistrates' Court, where they are represented by a s..............
They may then have to wait some time before their case is heard in the local
Crown Court or the Central C............. Court (The Old Bailey) in London,
where the d............. is represented by a b............. and the case is heard by a
j............. and a j............. of twelve men and women. At the end of the t.............
they may be found not guilty and a.............d or found guilty and s.............d.
They may be sent to jail, given a s.............d sentence or put on p............., or
perhaps made to pay a f............. . If they feel they have been wrongly
convicted they may a............. against their sentence.

▶ Describe the legal process in your own country, beginning like this:
  'In my country, if a person has committed a serious crime . . .'

D   In many English-language newspapers, especially in the tabloids, a special shorthand style is used in headlines.

Work in pairs. Look at these headlines, which appeared on successive days in a newspaper. Can you explain what happened each day? The first is done as an example:

Bus fares set to rise says report

A report has been published saying that bus fares are likely to rise.

'Buses to be axed in bid to cut costs' says bus chief

Clash over threat to axe buses – passengers slam bus chief

Minister backs bus chief

Bus chief quits over bus battle

Minister axed after Cabinet split over bus row

E   Work in pairs. Match these VERBS which are often found in newspaper headlines with the more common verbs in italics below:

axe/scrap   back   call   clash   curb   grab   loom
oust   quit   slam   soar   swoop   vow/pledge

*be imminent   confiscate   criticise   disagree   promise   raid
reduce/dismiss   replace   request   resign   restrict   rise   support*

F   Work in pairs. Now do the same with these NOUNS which are often found in newspaper headlines:

BATTLE/CLASH/FEUD/ROW   BID   BLAZE   CHIEF   DRAMA
FURY/OUTRAGE   LINK   RIDDLE   SPLIT   THREAT   WAR

*anger   attempt   connection   disagreement   division   fire
happening   mystery   person in charge / leader   possibility
rivalry*

G   After this lesson, buy an English-language newspaper and read it before the next lesson.

Tell the rest of the class about one article that particularly interested you.

21.2   The wrong Wolff   Reading

Find the answers to these questions in the articles opposite.

1 How many papers reported Professor Heinz Wolff's death?
2 How many papers reported Dr Heinz Wolff's death?
3 Why did *The Sun* confuse the two Heinz Wolffs?
4 Why was Joan Wolff particularly worried about *The Sun* report?
5 What did the two Heinz Wolffs have in common?
6 Why do you think every sentence is a new paragraph in *The Sun* report? How is the style of *The Guardian* report different?

Great Egg Race prof dies at 61

ZANY scientist Dr Heinz Wolff, who shot to fame in the BBC's loony inventions series The Great Egg Race, has died in hospital.

The balding 61-year-old professor founded a world-beating research unit at London's Brunel University.

But with his fly-away hairstyle, half-moon specs and bow tie, he became best known for his part in wacky computer adverts in which he was crushed under a ten-ton weight.

In 1939 his family fled from Berlin to start a new life in Britain.

Genius Dr Wolff, who spent 30 years with the Medical Research Council, once refused a place at Oxford and deliberately failed his Cambridge University entrance exams.

Wolff . . . TV star

(from *The Sun*)

Sun tribute cried the wrong Wolff

Ed Vulliamy

PROFESSOR Heinz Wolff, the distinguished director of the Brunel Institute for Bio-engineering, whose tragic death was reported in the Sun last Monday, spoke cheerfully enough to the Guardian yesterday, using not a ouija board or spirit medium but a telephone from a Dutch seaside town called Noordwijk.

"Great Egg Race Prof Dies at 61," announced the Sun, referring to Professor Wolff's role in what the paper called the "loony inventions series" on BBC TV – and sparked off a bizarre chain of events throughout which Professor Wolff remained alive and well.

Within days of the Sun's story, two obituaries appeared in the Times and the Independent, detailing the career of a Dr Heinz Wolff, a leading psychodynamic psychiatrist, who had died at 73.

Dr Wolff had, sadly, died – but the Sun had got the wrong Heinz Wolff.

Professor Heinz Wolff was in Holland yesterday to make a presentation to a research laboratory. "I have started to receive cards in the post saying 'I'm glad you are still alive'," he said. "The main thing has been the tremendous number of phone calls I've had to make – family, friends, people who ask me to lecture to them or make videos; I'm still doing it."

When his death was announced, organisers of a meeting he was due to attend decided to cancel, out of respect, and telephoned his home to offer condolences. His wife, Joan, said yesterday: "The switchboard at Brunel was jammed with people ringing up on Monday morning. But our first thoughts were for the family, and the terrible worry that people would hear second hand – I mean, most of our friends don't read the Sun."

Both Professor Heinz Wolff and Dr Heinz Wolff were born in Berlin and settled in London. At one time, when Professor Wolff lived in Hampstead Garden Suburb and Dr Wolff lived in Hampstead, their telephone numbers differed by one digit.

Professor Wolff is a graduate of University College, London; Dr Wolff trained, and later became a department head, at University College Hospital. "We have been confused before," said Professor Wolff, "but never in such a horrifying way."

Several famous names have read of their own deaths in the newspapers, the most celebrated being Mark Twain, who complained that "reports of my death are grossly exaggerated". George Bernard Shaw read his own obituary and Ernest Hemingway was killed in print twice before he died. The Guardian also paid last respects to the writer Ngaio Marsh before she was quite ready to accept them.

(from *The Guardian*)

30 May 📼 You'll hear the early evening radio news. Listen to the recording at least twice:

1 Decide what the attitude of the broadcaster is to the hippies.
2 What actually happened? Note down what you consider to be the THREE most important points.
3 Compare your notes with a partner.

31 May   Now read the press report on the next page of the same events:

1 Decide what the attitude of the writer is to the hippies.
2 Note down what you consider to be the THREE most important points made in the article.
3 Compare your notes with a partner.
4 What are your reactions to the points of view expressed by Tony?

Travelling tribe of 300 individuals tries to leave 'rubbish society' behind

Andrew Moncur

Home for Tony and his four-year-old daughter, Emma, is a tarpaulin tent, now packed into a Jaguar with chronic engine fatigue.

It, and possibly 99 other irregular mobile homes, were in the process of eviction from a Somerset farmer's land yesterday. Tony and Emma were resuming their barefoot journey through the byways of an England whose conventional society they reject. Society has returned the sentiment, in full measure, since they took to the road two years ago.

This mutual antipathy had its expression yesterday when the convoy's children, who have shocked local people and been widely criticised, took the chance to throw a little mud (literally) at the local Tory MP, who came to inspect the site of their mass trespass. Mr Robert Boscawen, MP for Somerton and Frome, was not greatly put out.

Tony is not typical of the 300-odd travellers whose sojourn in farmer Les Attwell's grass field at Lytes Cary near Somerton has been front page news this week.

This is because the typical traveller does not really exist. The convoy consists of disparate groups.

The age of the adults ranges from 16-60; backgrounds are widely varied, from the painfully respectable to the more painfully deprived.

Tony, aged 23, was set on a life of utter normality in a North Wales town before he gave up his shoes and his trade as a time-served plumber.

"I saw what society was, just rubbish. You could say it's a paranoid view but I don't think so – George Orwell's 1984 has happened already," he said yesterday.

"This is my family. Where else can you go where there are 300 members of a family all in one place? It is a lot closer than it is in the city, where you never get close to anybody.

"In my bender I have probably got everything you have in your house; gas cooking, heating, even a kitchen table. I prefer it to living in a house. I believe in doing what I want to do.

"Put Emma with a kid in London who might be three or four times as old as her, and she's the same age as them. She learns what she wants to learn, what she needs to learn.

"It is like a tribe, if you like. She can read and write. She has been on the road since she was two and she is healthier here than she was anywhere else.

"I don't wear shoes and she doesn't either. One day there was snow and I took about four steps outside and bloody felt it. She was out there, sitting in the snow and making a snowman. She doesn't feel it.

"I think we are people who have seen society for what it is. It takes a lot of courage to make that move, to give up everything you know. It takes about three days to adjust."

---

31 May to 9 June 📼 You'll hear a sequence of early evening radio news broadcasts for each day between 31 May and 9 June.

As you listen, mark the route that the 'peace convoy' took on the map overleaf.

Note down what you consider to be the SINGLE MOST IMPORTANT EVENT reported on each day.

Compare notes with a partner halfway through the sequence and at the end.

Map labels:
SOMERSET — Compton Dundon • — Somerton • — Lytes Cary • — Yeovil / — DORSET — Dorchester • — Corfe Castle• — Upton • Poole • — Bournemouth — Stonehenge ∴ — WILTSHIRE — HAMPSHIRE Southampton • — Stoney Cross • — New Forest — Ringwood • — Calshot • — Bournemouth

Your reactions?
Work in groups. Find out how your partners would feel if the peace convoy had set up camp in THEIR fields or in a field next door to THEIR home. Do they approve or disapprove of what the police did on 9 June? What do they think the police (or government) should have done sooner?

10 June and 12 June

Now read this editorial and the letter to the editor on the next page.

Operation Overkill

Nothing better illustrates the bizarre pointlessness of the current persecution of the Peace Convoy than the sight of dozens of police marching dozens of hippies along the A31 in the drizzle yesterday after the Stoney Cross campsite was broken up at first light. Sure, the Convoy members are not all sweetness and light, free love and lentils. Sure, they leave a lot of litter and they drink too much. Sure, they have messed up some fields and a disused airfield and blocked some roads for a while. But that hardly makes the Convoy the public enemy that it has now become, commanding headlines, parliamentary statements and emergency ministerial committees. It doesn't make Stoney Cross "the world's most famous blot on the landscape," as one tabloid had it yesterday. And it doesn't justify the absurd waste of police time and public money (500 police officers on overtime at four o'clock in the morning don't come cheap) that was involved in ludicrous Operation Daybreak launched yesterday.

Nothing that the police either did or said yesterday was remotely proportionate to the problem posed by the Peace Convoy. First, there was no need to go in at 4am, rather than in mid-morning. It wasn't as though the hippies were planning on going anywhere; on the contrary. Second, there was no need to have so many officers, drawn from four different forces. The country is supposed to be short of police in the war against crime. The Convoy has consistently acquiesced when it has been evicted in the past and there was no reason to suppose that this time would be any different; nor was it. Third, it is clear that the main object of the

operation was to separate the hippies from their vehicles, thus in the words of the Hampshire chief constable "neutralising" and "decommissioning" the Convoy. Fine – but then what? People don't just disappear, however much you may want them to. Given the importance of the summer solstice to this particular group, it is obvious that they will soon be back in some way. Does that mean that hundreds of police are to spend the next fortnight marching around the lanes of southern England in case someone makes a fraudulent social security claim or someone else steals some firewood? Chief Constable Duke talked yesterday as though he had solved the problem. Alas, he has merely displaced it.

Sooner or later, someone is going to have to be a bit sensible. The Peace Convoy is an environmental problem, it is true, but is it really as great an eyesore or disruption as all the Ministry of Defence's convoys, ranges and no-go areas? Has the Peace Convoy destroyed rural England on a scale to match the grain baron farmers? Are all the road traffic, drugs and criminal damage offences that have piled up around the Convoy really so overwhelmingly serious that everyday crime prevention across large tracts of the south-west needs to be suspended to deal with it? If there was one person in Whitehall with a fraction of the public spirit of the Cornish landowner who has now offered asylum to some of the Convoy, then the whole problem could have been solved weeks ago by the provision of a site. Instead Government seems much happier aimlessly stoking up a mood of intolerant over-reaction which does no credit to anybody and which ensures that the trouble and expense of this whole pathetic business is perpetuated far longer than it ever needed to be.

186

Why the police officers of Stoney Cross deserve bouquets from the convoy

IN THE interests of accuracy about our operation at Stoney Cross, I feel bound to take what is for me a most unusual step in writing to you.

The previous violence of the convoy when its members drove heavy goods vehicles and coaches at police officers endeavouring to enforce the law, when vehicles from the convoy were driven forcefully at police road blocks, have in the past led to scenes that I would certainly not like to see repeated.

It was for those reasons that such a large number of officers was drawn together so early in the morning, to ensure a peaceful containment of the site without risk of further violence which would have required a police response. That no injuries or damage occurred during the taking of the site is clear justification for that decision.

Recognising that at the end of the operation a large number of people, including children, would be effectively displaced, it was *police officers* who took the initiative to draw together the relevant groups of the social services in order that those caring agencies, including police, could play their part in taking care of members of the convoy.

Police officers laid on coaches to provide transport to the social services; *police officers* offered and provided refreshment to members of the convoy; *police officers* persuaded members of the convoy to take the obvious advantage of the caring agencies.

Police did not march dozens of "hippies" along the A31; the "hippies" themselves decided to set off in that direction without any consultation with or direction from police. The police officers went with them to ensure their safety and that of other road users.

As to your frivolous comment, (Leader, June 10) about fraudulent social security claims and the theft of firewood, I am sure you realise that the unlawful behaviour of the convoy is far greater than this.

Yes, of course the convoy is a social and environmental problem, as well as a legal one. For my part I have no hesitation in applying the law to ensure the safety and protection not only of the public but also of the convoy members themselves.

As for the order of the High Court, are you really suggesting that it should be ignored, or would you expect me to sit back and contemplate another series of offences and disruption for other communities? I am confident that the firm, caring operation by police, coupled with its shared and overtly caring aspect, was justified and proper.

John Duke,
(Chief Constable),
Hampshire Constabulary,
Winchester.

Work in pairs. Discuss these questions with your partner. Then write your answers in no more than ONE sentence each.

1 What is *The Guardian*'s attitude to the convoy members?
2 What, according to *The Guardian*, were the three main mistakes of the police operation?
3 What does *The Guardian* think should be done?
4 Why, according to John Duke, did the police move in at 4 a.m.?
5 What is John Duke's attitude to the 'hippies'?
6 What is the main point of John Duke's letter?
7 Whose views do you side with and why?

21.4 Semantic markers   Effective writing

A [ht] Work in pairs. Look at the editorial opposite and highlight the following words and phrases in it:

Sure, ... Sure, ... Sure, ...	ANTICIPATING OBJECTIONS
But ...	COUNTER-ARGUMENT
It doesn't ... And it doesn't ...	ADDING FURTHER POINTS
First, ... Second ... Third ...	LIST OF POINTS
Sooner or later, ...	TIME RELATIONSHIPS

[ht] Now highlight the 'rhetorical questions' that were used in the editorial – what answer (if any) is expected to each question?

⟫→

187

B   These expressions can be used (rather like 'signposts') to connect the ideas in a piece of writing and show the reader which way you're heading.

Anticipating objections:
>   While it is true that   Although it must be admitted that   Certainly   Although

Counter-argument or contrast:
>   On the other hand   Nevertheless   Nonetheless   In spite of this   All the same
>   After all   At all events   In any case

Adding further points:
>   Furthermore   Moreover   Besides   What is more

List of points:
>   Firstly   First of all   In the first place   To begin with
>   Secondly   In the second place

Time relationship:
>   Meanwhile   At the same time   In the meantime   For the time being
>   Eventually   One day   Until then

Giving reasons:
>   The reason for this is   The cause of this is

Stating or anticipating consequences:
>   As a result of this   Consequently   Because of this   And so   This means that
>   Therefore   That is why   It follows that   If this happens   If this happened

Summary or conclusion:
>   To sum up   In other words   In short   After all   When all's said and done

▶ Work in pairs. Decide which of the expressions you could use in place of the phrases you highlighted in the editorial.

C   Fill the gaps and then continue this article in your own words.

.... hard drugs can never be totally defeated, there are a number of steps that should be taken to reduce their use. .... these steps must be taken at once – before it is too late.

.... , national governments throughout the world must control the use and supply of drugs within their borders. .... international organisations must coordinate individual states' policies. States which 'supply' drugs may be pursuing contradictory policies to states that 'consume' them and .... time and effort is frequently wasted.

Secondly, ...

21.5   Reports and opinions   Creative writing

A   Work in pairs. Look at the news photos on the next page and discuss these questions:

- What do you imagine has happened and what do you think is going to happen later?
- Why are such events considered to be 'newsworthy'?
- What can be done to prevent this kind of thing happening?

Make notes. Then join another pair and share your ideas.

B Choose ONE of the photos on the previous page and, using the notes you made in **A**, write TWO articles about it:

1 An on-the-spot report from a correspondent describing the events shown.
2 A newspaper editorial, giving your views on what should be done to prevent it happening again.

21.6 *Back, front* and *side*

Idioms

Fill the gaps in these sentences with *back*, *front* or *side*.

1 The peace convoy was ....-page news for two weeks.
2 The interviewer tried to find out more about the candidate's ....ground.
3 He is a civil servant but he moonlights as a plumber on the ....
4 They are such good friends that they always sit ....-by-..............
5 I don't like it when people criticise me behind my ....
6 The Vice-President is the ....-runner in the Presidential contest.
7 Most tennis players have a stronger forehand than ....hand.
8 If you need some support, let me know and I'll .... you up.
9 They were going to take part in the scheme but they've ....ed out of it.
10 The guerillas are members of the National Liberation ....
11 Computers can crash, so always keep a ....-up copy of your data.
12 We were scared when the car started moving ....wards down the hill.
13 A ....-bencher is an MP who isn't a minister or a shadow minister.
14 Drowsiness is a ....-effect of taking these tablets.
15 I didn't realise that I had my jumper on .... to ....
16 The laundry business was a .... for the gang's criminal activities.
17 A reference book has its contents in the .... and an index in the ....
18 We all felt sick as the train moved from .... to ....
19 When I challenged her, she .... down and changed her mind.
20 What was I talking about before I got ....tracked?

'Did Esme Drycott really go to her lover that night? Is Selwyn Plunkett dead, or alive and well in Peru? Was Melanie Frayle asleep or drugged? Who was the man in the green Mercedes? Stay with us for Part Two, after the break.'

22 Education

22.1 Schools and colleges   Vocabulary and listening

A   Work in groups. Ask your partners to tell you about all the schools and educational institutes they have attended.

B   Fill the gaps in these sentences.

1 Before they start school, very young children in Britain may go to a .... where they play with other children and learn to socialise.
2 British children start .... school at the age of 5 and move to a .... school at 11 or 13. At the age of 18 or 19 they may go on to .... education at a university, polytechnic or college.
3 At the age of 16, British pupils take GCSE (...............) exams. They may stay on at school to take GCE A levels (...............) two years later when they are in the .... form.
4 A British school or university year is divided into three ....s; in America the year is divided into two ....s.
5 In Britain private boarding schools are known as .... schools – in the USA this term refers to the normal kind of state school.
6 At the end of a university course, graduates are awarded a .... – probably a BA (...............), BSc (...............) or BEd (...............); post-graduates can take a further course or do research and write a .... in the hope of getting an MA (...............) or a PhD (...............).

C   The National Curriculum in England and Wales consists of ten subjects which all children must study at school:
English, technology and design, music, mathematics, history, art, science, geography, physical education, a modern foreign language.

Work in groups. Make a list of the school subjects which are/were your favourites AND the ones you dislike(d). Explain to your partners why you enjoy(ed) or don't/didn't enjoy them.

D   Work in pairs. What do you already know about the education systems in Britain, the USA or Australia?

You'll hear short descriptions of the education systems in England, the USA and Australia. Make notes on how a 'typical' pupil passes through the system in each country. Compare your notes with your partner.

★ Private education doesn't operate in quite the same way as state education and there are regional variations in all three countries.

E   Work in groups for this discussion.

- If the members of your group come from different countries, find out about the education systems in their countries.
- If you all come from the same country, what are the main differences between the education system in your country and those in England and the USA?

What improvements should be made to your country's education system?

F   Work in groups. Find out from your partners what they think about the following topics:

- Private education
- Boarding schools
- Coeducational schools v. single-sex schools
- School uniforms
- If it's a good idea for pupils to specialise in their 'best' subjects at school
- Pupil power – pupils participating in the running of schools
- The best age for children to start primary school – 4, 5, 6 or 7?
- Whether students should stay at school till they're 18 or 19

22.2   *-ing* and *to* __   Grammar

A   Work in pairs. Discuss the difference in meaning (if any) between these sentences and decide how each sentence might continue:

1 We stopped to eat our sandwiches when . . .
   We stopped eating our sandwiches when . . .

2 I won't forget to meet her because . . .
   I won't forget meeting her because . . .

3 Sometimes she didn't remember to hand in her work because . . .
   Sometimes she doesn't remember to hand in her work because . . .
   Sometimes she doesn't remember handing in her work because . . .

4 The lecturer went on to tell the audience about . . .
   The lecturer went on telling the audience about . . .

5 We tried to get through to her on the phone but . . .
   We tried getting through to her on the phone but . . .

6 I used to write a lot of 250-word essays but . . .
   I'm used to writing a lot of 250-word essays but . . .
   I usually write a lot of 250-word essays but . . .

7 I regret to tell you that your application was unsuccessful because . . .
   I regret telling you that your application was unsuccessful because . . .

8 He'd like to study alone because . . .
   He likes studying alone because . . .
   Studying alone is what he likes because . . .

B   Work in pairs. Correct the errors in these sentences.

1   Although I was looking forward to meet her, I was afraid to make a bad impression.

2   To smoke is not allowed in the classroom but students are permitted smoking in the cafeteria.

3   Everyone was beginning getting nervous before the exam, but once we began realising that we were all in the same boat we began to feel better.

4   The man denied to have committed the crime but he failed convincing the magistrate.

5   They made me to sit down and wouldn't let me leaving without to apologise for being rude to them.

6   To get into university you have to having the right qualifications.

7   Don't forget making notes before you start to write the essay, and remember checking your work through afterwards.

8   You can't expect achieving success without to work hard.

C   Work in pairs or, preferably, prepare this exercise before the lesson. Decide which of these sentences the verbs below can be used in – some of them can be used in more than one sentence. Make sure that you use the correct PAST form of the verbs.

Anne	to read *War and Peace*.
Bill	me to read *Crime and Punishment*.
Cathy	reading *Don Quixote*.
Dennis	me reading *A Tale of Two Cities*.
Elaine	that I was reading *Emma*.

admit   advise   agree   allow   appreciate   arrange   ask
assume   attempt   avoid   begin   can't help   choose
consent   consider   contemplate   continue   decide   delay
deny   detest   discover   dislike   dream   encourage   enjoy
expect   fail   feel like   find   find out   finish   forbid
force   forget   get   give up   guess   happen   hear   help
hesitate   hope   imagine   intend   invite   know   manage
mean   miss   notice   order   persuade   postpone   practise
prefer   pretend   prevent   promise   propose   realise
recommend   refuse   resent   see   spend an hour   suggest
teach   tell   think   try   understand   want   watch   wish

D   [ht] Highlight the verbs in **C** you found difficult or made mistakes with. Then write sentences to illustrate each of the 'problem verbs' – making sure you illustrate more than one use if necessary. For example, with *imagine*, you might write these examples:

In my dream I imagined myself being chased down a long dark corridor.
I imagine that they were very pleased to pass their exams.
I can imagine her finding out about the mistake and being really angry.

A Read this newspaper article (preferably before the lesson) and find the answers to the following questions:

1 What is the main underlying principle of American education?
2 How many students take part in higher education in the USA?
3 Why do students take Scan-Tron exercises?
4 What is the Sat? At what age do students take it? What is its purpose?
5 What is the Cat? At what ages is it taken? What is the purpose of it?

The Cat Sat on the test

School testing, like baseball, is crucial to the American way of life. **Michael White** in Washington offers a parent's view of the results

NOT MANY days pass without one or other of my kids getting out a number 2 pencil in their American suburban classroom and shading in the dots of a Scan-Tron paper in the correct number 2 lead so that the computer can read it.

And what is this Brave New World all about, you may be wondering? The answer is standardised testing, a national passion in this vast country of endless diversity.

So a Scan-Tron paper is what you use to answer the multiple-choice questions you get in maths, science, world studies (history and geography) or whatever it happens to be. Why did denim trousers become popular in the 1850s? Because they were (a) blue; (b) durable; (c) attractive; (d) inexpensive? Shade in the correct letter (incidentally it is (b)) in this 13-year-old's comprehension test and the computer will machine-read it.

British parents, teachers and pupils may already be fuming – or jeering – at the mention of pernicious multiple-choice techniques, let alone no. 2 pencils. But American education has its own ends: a system democratically

designed to educate the many rather than nurture the brightest few. Even though its public (i.e. state) as well as private schools actually do nurture an elitist core an astonishing near-50 per cent of Americans go on to some form of higher education. And there are 240 million of them.

Tests are part of the means to that end. Education is primarily a state and local function administratively and financially. Rich Massachusetts can and does spend more than poor Mississippi.

So there has to be some way of objectively evaluating Boston and Biloxi's idea of an A-student in the name of both progress and value for money. Americans are practically-minded. Education is utilitarian. The consumer's parent is king – and can vote out the school board. Quantification is a national instinct which finds expression in both IQ and baseball scores.

There is another reason why routine testing and published results matter so much. The US boasts no national exam system, no Himalayan range of GCSEs, A levels or Baccalaureates to scale. Pupils

are evaluated in two ways: in a process of continuous assessment by their teachers, via class work, homework, occasional essays and Scan-Tron exercises which produce term grades; and by national tests conducted at the ages of 8, 10, 13 and 17 – at least in our state, though practice varies.

For college aspirants there is the Scholastic Aptitude Test (Sat) taken by about 1 million 17-year-olds a year, plus anyone younger who wants a practice run. Even at graduate level a host of tests exist.

Susan Sullivan, who teaches at one of Washington's best schools, regrets this emphasis. "In the British system the teacher is a coach. You work towards the same goal and the enemy to be overcome is the A level. In our system the end of year assessment is so important, the teacher can be the enemy." And the multiple-choice test can be the enemy of real learning, the crucial technique being how to spot the "right" answer.

My 13-year-old at the local Junior High School offers a few basic tips on multiple-choice technique, "Statements are more usually 'true' than 'false' in these tests. If in doubt pick (c) or the longest answer." He does not have to write many essays and idiosyncrasy/creativity sits uneasily in the system. On the other hand he is in the fast stream, laden with homework and kept busy.

That too is a function of early diagnostic and formative

testing, bolstered by teacher evaluation. In the restless, anxious debate about the quality and direction of US education ("Why are the Japanese winning?") one familiar complaint is that the strongest and the weakest are identified and helped: but it is the 80 per cent in the middle whose fate is vital to the nation's social and economic health.

We happen to live in Maryland suburbs but the standardised national test our kids take at 8, 10, 13 and 17 is the California Achievement Test (Cat) widely used, as are the comparable Iowa and Stanford tests in some states. Covering such basics as reading vocabulary, spelling, language expression and math computation, they produce results expressed in stanine bands (1–9) and national percentiles. If you are bright, white and middle class your scores will probably be in the 90 per cent band: 60 per cent is the high school failure rate. If you are a poor black or Puerto Rican your scores may lag horribly.

Contemplating the jungle of American testing systems Britons might usefully note that anxiety about the efficacy of testing has produced more and more tests and refinements of tests. In college selection it has also produced greater reliance on teacher assessment.

The much-vaunted Sat scores may be helpful to the top 50 colleges in weeding out lesser applicants for entry. Most US colleges don't suffer heavy over-subscription and some publish misleading Sat scores, gleaned from their freshman intake, to boost their image in the marketplace. Good for business, say the critics, bad for education. "The tyranny of the Sats" frightens away promising students.

B   Answer these more detailed questions by referring back to the article.

1 Why does a particular kind of pencil have to be used?
2 Who controls and pays for education in the USA?
3 What are the US equivalents of GCSEs and A levels?
4 How are pupils in the USA evaluated by their teachers?
5 Why is the relationship between pupils and teachers different in the UK and USA?
6 Which answers in a 'true or false' test and in a multiple-choice test are the ones to pick if you don't know?
7 What other tests are equivalent to the Cat?
8 What skills does the Cat cover?
9 Which pupils do less well in national tests?
10 Why do some colleges publish misleading Sat scores? What is the consequence of this?

C   Highlight the following words and phrases in the article and try to work out their meanings from the context.
Match their meanings to the synonyms below.

*fuming   pernicious   nurture   A-student   utilitarian
quantification   continuous assessment   grades   aspirants
idiosyncrasy   fast stream   efficacy   much-vaunted*

bright pupil   cultivate   effectiveness
evaluation throughout the course   harmful
hoping to be admitted   marks   measurement   over-praised
practical   top class   unconventional behaviour   very angry

D   Work in groups. Ask your partners to talk about their experiences and to give their opinions on the following topics:

• National and international exams
• Regular performance tests
• Continuous assessment by teachers/lecturers
• The use of computers to assess learning
• The use of computers in education – to assist learning

A   You'll hear two accounts of a first day at school – one from a little boy's point of view, the other from a young teacher's point of view.
Read this extract before you listen to the recording.

> The village school at that time provided all the instruction we were likely to ask for. It was a small stone barn divided by a wooden partition into two rooms – The Infants and The Big Ones. There was one teacher, and perhaps a young girl assistant. Every child in the valley crowding there, remained till he was fourteen years old, then was presented to the working field or factory with nothing in his head more burdensome than a few mnemonics, a jumbled list of wars, and a dreamy image of the world's geography. It seemed enough to get by with, in any case; and it was one up on our poor old grandparents.

(from *Cider with Rosie* by Laurie Lee, 1959)

Now listen to the recording. You'll hear about Laurie's first day at the local village school.

B   Listen to the second extract, which is from *Decline and Fall* by Evelyn Waugh (1928):

Paul Pennyfeather is a new teacher at public school in Wales. The bell for the first lesson has just rung. Paul and two other masters are on their way to their classes . . .

C   Work in groups. Discuss with your partners how your own experiences of school compare with Laurie's and Paul's.

D   Write an account of your own first day at a new school or in a new class. Or, perhaps, write about your first day in this class.

22.5   Making an emphasis

A 🖺 Work in pairs. Highlight the words in this paragraph which emphasise or intensify the meaning of the nouns and adjectives used. What would be the effect of omitting these words?

Our class picnic very nearly turned out to be a big disappointment because of the heavy rain and the large number of people who dropped out at the very last minute, but to everyone's total amazement it was a great success and we all had an extremely enjoyable time. The people who had decided not to come must have been absolutely furious.

B Work in pairs. Which of these emphasising adverbs would normally be used with each of the adjectives below? Refer back to 3.4 on page 22 if necessary. Look at these examples first:

very/extremely   angry   disappointed
absolutely   astonished   furious

amazed   amazing   brilliant   catastrophic   clever   cross
different   disappointing   disastrous   enjoyable   fantastic
happy   helpful   idiotic   perfect   powerful   proud   sleepy
surprised   wonderful

C Work in pairs. Which of these emphasising adjectives would normally be used with each of the nouns below? In cases where there is more than one possibility, just choose one. Look at these examples first:

great   achievement   disappointment   number
deep   admiration   sleep
big   decision   disappointment
large   number   proportion
heavy   sleeper   rain
high   cost   level
strong   feeling   taste
absolute/complete/total   amazement   astonishment   disaster

amount   anger   catastrophe   detail   difference   drinker
enjoyment   excitement   failure   fool   friend   fun
happiness   help   idiot   improvement   love   nonsense
opinion   power   pressure   price   pride   proportion
quality   quantity   sense of humour   show   sigh   skill
smell   smoker   snow   speed   strength   success   surprise
traffic   trouble   understanding   wealth

D Work in pairs. Write six sentences, each containing at least one of the adjectives or nouns used in **B** and **C**. Leave a gap for the appropriate emphasising adverb or adjective. Pass your sentences on to another pair and get them to fill the gaps. One is done as an example:

We were ………… amazed at the ………… number of people who came.

22.6　Using stress

A Notice where the main stress is placed in each of these words.

quálified　/ˈkwɒlɪfaɪd/　qualificátion　/ˌkwɒlɪfɪˈkeɪʃən/
exám　/ɪgˈzæm/　exáminer　/ɪgˈzæmɪnə/　examinátion /ɪgˌzæmɪˈneɪʃən/

B Work in pairs. Take it in turns to say each of these words aloud and
mark the main stress in each one. Listen to the recording afterwards.

acádemy　académic
art　artistic
biology　biological
botany　botanical
chemist　chemistry　chemical
consult　consultation
economics　economical　economy
educate　educational
examine　examination
geography　geographical
grammar　grammatical
history　historical

lecture　lecturer
literature　literary
maths　mathematics　mathematical
physics　physical
politics　political
second　secondary
secretary　secretarial
society　sociology
special　specialise　specialisation　speciality
statistics　statistical
zoology　zoological

C Work in pairs. Take it in turns to read each of these sentences aloud,
paying attention to the word stresses. The first is done as an example:

1 She's stúdying pólitics at univérsity and hópes to becóme a politícian.
　/ʃiz ˈstʌdijɪŋ ˈpɒlɪtɪks ət ˌjuːnɪvˈɜːsɪti ənd ˈhəʊps tə bɪˈkʌm ə ˌpɒlɪtˈɪʃən/
2 Maths is an interesting subject but I don't want to be subjected to a long lecture about
　it, thank you very much!
3 What a lovely present! I was present when they presented her with the award.
4 Wait a minute – I just need to make a minute adjustment to this machine.
5 When are you permitted to use the emergency exit?
6 You need a special permit to use this entrance.
7 I've read the contents of the book and now I feel quite content.
8 After our dessert, we watched a film about some soldiers who deserted and escaped into
　the desert and joined a group of rebels.
9 When a metal object cools down it contracts.
10 This contract is invalid because it hasn't been signed.
11 The people rebelled because they objected to the government's policies.
12 I don't normally mind being insulted – but I do when such dreadful insults are used.

A   Read this newspaper article and then, working in groups, discuss these questions with your partners:

- How old is the writer of the article?
- Why is he not looking forward to his next year at school?
- What does he think he *will* enjoy about next year?
- How are your own experiences similar or different to the writer's?
- What advice would you give the writer?

That sixth sense of plus and minus

Tom Smithies

MY LAST exam was history and finishing it signalled the completion of 12 years that I once thought would never end.

For over a decade I have had to trudge off to school five times a week, 39 weeks a year. As the day I had looked forward to for years approached I expected a feeling of elation, of breaking free – just think: old So-and-so cannot criticise my homework ever again. Yet in the event it was rather sad. I am going into the sixth year for A-levels, but so many of my friends have left, and the sixth form, while being a whole lot groovier, won't be the same without my old mates.

It has taken until now for me to understand how important these friendships are. Some have taken years to build up, and it was a jolt to realise that some people whom I knew and liked had decided to leave, and it is possible that our paths will not cross again. Just two months ago they were lending me their calculators or sharing a bag of crisps and the latest joke. Now they will go off to work in banks, garages, farms and shops.

The comradeship was built not just on similar interests and common attitudes: we were all victims of circumstance, lumped together because of where our parents chose to live. In such an environment there are bound to be disagreements and fights – adolescence is nothing if not volatile, and those who tell us to grow up fail to understand that that is exactly what we are doing, learning by our mistakes and experiences. By sharing the things that naturally befall you, companionships spring up, quietly binding alliances of black and white, male and female.

Luckily, there are also some who are staying on for the sixth form, so why should I feel saddened at leaving the fifth year when a lot of my friends will stay on? Well, I consider myself lucky in that I have friends in every year of the school, but sixth-formers rarely seem to socialise with any year below the fifth.

It is one of those peculiar conventions, caused, I suspect, by the sixth form's wish to seem aloof from the rest. It is a custom that next year, like the insensitive tourist, I shall have great fun disregarding entirely.

So now I return to school to begin the A-level trail. There will be some new faces – my school has the sixth form for a wide area – and the teachers are said to regard you as halfway human, so it should be an enjoyable two years. And once they are over it will be up to me whether I sink or swim. There is no one to copy homework from in big business.

B   Imagine that the writer of the article is a friend of yours. Write him a letter, telling him that you have read his article and giving him your reactions to it.

22.8 *Pick, pull, put* and *set*　　　　　Verbs and idioms

A　Fill the gaps with suitable forms of *pick*, *pull*, *put* or *set*.

1 It takes most people a long time to .... up a new skill.
2 Was it her own idea or did someone .... her up to it?
3 Can you .... me up at the station tomorrow? But please don't .... yourself out – if it's not convenient I'll get the bus.
4 In the USA if someone doesn't believe you they might say, 'You're .... me on!', whereas in Britain they'd say, 'You're .... my leg!'
5 We didn't expect him to succeed, but to our surprise he .... it off.
6 Building work on the tunnel has been .... back by the bad weather and the opening will have to be .... back.
7 In a crowded place it's quite easy for someone to .... your pocket.
8 I bought a new desk yesterday and it took me all day to .... it together. Now that it's .... up, I'm very pleased with it.
9 It looks as if the bad weather has .... in for the rest of the week, so we may have to .... off our trip till next week.
10 If they ask us to .... them up for the night, what can we say to .... them off?
11 At the end of the meal, while I was still .... my teeth, she insisted on .... up the bill.
12 Just as I was .... out from the car park a farmer in a red ....-up ran into the back of my car. I .... in to the side of the road but instead of .... up, the farmer .... up speed and disappeared into the distance.

B　Fill these gaps with suitable forms of *pick*, *pull*, *put* or *set*.

After she had .... our brains on the feasibility of the idea she .... about .... forward her plans to the committee. Unfortunately, she didn't .... the ideas across very well. As soon as she sat down, people began to .... holes in her arguments. They said she was trying to .... the wool over their eyes. She felt that everyone was .... on her unfairly and she knew that she was being .... down. She .... this down to her poor presentation and she felt terribly up..............., but she had to .... herself together, ... on a smile and .... up with the humiliation.

C　Work in pairs. Write a mini-exercise with SIX sentences with gaps (...............) using the phrasal verbs from **A** and **B**. Pass your exercise to another pair and get them to fill the gaps.

23 Science and technology

23.1 Scientists and engineers

Vocabulary and listening

A Work in groups. Find out from your partners:
– which were/are their favourite science subjects at school
– if both girls and boys are encouraged to become scientists or engineers in their country
– what technical subjects are taught at schools in their country

B Work in pairs and answer the questions:

1 What are these things (used for fixing things together) called?

2 What are these controls called?

3 What are these tools called?

C Work in pairs. Take it in turns to say what these pieces of equipment or products are used for. The first is done as an example.

A pencil sharpener is a device/gadget/thing you use for sharpening pencils.

a pencil sharpener   a zip   a ruler   a spirit level
a bicycle pump   a torch/flashlight   a safety pin   a rubber band
a stapler   a corkscrew   a penknife   a test tube   a tin opener
a fuse   a plug   a padlock   a telescope   a microscope
a pair of binoculars   a rubber stamp   a postage stamp
an air conditioner   hair conditioner   a toolbox
a chest of drawers   a drawing pin/thumbtack   a drawing board

D You'll hear ten short spoken extracts. As you listen, note down:
• The subject the speaker is talking about.
• The tone of voice he or she is using (patronising, bored, enthusiastic, etc.).
• Who you think he or she is talking to (a group of students, a child, etc.).

For example, the first speaker is talking about bicycles in a kind, unpatronising tone of voice and she seems to be talking to a group of adults.

23.2   Astronaut wanted

A Find the answers to the following questions in this article:

1 What kinds of tests are the applicants having to take?
2 Who is Mr Glazkov?
3 How many people applied to be astronauts?
4 How many applicants are being tested this week?
5 What do the people being tested have in common?
6 How many will there be on the final shortlist?

Hale and hearty reach for the stars

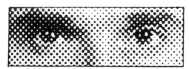

Eyewitness

. . . .

Shyama Perera

"THE training will be ad-nauseam. You could even teach a monkey to do it," said the aspiring British astronaut. "You should not think we are superhuman, we do not need to be anything more than hale and hearty. There are no treadmills in space."

Juanita Lofthouse, 5ft 3ins tall and a bantam weight 7st 2lbs – "There won't be excess baggage if I go up" – was, in fact, preparing to run a tread-mill during her medical fitness test in London yesterday.

A veteran of the London Marathon, she envisaged no problems but was apprehensive about the afternoon's psychological tests. "You could be the world's greatest scientist but if you are going to crack up, then you're no good for these purposes."

In a windowless room near King's Cross, Juanita and 15 other budding astronauts saw the future – and it was deadly dull. Cooped up and sweating under the camera lights, they answered inane questions while waiting for check-ups.

"I should have brought a script, shouldn't I?" asked fresh-faced Dr Keith Waldron, one of those with a track record of work on micro-gravity, and almost certain to make the final shortlist for the Anglo-Soviet Juno space mission.

Juanita was slightly more cynical: "At the moment, we've all got novelty value because we are all serious scientists who also speak a foreign language – there are very few people with that combination."

Actually, Keith had only O-level French, but the cosmonaut overseeing the tests, Mr Yuri Glazkov, was using an interpreter anyway, so it didn't seem to matter that much.

Mr Glazkov, short, rotund, and hot in his navy suit, was dealing with the media circus as politely as possible. He ran through the perfect space traveller's attributes for the umpteenth time.

A veteran of the 18-day Soyuz 24 space mission in 1977, he described his feelings on his return. "The first feeling is joy to be back safely on earth, but to be honest, adapting to normal life was not easy.

"The other feeling was that this was enough and I did not want to do any more, but after about two days, like any sailor or pilot, the urge to go back came over me."

However, while Russians have traditionally been aware of opportunities within their space programmes, space travel is something new to the British, who have enough of a problem finding a train to take them from Newcastle to Lowestoft, let alone trying to decipher the timetables.

Miss Lofthouse, the first person in her family to go to university, is finishing a PhD on the structure and function of the red blood cell cyto skeleton.

She and Dr Waldron are among 150 people who will be tested this week for their suitability for space travel. They were picked from 3,500 applicants who qualified after answering "yes" to four questions: are you aged between 21 and 40; do you speak a foreign language; are you a British subject; and do you have a degree in science, medicine or engineering.

A final shortlist of four will be sent to Moscow to be checked by the Soviets, from which two people will be picked after intensive testing. However, only one will make it on the Juno mission, which is scheduled for the spring of 1991.

ASTRONAUT WANTED
NO EXPERIENCE NECESSARY.

GLAVCOSMOS, the Soviet Space Administration, has offered a place to a British astronaut on a space flight in 1991.

Whoever is chosen will have had no experience because no Briton has ever flown in space ■ He or she will automatically write themselves into the history books ■ It is fitting that the flight is scheduled to take off on the 30th anniversary of Yuri Gagarin's historic first manned space flight on the 12th April 1991. It will be called the 'Juno' Mission.

The flight touches down eight days later.

The First ANGLO-SOVIET *Space Mission.* The eight days in space will be spent on the Soviet Space Station MIR from which the British astronaut will conduct scientific experiments ■ The

experiments will be carried out in order to advance our knowledge in basic science, others will demonstrate important principles in education and a few will test advances in space technology ■ The work will encompass biological experiments involving plants, cells, bacteria, and the astronaut.

Experiments in mater science will include the growing of crystals, p cularly of proteins, pos the development of a and the study of under conditions wh is not possible to re on Earth.

The mission is the first commercial joint venture between the Soviet Space Administration and British industry.

In fact it's the first ever

...for it is Perestro...

The mission will raise £16M in revenue from the

...and universities, ... acts a... in the ... experi... which ... a lab... launch...

...nal ...her ...cine, ...anual ...icants ...ility to ...uage ...ndard of ...They will also have the ability to work

two fi... selecte... ...ched... ...oviet Centre... candid... missio...

H...
Al...

The... MSL Limit... consul... 32 Ay... W1M applic... phone between weekd... at wee... remain...

B Refer back to the article and answer these more detailed questions.

1 How did Juanita Lofthouse feel about the morning's tests and about the afternoon's tests?
2 Why were the members of the group sweating?
3 Why is Keith Waldron very likely to make the shortlist?
4 How well do the applicants have to speak Russian?
5 Why does Juanita Lofthouse think the press are interested in her and her fellow-applicants?
6 What is the writer's opinion of the British public transport system?

C Work in groups. Decide which of these research projects should, in your opinion, have the most government money spent on them:
- nuclear weapons research
- conventional weapons research
- medical research
- scientific research
- educational research
- space exploration

▶ Give an example of each type of research and say why you believe it is worthwhile OR pointless.

23.3 How does it work?

A Work in pairs. Before you listen to the recording, check how much your partner already knows about how a video recorder and CD player work.
Which of the missing information in the diagram below can you fill in?

B 🖭 Listen to the recording and fill the gaps in the diagram.

VHS VIDEO RECORDER

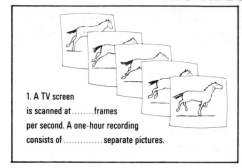

1. A TV screen is scanned at .... frames per second. A one-hour recording consists of .... separate pictures.

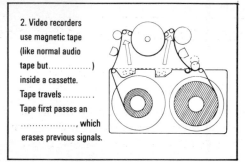

2. Video recorders use magnetic tape (like normal audio tape but ....) inside a cassette. Tape travels .... Tape first passes an .... , which erases previous signals.

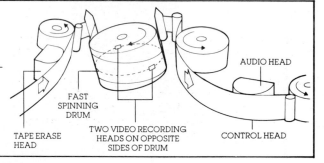

3. Then it travels round a fast spinning drum. There are two video recording heads on opposite sides of the spinning drum. The drum is .... slightly – as the tape goes past the drum the recording heads pass the tape many times, leaving a message in .... 'stripes'.

TAPE ERASE HEAD

FAST SPINNING DRUM

TWO VIDEO RECORDING HEADS ON OPPOSITE SIDES OF DRUM

AUDIO HEAD

CONTROL HEAD

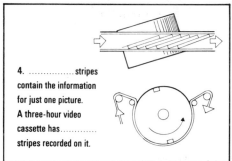

4. .... stripes contain the information for just one picture. A three-hour video cassette has .... stripes recorded on it.

5. After it has left the spinning drum the tape passes the .... and .... heads. The soundtrack is recorded along the top edge of the tape, and the control track, which .... playback speed to recording speed, is recorded along the bottom edge of the tape.

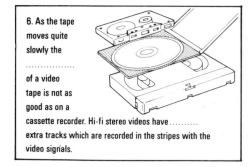

6. As the tape moves quite slowly the .... of a video tape is not as good as on a cassette recorder. Hi-fi stereo videos have .... extra tracks which are recorded in the stripes with the video signals.

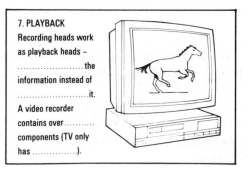

7. PLAYBACK
Recording heads work as playback heads – .... the information instead of .... it. A video recorder contains over .... components (TV only has ....).

C Listen to the second part of the recording and make notes on how a CD player works.

Compare your notes with a partner.

D The class is divided into an EVEN number of pairs. Half the pairs should look at Activity 62 (how a MOVIE PROJECTOR works), the other half at 56 (how a MOVIE SOUNDTRACK works).

When you have familiarised yourselves with the process, join another pair who were studying the other information and share your knowledge.

23.4 A good introduction and conclusion   Effective writing

A Work in pairs. Look at the OPENING paragraphs of the reading passages in Units 20 to 23. Discuss these questions with your partner:

- What effect does each opening paragraph have on you as readers?
- Which of the paragraphs encourages you to read on and find out more?
- Does the very first sentence of each passage catch your attention?

Decide which of these opening sentences you prefer for an article on 'How a movie projector works':

```
Have you ever wondered how a movie projector works?
Did you know that a movie projector shows 24 frames every
    second?
There are 1,440 individual frames in one minute of a movie.
Not many people know how a movie projector works.
A two-hour movie consists of 172,800 frames.
Everyone's been to the cinema, but not many people know what
    happens in the projection room.
```

B Work in pairs. Draft a short opening paragraph (two or three sentences) for an article or essay on each of the following topics:

1 Space exploration
2 Genetic engineering
3 Studying science
4 How compact discs work
5 How a movie projector works
6 How a video recorder works

▶ Show your paragraphs to another pair and ask for comments on how effective they are.

C Work in pairs. Now look at the CONCLUDING paragraphs of the same reading passages. What is the effect of each one on the reader? Which of them leave you feeling better informed and satisfied?

D Work in pairs. Draft a concluding paragraph (two or three sentences) for each of the articles or essays you began in **B**.

Show your paragraphs to another pair and ask for comments on how effective they are.

23.5 Where next?

A Read this article (preferably before the lesson) and find the answers to the following questions:

1 When was this article written?
2 How many earthquakes are there every year?
3 What determines the amount of damage caused by an earthquake?
4 How can scientists tell that an earthquake may be about to happen?
5 How certain can scientists be about the likelihood of an earthquake?
6 Why were engineers relieved after the 1989 San Francisco earthquake?

WHERE NEXT?

Our Science Correspondent, **Robert Matthews**, examines seismologists' efforts to forecast tremors and looks at the latest building techniques to resist earthquake damage

NO natural phenomenon brings home more clearly the piffling scale of human activity than an earthquake. Last Tuesday evening, San Franciscans saw their most impressive skyscrapers rocking to and fro like cocktail twizzle-sticks.

At a time when scientists can usually be relied on to come up with at least an explanation, if not a cure, for virtually every blight on man's existence, it comes as a shock to learn that the study of earthquakes is still in its infancy, and that predicting them with any reliability is still years away.

The cause of earthquakes is easy to understand. If all the world's oceans were drained away, the Earth's surface would look like a giant egg-shell criss-crossed with huge cracks.

These cracks mark the boundaries between so-called "tectonic plates": vast slabs of rock as much as 4,000 miles across and 18 miles thick. Despite their immensity, these plates are far from static. They float on a bed of molten, lava-like material known as magma.

Thermal currents in the magma rise up under the plates and slowly, but inexorably, force them against one another. The grinding of the plates gener-ates enormous tension in the rock. When it can take no more, the rock tears, releasing huge amounts of energy. An earth-quake is the result.

In any one year, the number of earthquakes around the world stays roughly constant. About 3,000 earthquakes of at least moderate intensity are usually detected.

Most of these cause relatively little damage; despite the com-mon fixation with the Richter scale strength of a particular earthquake, it is where, rather than how powerful, an earth-quake is that determines the amount of damage caused.

Even a moderately strong earthquake in, say, China can cause immense devastation. Just after the San Francisco quake, a considerably weaker one struck northern China, making 50,000 people homeless. The trouble is hundreds of millions also live in coastal regions: precisely where the tectonic plates perform their tug-of-war.

This has led scientists to seek ways of predicting when and where an earthquake will strike. These range from looking for jumps in the level of radon, a radioactive gas, released from rock about to give way, to an investigation of folklore that insists earthquakes are preceded by odd behaviour in animals.

According to Dr Russ Evans of the British Geological Survey in Edinburgh, the most promising prediction method seems to be the use of "foreshocks" – tiny creakings in the earth that pre-sage a major quake.

These enabled the Chinese, in 1975, to make the first, and so far only, useful prediction of an earthquake. They evacuated part of Manchuria 24 hours before a quake, which would have killed thousands, struck.

However, the success followed weeks of shuttling the local population in and out of the area as the scientists made, and then withdrew, their predictions. San Franciscans could hardly be expected to endure similar treatment.

Not surprisingly, the Ameri-cans have brought the full weight of science to bear on the problem. On part of the notor-ious San Andreas fault in Cali-fornia, about 100 miles south of the epicentre of last week's quake, the US Geological Survey runs the Parkfield Earthquake Prediction project. Boreholes containing extremely sensitive pressure and move-ment sensors, detect even very weak "foreshocks".

The problem is that the Earth is always creaking quietly away, but only occasionally produces a major earthquake. Trying to separate out the creaks from the quakes demands large amounts of data, which take years to accumulate.

Dr Evans maintains accurate earthquake prediction is still a scientific pipe-dream. A wrong, or even slightly mis-timed pre-diction would prove worse than useless, he points out. Dr Evans pictures the scenario of the two-tier highway to Oakland, which collapsed last week, being jammed with citizens fleeing a predicted earthquake which came an hour too soon.

If prediction is impossible, minimising the damage must be the next priority for scientists and engineers. Huge sums have been spent on designing earthquake resistant structures.

The San Francisco earthquake proved that the engineers had got their sums right. The slender pyramid of the Transamerica building and its skyscraping neighbours survived virtually unscathed, despite swaying by as much as three feet during the quake.

The usual approach is to make the building as rigid as possible, and betting that sheer strength will enable the building to withstand the tremors.

To resist the side-to-side "longitudinal" tremors which put the most strain on the building, engineers reinforce the central core of the structure.

Some engineers, particularly in earthquake-prone Japan, want to isolate the main structure from its foundations. The simplest way of doing this is to

Horror of the Cypress Freeway sandwich

put the building on shock-absorbing bearings made of lead or rubber.

The most sophisticated technique under study involves "active vibration control". A building struck by a quake responds rather like a huge, upside-down pendulum, swaying from side to side. By changing the weight distribution of the building, it is possible to damp out the worst swaying.

A computer senses the onset of the quake and sends instructions to weights on the building's roof. These are positioned so that the amount of swaying is minimised.

Japanese engineers reckon that as much as three-quarters of the movement can be countered using this technique.

B   Answer these more detailed questions by referring back to the article.

1   How are earthquakes caused?
2   Where do most earthquakes occur and what is the result of this?
3   Why is it so difficult to predict exactly when a major earthquake is about to happen?
4   How does Dr Evans think that a slightly mistaken prediction could be more dangerous than ignorance?
5   How do some Japanese engineers want to protect modern buildings from earthquakes?
6   What is the very latest idea for protecting buildings from earthquakes?

C   Highlight the following words in the article – if any are unfamiliar, try to work out their meanings from the context.

blight   inexorably   fixation   tug-of-war   presage   pipe-dream
scenario   two-tier   unscathed   earthquake-prone   countered

D   Work in groups and discuss these questions:

• Have you ever experienced an earthquake? What was it like?
• What earthquakes have happened recently in your country – and in other parts of the world? How serious were they?

A Work in pairs. Find out your partners' reactions to this advertisement:

JUST SAY NO.

America is hooked on foreign oil. Today, we import almost 40 percent of the oil we use—even more than in 1973, when the Arab embargo plunged us into gas lines, rationing, and recession.

The more we can use nuclear energy, instead of imported oil, to generate electricity, the less we have to depend on foreign nations.

The 110 nuclear plants in the U.S. have cut our foreign oil dependence by over three billion barrels since 1973. And they have cut foreign oil payments by over one hundred billion dollars.

But 110 nuclear plants will not be enough to meet our growing electricity demand. More plants are needed.

To help kick the foreign oil habit, we need to rely more on our own energy sources, like nuclear energy.

For a free booklet on nuclear energy, write to the U.S. Council for Energy Awareness, P.O. Box 66103, Dept. SN01, Washington, D.C. 20035.

Nuclear electricity and energy independence

U.S. COUNCIL FOR ENERGY AWARENESS

Nuclear energy means more energy independence.

©1989 USCEA

B Write an essay giving your reactions to the advertisement. Before you start writing, make notes and decide:
– how you will begin (your opening paragraph)
– what your main points will be
– how you will end (your concluding paragraph)

▶ Check your work through and correct any mistakes you notice.

C Show your work to a partner and ask for feedback.

23.7 *First, second, third, last* and *late*   Idioms

A Work in pairs. Discuss the difference in meaning (if any) between these phrases:

1 I decided to catch a late train.   I decided to catch the last train.
  I decided to catch the first train.   I decided the train was late.
  I decided to catch the early train.   I decided to catch an early train.

2 Her first husband   Her second husband
  Her last husband   Her late husband
  Her latest husband   Her former husband
  Her ex-husband   Her husband is late

3 A second-hand watch   The second hand on a watch

B Fill the gaps in these sentences with suitable forms of *first, second, third, last* or *late*:

1 If this awful weather .... till the weekend it will be the .... straw.
2 Right, ... things ....: when shall we meet tomorrow? I think I'd better call for
  you .... thing in the morning – no, on .... thoughts, it's better if you call for me
  by 8 o'clock at the ....
3 There are only a few left unsold, so it's .... come, ... served.
4 They didn't get on very well at .... but by the end of the course, which .... six
  months, they were the best of friends.
5 It seems to be .... nature to many American people to be on .... name terms
  with everyone.
6 I expected there would be a lot of ....-minute preparations to make but .... on I
  found that nothing at all needed doing.
7 Well, I haven't dealt with ACME plc at .... hand but they have a ....-rate
  reputation. You should certainly apply for the job.
8 On the other hand, Zenith International are a ....-rate company – I'd only apply for
  a job with them as a .... resort.
9 He's never satisfied unless he has the .... word in an argument.
10 Everyone is entitled to one mistake, please give me a .... chance.
11 The doctor wasn't sure what to do, so she asked for a .... opinion.
12 My aunt's children are my .... cousins but my mother's cousin's children are my
  .... cousins.
13 The .... news is that, at long ...., the problems have been solved.
14 I attended a .... aid course the week before ....
15 Most novels are written in the .... person but some, where the narrator is the main
  character, are written in the .... person.

C Work in pairs. Write a mini-exercise with six sentences with gaps
(...............) using the phrases from **A** and **B**. Pass your exercise to another pair
and get them to fill the gaps.

24 Utopia

24.1 The perfect society

Reading and listening

A Read this magazine article, preferably before the lesson. MAKE NOTES (like those shown below) on what you think are the most desirable and least desirable features of Aldous Huxley's Pala.

Compare your notes with a partner.

> NAME OF UTOPIA: Aldous Huxley's PALA (1962)
>
> **Good points**   **Bad points**
>
> Voluntary daily digging
>   for intellectuals
>
> No army

Island
. . . being the book that spelled out the ingredients for Utopia

LONG BEFORE JOGGING in Central Park became the fashion, intellectuals on the tropical island of Pala used to put in a couple of hours hard digging every day. They weren't obliged to. But the Palanese were very advanced in matters of health: they didn't separate minds from bodies, venerating brains at the expense of the whole human organism.

In economic matters too, Palanese thinking was very advanced. Export crops were discouraged: the islanders were fed first. Money was wasted neither on status symbols nor on weapons. The government bought no armaments: there was no army.

Where was this utopia? Only, unfortunately, between the covers of **Island**, Aldous Huxley's final novel. In it he detailed his prescription for a sane society – especially for Third World countries short on money but rich in human resources.

Huxley showed how colonialism had carved out a false channel for most developing countries, draining them of their wealth and their culture. He advocated a siege economy, to stop the leakage. Pala was closed to the outside world, especially out of bounds to merchants, missionaries and mediamen, the usual links between the developing world and the West.

Within the walls of the island fortress, radical changes were brought about. For example, wealth was shared more equally – the richest Palanese earning not more than four or five times as much as the poorest. And jobs didn't define personal worth, since the Palanese swapped jobs regularly. Being a doctor for six months

and then a farmer for the rest of the year not only made a Palanese a more rounded person, but also made sure he didn't consider himself superior to people who got their hands dirty. The personal and social integration achieved were, for the Palanese, worth more than the time and money spent on making the changeover.

Huxley takes, one at a time, every important social ingredient that he can squeeze into a 300 page novel – schools, newspapers, politicians, religious and scientific beliefs, ideas about family life – and examines it to find its value. What, for example, is there worth saving in family life? And what is constraining about it? Huxley doesn't polarise the issue into pro-family or anti-family camps. He concocts his own variation of a family that accommodates both the closeness and security that come from a two-parent set-up, as well as the variety and freedom that come from a child having several homes to choose from. Palanese society, therefore, is an amalgam of the best in every society that Huxley knows.

First published in 1962, **Island** had a powerful influence on the young idealists of the day. Many of the ideas were so advanced that they are only now being widely recognised – like Huxley's insistence that Western medicine and holistic health care techniques should be allies, not enemies.

But there is one huge snag. Pala is fiction. Huxley is the God of Pala. How are real people in real countries to shift to this paradisal willingness to live cooperatively? For instance, it might not help a real country to adopt a siege economy: who would stop the big bad unequal world outside the fortress walls from being reproduced within the walls as a small bad unequal world?

Huxley's answer leads him out of the political realm into the realm of spiritual values. His islanders have evolved inwardly. They have all experienced a transpersonal dimension where they are part of a universal oneness; when they return to the material world, they remain inspired by the glimpse of the ideal.

Dangerous waters. Perhaps to forestall critics tempted to dismiss Huxley as a dreamy 1960s mysticism-junkie, he included among his cast of characters a group of spiritual fakes, charismatic guru figures who use their followers' gullibility to gain political power and line their pockets. Huxley sets these vigorously apart from the genuinely spiritual, whose spirituality is infused matter-of-factly into their everyday lives, in everything they do – eating dinner,

making love, coping with an injury. It is their constant awareness of the here and now – a phrase popularised more by **Island**, surely, than by any other book – that does the trick.

In Huxley's **Brave New World**, everything from muzak to mechanical sex was used to blot out consciousness and turn people into manipulable zombies. The result was a hell on earth. In **Island**, everything, including sex and drugs, is partaken of consciously to heighten individual consciousness still further. The result is Pala, Huxley's heaven on earth.

Anuradha Vittachi

Island
by Aldous Huxley (1962)

Granada (pbk)
UK: £1.95/Aus: $7.50

B   You'll hear some people giving short talks about four more fictional perfect societies. MAKE NOTES of the good points and bad points of each one, in the same style you used in **A** above.

Plato's REPUBLIC (about 360 BC)
Thomas More's UTOPIA (1516)
H.G. Wells's A MODERN UTOPIA (1905)
James Hilton's SHANGRI-LA (1935)

C   Work in groups and compare your notes with your partners. Then decide together which of the features of each perfect society you might include in your own version of Utopia.

24.2   Special uses of the Past   Grammar

A   Work in pairs. Discuss the difference in meaning or emphasis (if any) between these sentences:

1 I was hoping we could have a talk today.   I hope we can have a talk today.
  I had hoped we could have a talk today.   I'm hoping we can have a talk today.

2 I wonder if you could help me.   I wondered if you could help me.
  I was wondering if you could help me.

3 Were you wanting to see the manager?   Did you want to see the manager?
  Do you want to see the manager?   Didn't you want to see the manager?
  Don't you want to see the manager?   Would you like to see the manager?

4 I wish there was more time.   I wish there were more time.
  I wish there had been more time   If only there were more time.

211

B Fill the gaps in these sentences. The first is done as an example.

1 He always talks to us as if we ...*were*... children.
2 I'd rather you .... smoke in here, if you don't mind.
3 It's time you .... to the station to catch your train.
4 I wish I .... better at putting a name to a face.
5 If only I .... the solution to the problem.

C In these sentences most of the continuations are grammatically correct, but some are wrong. Mark the ones that are correct with a tick ✓.

1 It's past midnight and I think it's time ...
... I went to bed   ... for me to turn in.   ... I call it a day.
2 It's terrible, she behaves as if ...
... she owned the place.   ... she weren't a guest.   ... it was her own home.
3 He spoke to me as if ...
... I were a half-wit.   ... I was simple-minded   ... I have no brains.
4. I wish ...
... she were less outspoken.   ... she wouldn't speak her mind so frankly.
... I was less sensitive to disapproval.   ... I can tolerate criticism better.
5 I'd rather ...
... you didn't tell me off.   ... you don't scold me.   ... not to blame me.
6 I wouldn't mind if ...
... he isn't such a daydreamer.   ... he weren't so forgetful.
... he was less absent-minded.
7 If only ...
... the world is a better place.   ... the world were a better place.
... the world be a better place.   ... the world should be a better place.

D Now use your own ideas to continue these sentences:

1 It's high time ...   4 I'd like to suggest that ...
2 I'd much rather you ...   5 It'd be much better if you ...
3 She looked at me as if ...   6 I do wish ...

E Work in pairs. Here are some ideas that can be expressed by using different structures. Put a tick ✓ beside the continuations that 'feel' suitable to you. Again several are correct. The first is done as an example.

1 It is absolutely essential that these letters ...
... are posted today. ✓   ... were posted today. ✗
... should be posted today. ✓   ... be posted today. ✓
2 If any unforeseen problems ...
... should arise, let me know.   ... were to arise, keep me in the picture.
... arise, don't keep me in the dark.   ... are to arise, tell me at once.
3 I insist ...
... that she should be informed.   ... that she is given the information.
... she be informed.   ... to inform her.
4 It's important ...
... that we were on our guard.   ... that we are as careful as can be.
... to be extremely careful.   ... that we should show the utmost care.

5 I propose that …
    … we take a vote on it.   … we should ask for a show of hands.
    … the matter be put to a vote.   … we held a ballot.
6 We demand …
    … that payment is made at once.   … that payment be made at once.
    … to be paid at once.   … that payment was made at once.

Highlight ONE continuation for each sentence that you feel most 'comfortable' with.

Which of the continuations would you use in a more formal style?

24.3   *Lay, lead, leave, let* and *lie*   Verbs and idioms

A   Fill the gaps with a suitable form of *lay, lead, leave, let, lie* (lie/lay/lain) or *lie* (lie/lied/lied) and complete each sentence in your own words:

1 He ……………… about his age but as we knew he was ……………… about this we …
2 I began to ……………… the table for lunch but while I was ……………… the table …
3 I was so tired that I ……………… down on the bed and while I was ……………… there …
4 They ……………… the room together and as they were ……………… the room …
5 We didn't expect them to ……………… us in because …
6 One thing ……………… to another: if we'd known what it was ……………… to, we might have …

B   Fill the gaps with a suitable form of *lay, lead, leave, let* or *lie*.

1 After a slow start she took the ……………… and finished first.
2 This really is unfair and I'm not going to take it ……………… down – they ……………… me on by saying I'd get a rise this year and now they say I won't.
3 I can't get interested in this subject – it ……………… me cold.
4 I wouldn't even want to spend one night there, ……………… alone work there.
5 According to the ……………… article in the paper the reason the management gave for so many workers being ……………… off was a pack of ………………
6 If you're feeling tense or angry, it's a good idea to ……………… off steam.
7 The glass was so slippery that I couldn't help ……………… go of it.
8 The city of Salisbury ……………… in a valley, near the south coast.
9 It's best to ……………… it be – if the system's working well it's best to ……………… well alone, making an adjustment may ……………… to problems. 'If it ain't broken don't fix it', as the saying goes.
10 I'm going to ……………… my cards on the table and tell you quite frankly what my plans are.
11 She wants her boss to ……………… her take three months' ……………… of absence (unpaid) as well as the four weeks she has ……………… over from last year's holiday entitlement. She hopes her boss won't ……………… her down by refusing to ……………… her go.
12 He explained the ………………out of the factory and the manufacturing process very simply, in terms a ……………… person could follow.
13 If you'll ……………… the arrangements to me, I'll ……………… on all the necessary equipment and make sure nothing is ……………… out.
14 We wanted to go out for a walk but the rain didn't ……………… up all day.
15 What are all these questions ……………… up to? Why don't you ……………… me alone?

24.4 Reading aloud Pronunciation

It's always more efficient to show someone else a written text or give them a photocopy – it's usually only necessary to read something aloud when you're on the phone or when you have to give a group of people some information and they don't have copies to look at.

A   Work in pairs. Arrange these ideas about reading aloud in order of importance:

1 Pause frequently for questions from your listeners.
2 Summarise the less important parts to save time.
3 Don't read too slowly.
4 Decide in advance how to pronounce any difficult names or words.
5 Read the passage through to yourself first.
6 Don't read too fast.
7 Spell out important names, if necessary.
8 Think about your listeners as you read.

▱ Now listen to the recording about Brasília. To what extent did the reader seem to be following the ideas above?

B   ▱ Listen to the first paragraph of the article again. Mark the catenation below (i.e. the way the words are joined up – and   not   spoken   with   a   pause   between   each   one   ). The first line is done as an example:

BRASILIA – UTOPIA IN THE HEART OF BRAZIL

Brasília, the capital city of Brazil, was designed as a futuristic Utopian city in the 1950s by Lúcio Costa and Oscar Niemeyer, both followers of the great French architect Le Corbusier. Brasília is a purpose-built city twelve hundred kilometres from the coast on a red dirt plateau where no one lived – or wanted to live. It's the most photogenic city in the world with sweeping avenues, beautiful ceremonial buildings and fantastic sunsets.

The parliament building, shops, hotels, flats, leafy suburbs for the

---

C   ▱ Work in pairs. One of you should look at Activity 52, the other at 65, where you will see the middle and final sections of the article. Read it through to yourself and then read your section aloud to your partner.

Ask your partner to suggest how you could improve your reading.

A You'll hear a recording of a letter being read aloud. Make notes on the main points and compare your notes with a partner.

B Read this advertisement and highlight what you consider to be the most interesting points.

What would be the main advantages and drawbacks of life in Nosara?

Beach homesites for sale in beautiful Costa Rica...

Now you can own property along the beaches of Nosara in peaceful Costa Rica for just $6,450–only $150 down payment, and $150 a month at absolutely no risk!

Imagine a home tucked away in a secluded cove or on a lush green hillside within a 10 minute walk of a broad, white sand beach caressed by gentle ocean breezes . . . a nearby river . . . year around temperature that seldom goes below 72 degrees or above 82 degrees . . . plenty of room for horses, a few cattle, ample gardens, and located in a country with one of the most stable democratic governments in the world, where the military establishment has been banned by constitutional decree, the literacy rate and health care systems are among the best in the world, and where foreigners are genuinely liked and appreciated and afforded all the legal protections of citizens.

> "Costa Rica, sometimes called the Switzerland of Latin America, has been unscathed by the turmoil that typifies the rest of Central America. Its army was disbanded by constitutional decree in 1948, and most of the national budget goes into education and health care . . . There are four universities, and the nation boasts it has more schoolhouses than policemen. The literacy rate is above 90%, among the highest in the world, while the infant mortality rate is among the lowest . . ."
>
> The Los Angeles Times,

Dreams don't come true by themselves. There comes a time to take action, and if you want to someday live in paradise, that time is now.

We have more than 3,000 acres subdivided into homesites and farms that range in size from 1/3 to more than 12 acres, with 25 miles of all-year roads, electricity and water systems already in operation, and an ecologically sound master-plan that provides for parks and green areas.

Full title to the 1/3 acre homesites – all within a 10 minute walk of the beach – are being offered for only $150 down payment and 42 payments of $150 a month, with NO INTEREST CHARGE! But we don't want anyone to risk buying something they're not completely sure of, so we also provide a unique guarantee: If you visit Nosara at any time within one year of signing the purchase agreement and decide for any reason that you don't want the property, WE WILL REFUND EVERY CENT YOU HAVE PAID, with no questions asked! Or if you find another site you would prefer to own, we will be pleased to work a trade and apply the money already paid toward the new site.

Nosara is on the beautiful Pacific West Coast just 100 miles from San José, the capital city. There are already 65 homes built at the beaches of Nosara, and they range from comfortable $8,000 cabins to expansive villas of around $100,000 (construction cost averages only $25 per square foot). Hundreds of acres have been set aside for parks and wildlife refuges that abound with wild parrots and other birds, deer, pecary and other animal life. The beaches are without equal any place in the world, but remain tranquil and uncrowded.

Yes, you can find all the privacy you have ever dreamed of in Nosara, but there's no need to give up the amenities of the "good life". There are two luxurious hotels with a swimming pool and fine restaurants, tennis courts, horseback riding, some of the finest sportfishing in the world for marlin, sailfish, dolphin, wahoo, tuna, snapper and much more! If you crave the nightlife and shopping of a cosmopolitan city, drive to San José or fly by air service from the Nosara airport.

There's only so much time for dreaming . . .

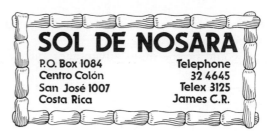
C Work as a team to design your group's own Utopia.

Discuss these questions with your partners:

- What will the physical environment of your Utopia be like?
- How will the government be organised?
- How will work and possessions be divided among the people?
- What part will science and technology play?
- How will public and private transport be organised?
- What family structures will exist?
- What will the education system be like?
- How will crime be prevented or punished?
- Why isn't life like this now?

D Give a joint presentation of your plans to the whole class – each member of the team should participate in the presentation, perhaps covering different aspects of the topic.

'Have you been hoovering again?'

Communication activities

—— 1 ——————————————————————

THE BLUE LAGOON by H. de Vere Stacpoole (1909)

- Dick (age 9) and Emmeline (age 8, his foster sister) were on a ship with Dick's father when their ship was wrecked in a storm. Only Dick and Emmeline escaped to an island, with Paddy Button, one of the crew.
- Island had fresh water and fruit. Paddy warned them not to eat some red berries as they would 'send them to sleep'.
- Passing sailors landed on island: children were afraid and hid – sailors took away small box belonging to Emmeline.
- Paddy was drowned – Dick had to learn to find food and catch fish – one day he was nearly caught by a giant octopus.
- Years passed. One day, Emmeline went off into forest. Next day, to Dick's surprise, she came out with a baby in her arms.
- Later they made a boat, wanting to get to the other side of the island. Strong current carried the boat away from the island. They ate red berries they had with them and went to sleep, expecting never to wake up.
- Meanwhile Dick's father, who had also survived the shipwreck, was living in San Francisco. He had bought Emmeline's box from a sailor, found out where he had got it and set sail to find them. Near the island, found a young couple and a child in tiny boat apparently dead. But, happily, they weren't dead – just sleeping.

—— 2 ——————————————————————

Find out what your partners think about these questions:
- What's your attitude to the widening gap between the rich and the poor in the world today?
- Should rich people feel guilty about their good fortune?
- What would it be like to be world famous?

3

You are the MANAGER of the Excelsior Restaurant. You'll receive a booking enquiry. Study this information before answering the phone:

- Private room (capacity 40 persons) available on 18 and 19 December but only if 36 persons book, not for smaller number.
- Five-course Xmas dinner costs £18.50 per person, including aperitif and coffee but not wine. House wines @ £7.95 per bottle.
- Guests should arrive at 7.30 p.m. for 8 o'clock.
- You require confirmation in writing with 25% deposit within 24 hours.

▶ When the 'observer' has given his or her feedback, turn to Activity 14.

4

AFTER 60 or more hours a week of helping to build Japan Inc, a couple of thousand young Japanese strap on battery packs and helmets, draw phaser guns, and enter the world of high-tech wargames.

Photon is billed as the ultimate game on planet Earth, but for those who come back again and again to Tokyo's Photon base it is much more than a game.

One young banker said he tries to play at least once a week. "I think the enemy is my boss, or maybe a bad customer. It gets rid of tensions from my job," said Mr Hiroshi Matsumoto.

"Baseball, golf, nothing is as good as coming here," said another banker.

The Photon base is a huge warehouse in suburban Tokyo. Inside is a giant two-storey maze with pulsating neon lights, ramps, bunkers and barriers.

It is dominated by two team-based targets at either end of the room. S─ people are the g── p──

5

Paragraph 1 is from *Emma* by Jane Austen (1816).
The delightful Emma's mismanagement of other people's affairs leads to consequences she could not have foreseen. A comedy of self-deceit and self-discovery. Jane Austen's elegant, gently ironic style makes her one of the greatest English novelists, whose work still appeals strongly to the present-day reader.

Paragraph 2 is from *A Tale of Two Cities* by Charles Dickens (1859).
One of Dickens's most popular stories. The action takes place against the turmoil of the French Revolution in the two cities of Paris and London. The three main characters, Charles Darnay, Sydney Carton and Lucy Manette are projections of Dickens himself.

	Location	Length (km)	Opened
The St Lawrence Seaway	USA/Canada	3,769	1959
	– from Duluth, Minnesota, via the Great Lakes and St Lawrence River to the Atlantic Ocean; closed during the winter because of ice		
Berlin Wall	Germany	105	1961
	– used to separate East and West Berlin; part of the 'Iron Curtain'		
Humber Estuary bridge	UK	1.4	1980
	– nicknamed 'bridge to nowhere' as it is so little used; cost £250 million		
Seto Osashi bridge	Japan	1.8	1989
	– suspension bridge connecting Honshu with Shikoku		
Seikan rail tunnel	Japan	54	1989
	– bullet train line between main island of Honshu and Hokkaido		
St Gotthard rail tunnel	Switzerland	15	1880
	– first Alpine tunnel; during construction 310 men killed: two deaths per month		

7

WHAT IS THE BODY SHOP?

To the hundreds of thousands of people all over the world who visit The Body Shop every week, it is, quite simply, the place where they choose to go to buy their skin and hair care products. They enjoy the experience: the smell, the sights, the sounds, the atmosphere. . . And they like and trust the products: they work well.

"IF YOU'RE HAVING A DOWN DAY OR IT'S POURING WITH RAIN OUTSIDE IT'S ALMOST LIKE SUMMER WHEN YOU STEP INSIDE" A BODY SHOP CUSTOMER

The Body Shop is the shop on your High Street. It is also an international company, with its headquarters in West Sussex, UK. We research, develop, manufacture, distribute and finally sell products for both women and men, of all ages.

The Body Shop approach is different from that of the mainstream cosmetics industry. We follow the route of health and well-being, rather than the obstacle-strewn path to 'beauty'. You will not find images of idealised women in our shops or our literature.

The Body Shop approach is non-exploitative. Our shops are self-service. Customers are not pressurised into buying something they do not really need or want by either advertising or forceful sales staff.

We back up our products with information: information readily available directly, or indirectly through our staff: Body Shop staff are trained to help you when you need or want it.

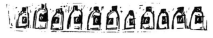

We offer choices: a choice of products that care for your skin and hair, and a choice of how you buy them.

1 Work in pairs. Rewrite this passage as reported speech.

> My friend Max spoke to me last Tuesday and said:
> "It's my birthday today. I got a card from my uncle in Australia
> yesterday and one from my aunt in Canada today. I know you
> can't come to my party tomorrow, so would you like to join
> me for a drink now or maybe we can meet later this evening?"

2 Now rewrite this passage using the exact words Susan used.

> Last Wednesday, my friend Susan spoke to me on the phone
> and told me that she wouldn't be able to see me this week.
> She had had a call from her brother ten minutes earlier and
> had heard her grandfather would be arriving there at the end
> of the week and this would be the first time she'd have seen
> him since he went to New Zealand in 1988. She hoped I
> wouldn't mind if we changed our meeting from this week to
> next week.

3 When you've finished, compare your versions with what your partners (in
the other pair) have written and with the passages in Activity 44.

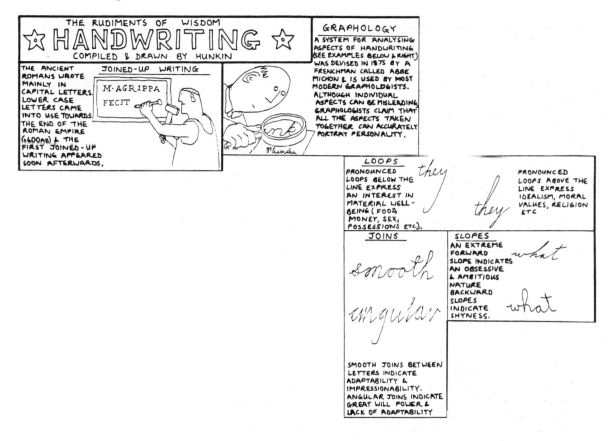

— 11 —

That was it, more or less. I had been to Brighton so many times I had no desire to linger. Much better, I thought, to push on to Bognor, where I had never been. But I had someone to see in Brighton – Jonathan Raban was there on his boat, the *Gosfield Maid*, moored at Brighton Marina, just beyond Kemp Town and the nudist beach ('Bathing Costumes Are Not Required To Be Worn Past This Sign'). Jonathan had said that he was taking a trip around the British coast and was planning to write a book about it. This interested me. All trips are different, and even two people travelling together have vastly different versions of their journey. Jonathan was doing his coastal tour anti-clockwise, stopping at likely ports in his boat.

He seemed contented on his boat. He had framed prints and engravings on the walls, and Kinglake's *Eothen* was open on a table under a porthole. It was strange to see a typewriter and a TV set on board, but that was the sort of boat it was, very comfy and literary, with bookshelves and curios.

'This must be your log,' I said, glancing down. The entries were sketchy ('. . . light rain, wind E S E . . .') – nothing very literary here, no dialogue, no exclamation marks.

He said, 'I keep planning to make notes, but I never seem to get round to it. What about you?'

'I fiddle around,' I said. It was a lie. I did nothing but make notes, scribbling from the moment I arrived in a hotel or a guest house and often missing my dinner. I hated doing it. It was a burden. But if I had been in Afghanistan I would have kept a detailed diary. Why should I travel differently in Britain?

(from *The Kingdom by the Sea* by Paul Theroux, 1983)

— 13 —

Shock

1 Move the patient as little as possible. Call for a doctor or ambulance.
2 Position the patient with his or her head low and feet raised – do not move any part that may be fractured.
3 Loosen tight clothing.
4 Keep the patient warm – cover them with a coat or blanket.
5 Reassure the patient by being calm, sympathetic and confident. Even if the patient appears to be unconscious they may be able to hear any unfavourable comments you make.
6 DON'T give the patient anything to drink, not even water and definitely not alcohol.
7 DON'T give the patient anything to eat.

— 14 —

You are the 'OBSERVER'. Make notes on the call. After you have given the callers your feedback, turn to Activity 30.

— 15 —

The things you know to be true are shown with a tick √ and the things you are unsure about are shown with a question mark ?.

Adrian had a cold ?	Chris overslept √
Flora had to go to hospital for an X-ray ?	Diane had hayfever √
Bill had a hangover √	Claire had a dentist's appointment ?
Frank had a headache √	Emma had a job interview √
Anne hurt her foot √	Dennis had flu ?
Betty was suffering from sunburn ?	Eric's car wouldn't start ?

16

PRINCE Charles intensified his crusade against the "huge, blank and impersonal" legacy of much post-war architecture in two new initiatives yesterday.

He published a book full of his strongest language yet on the issue, declaring that Britain had created "godforsaken cities from which nature – or, indeed, the spiritual side of life – has almost been erased."

He added, "It's a lucky city, especially in Britain, that doesn't have its heart torn out and thrown away."

Last night he also opened an exhibition which sets out his analysis at the Victoria and Albert Museum in London.

Amid displays reviling modern London as "a jostling scrum of skyscrapers" and modern Docklands as "the triumph of commercial expediency over civic values", a caption to photographs of tower blocks sums up: "Sometime during this century, something went wrong."

In the book, A Vi~i-- Britain (Doubl~-~ D~~~~

Study these instructions and secretly rehearse the trick together. Then join another pair and demonstrate the trick to them.

A member of the audience writes three names or words on a small piece of paper, putting the most important one in the *middle.* Tear the paper into three pieces and put it in a hat or box. Feel for the piece with no straight edges and pick it out. Read out the most important word that the member of the audience wrote.

Lindbergh is first to fly Atlantic solo

May 21 1927. A 25-year-old pilot became a new international hero tonight when he touched down in front of a crowd of 100,000 people at Le Bourget airport, completing the first solo non-stop flight between New York and Paris.

Boyishly good-looking, Captain Charles Lindbergh also needed great courage to fly his Ryan NYP monoplane, the Spirit of St Louis, across the Atlantic, sometimes dipping to within ten feet of the wave tops, and staying alert by munching home-made sandwiches.

His 3,600 mile flight was accomplished in 33 hours 39 minutes at an average speed of 107.5 mph. But until a few weeks ago Lindbergh was the dark horse in the race to win the $25,000 prize offered for the first non-stop flight from New York to Paris.

It seemed only his backers, a group of St Louis businessmen, believed in him. But he made a daring one-stop flight from California to New York to gain a lead over his rivals before taking off on the record-breaking flight from Roosevelt Field on Long Island at dawn yesterday.

His departure was big news on both sides of the Atlantic as the Spirit of St Louis, over-loaded with fuel, staggered drunkenly into the sky, after barely clearing the trees at the end of the runway. Alerted by radio and newspapers, large crowds gathered along the American coast to watch for the

Charles Lindbergh in front of the plane he flew across the Atlantic.

young captain's aeroplane as it flew north.

It turned west towards the Atlantic at St John's, Newfoundland at 7.15 pm New York time. From then on Lindbergh flew by dead reckoning, sometimes climbing as high as 10,000 feet.

He reported seeing the lights of Paris at 10 o'clock tonight and touched down at Le Bourget at 10.24 to the roar of the

crowd, who rushed forward to welcome the new hero, clearing two companies of French troops out of the way in the process. Lindbergh, born in Detroit and raised in Minnesota, is a quiet midwesterner, who appeared taken aback by the warmth of the reception. The race to be first across the Atlantic galvanised public interest so that the cause of aviation will also be boosted by this epic flight.

(from *Chronicle of the 20th Century*)

Paragraph 3 is from *Three Men in a Boat* by Jerome K. Jerome (1889).
Three friends decide to go for a holiday on the River Thames in a boat, taking with them plenty of food, a tent and J's dog, Montmorency. A series of hilarious mishaps occur during the voyage. One of the funniest books in the English language.

Paragraph 4 is from *Rebecca* by Daphne du Maurier (1931).
This outstanding romantic melodrama tells the story of an innocent young woman who marries the sophisticated aristocrat Max de Winter and goes to live in a remote country house called Manderley, with its sinister housekeeper, Mrs Danvers. Here she is caught up in the mystery of Rebecca, Max's beautiful first wife who died in strange circumstances.

20

THE topsy-turvy temporal life and times of disgraced TV evangelist, Mr Jim Bakker, took another sensational twist yesterday when a judge ordered the founder of the Praise The Lord Ministry to undergo psychiatric tests.

Mr Bakker, who apparently believes that "angry animals" are intent on attacking him, was discovered "lying in the corner of his attorney's office with his head under a couch, hiding," said his psychiatrist, Dr Basil Jackson. Mr Bakker had assumed the foetal position and was clearly hallucinating.

He was led crying from his lawyer's office by federal marshals and taken into custody after the order was issued by US district judge Robert Potter. "Please don't do this to me," he pleaded, before crawling into a car.

The presiding judge at Mr Bakker's trial in Charlotte, North Carolina, suspended proceedings yesterday pending the results of the tests.

Mr Bakker, aged 49, is accused, with other PTL executives, of diverting for their own use more than $4 million of the $158 million raised by selling holiday packages to supporters.

If convicted, Mr Bakker could be sentenced to 120 years in jail and fines of $5 million.

You work for Gamma Engineering and you want to book a private room for your staff Christmas dinner party. Telephone the Excelsior Restaurant to book a table. (You have already tried several other restaurants, but they were already booked up.) Study this information before you make the call:

- There will be 24 to 35 people in your party, but you may not know the exact number till the day before.
- Find out the inclusive cost of the Xmas menu.
- Dates: 1st choice Friday 20 December, 2nd choice Thursday 19th.
- Find out what time everyone should arrive.

▶ When the 'observer' has given his or her feedback, turn to Activity 42.

HOW DID THE BODY SHOP BEGIN?

This is a story that has been well-told many times over. In 1976, Anita Roddick opened a tiny shop in a side street in Brighton. She sold a range of twenty-five natural skin and hair care products in a variety of bottle sizes, labelled by hand. The shop had sprung from her idea that you ought to be able to buy as much or as little shampoo or skin cream as you wanted – just as you can do with apples or potatoes. . .

Today each Body Shop sells over 300 products. There are around 300 Body Shops, most of them franchised.

And we are still growing. . .

All the Body Shops across the world form part of a whole, that is held together by a common bond. It is underwritten by a common philosophy.

This is the strong foundation on which a thriving and successful international company has been built.

WHAT IS THE BODY SHOP PHILOSOPHY?

The Body Shop continues to trade today on the same principles that have held firm since its beginning in 1976.

We use vegetable rather than animal ingredients in our products.

We do not test our ingredients or final products on animals.

We respect the environment: we offer a refill service in our shops, all our products are biodegradable, we recycle waste and use recycled paper wherever possible, we use biodegradable carrier bags.

We use naturally-based, close-to-source ingredients as much as we can.

We offer a range of sizes and keep packaging to a minimum: our customers pay for the product, not elaborate packaging or for more than they need (and this helps keep the prices down too).

23

The chart shows the distribution of people under and over 25 in different parts of the world in 1970 and in 2000. Discuss these questions with your partner:

- What do the figures tell us about the probable numbers of older people in 2025 and later?
- How do people of your age fit into the pattern?

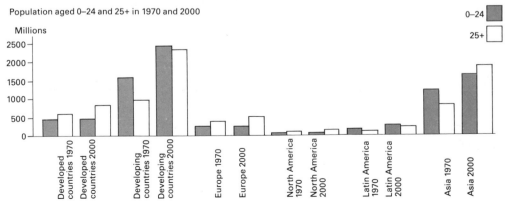

Population aged 0–24 and 25+ in 1970 and 2000

Millions

Join another pair and find out what they have discovered. Share your ideas and information with them.

	Location	Length (km)	Opened
Houston Canal	Texas, USA	91	1940

– Houston is America's third busiest port (after New York and New Orleans) even though it is 50 miles inland from the Gulf of Mexico

Rhine-Danube Wall	Germany	480	c. 90

– protected Roman Empire from hostile Germanic tribes

Chesapeake Bay Bridge-Tunnel	Virginia, USA	28	1964

– in mid-channel the road spirals down from bridges to a tunnel: US Navy insisted on tunnel to allow large ships unimpeded access to naval bases

Oshimizu rail tunnel	Japan	22	1981

– beneath the Japanese Alps for bullet train line from Tokyo to Niigata

Simplon rail tunnel	Switzerland-Italy	20	1906

– first tunnel dug from both ends simultaneously; when Swiss and Italian tunnels met misalignment was 9cm vertically and 20cm horizontally

25

James Dean (born 8 February 1931 – died 30 September 1955)
- Star sign: Aquarius.
- First words spoken to him in his first film *East of Eden*: 'Hello, pretty boy.'
- Symbolised tormented, rebellious middle-class youth.
- Famous for his looks: his slouch, the glance from beneath his hair, his vulnerable eyes.
- Only starred in three films, of which only *East of Eden* (1955) had been shown before he died. *Rebel Without a Cause* (1955) and *Giant* (1956) both released after his death.
- Killed in car crash outside Los Angeles on his way to a big race in his new Porsche in 1955 at the age of 24.
- Mass grief at his death – huge posthumous box office success of all his films.
- Reasons for his appeal even today: epitome of moody, vulnerable young man. Attractive to young women and men. Charismatic screen performances. He died so young that he remains a mystery.
- Quote:
  'To me the only success, the only greatness is immortality.'

You are the 'OBSERVER'. Make notes on the call. After you have given the callers your feedback, turn to Activity 31.

The next morning I made a couple of telephone calls from the marina office then spent a hasty hour tidying the saloon and polishing the brasswork on the wheel. I found a hiding place for my notebook in a drawer in the forecabin, under a pile of socks.

At noon, I spotted my visitor a hundred yards away across the catwalks. Focusing on him with the binoculars, I saw he was wearing an elegant pair of miniature binoculars himself. In his Papa Doc tinted spectacles, an L. L. Bean duckhunter's camouflage shirt, with a little brown backpack hoisted on his shoulders, Paul Theroux was on his travels.

"Hi – how you doing?"

Ten years before, Paul and I had been friends and allies, but the friendship had somewhat soured and thinned since. Nor had either of us been best pleased when each had discovered that the other was planning a journey, and a book, about the British coast. It was too close a coincidence for comfort. Paul was working his way round clockwise,

by train and on foot, while I was going counterclockwise by sea. At Brighton the two plots intersected briefly and uneasily aboard *Gosfield Maid*.

It took Paul less than five minutes to sum up the boat. He hunted through the saloon, inspecting pictures, books, the charcoal stove, the gimballed oil-lamps, the new, lavender-smelling gleam of the woodwork.

"Yeah," he said; "it's kind of . . . *tubby* and . . . *bookish.*"

The phrase rattled me. I rather thought that somewhere I had written it down myself.

"You making a lot of notes?"

"No," I lied. "I seem too busy with things like weather and navigation to notice anything on land. What about you?"

"No," Paul lied. "There's nothing to write about, is there? I don't know whether there's a book in this at all. I may turn out to have just spent the summer walking. Still, it keeps you fit –"

(from *Coasting* by Jonathan Raban, 1986)

28

Here are some basic principles of graphology:

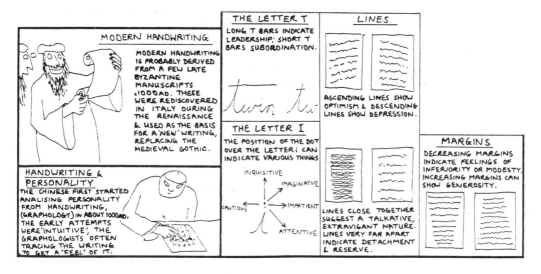

29

You feel VERY DEPRESSED because:

- Your two best friends are leaving the country and you won't see them again for a long time – if ever.
- You have a terrible headache – the aspirin you took hasn't had any effect.
- You don't think your English is getting any better.
- You feel sick – there's a flu epidemic and you think you may have caught it.

Explain your problems to your partners and try to resist their efforts to cheer you up.

30

You are Marketing Director of Zenith International. Phone your client, Mr/Ms Warner of Acme Enterprises. Study this information before you make the call:

- Ask after his/her family (you met them on your last visit).
- Arrange a meeting for the morning of Friday 13th February.
- Persuade him/her to allow a *whole* morning for your meeting.
- Invite him/her to have lunch with you.
- Ask him/her to recommend a good restaurant and book a table for you.

▶ When the 'observer' has given his or her feedback, return to page 165.

31

Study this information before starting the call. You are SALES DIRECTOR of Delta International. Phone the Hotel California to book a room for your four-day sales conference (65 people), preferably from 17 to 20 January. Find out:

- The cost of the room.
- About lunch arrangements – many of your sales people prefer to have a light lunch or snack, not a full meal at lunchtime.
- If bedrooms are available for delegates at a special rate.

Make a firm booking NOW, in case someone else books the room.

▶ When the 'observer' has given his or her feedback, turn to Activity 37.

32

THE SWISS FAMILY ROBINSON by J.R. Wyss (1813)

- A Swiss family (Father, Mother and their four sons: Fritz, Ernest, Jack and little Francis) were shipwrecked in the South Seas on a deserted island – with two dogs, sheep, cows and hens.
- Called the island New Switzerland. Built a tree house.
- Found a barrel of gunpowder, chests of clothes, boxes of books and even mirrors and chairs washed up on beach.
- Pineapples, sugarcane and all kinds of fruit growing. Salmon in the river and even oysters in the sea.
- Many unusual animals on the island: kangaroos, a huge snake (which Fritz killed), ostriches and elephants. Made butter and cheese from the milk of the cows they had brought with them.
- One day found an albatross with a message tied to its leg from Jenny, a girl shipwrecked on a nearby island. Fritz rescued her and they fell in love.
- Years passed: a ship came to the island. Father, Mother, Jack and Ernest decided to stay in New Switzerland. Fritz, Jenny and little Francis went back to Europe. Three of the passengers on the ship liked New Switzerland so much that they decided to stay there.

THE BODY SHOP PHILOSOPHY IN PRACTICE

HOW DOES IT WORK?

It works on many levels, some more visible than others.

Our *products* reflect our *philosophy*.

They are formulated with care and respect:

Respect for other cultures: Anita Roddick travels extensively each year and learns how people in different countries care for their skin and hair. Some of these ideas are incorporated into our products.

Respect for the past: we look to the past for experience and wisdom: many of our ingredients, such as honey and almond oil, have been used for centuries. 'Old' ingredients have a history of safety which we can rely on.

Respect for the natural world: many of our ingredients are naturally based, obtained as close-to-source as possible. We look to the plant world for our sources and inspiration.

And The Body Shop respects its customers, offering them choices, and providing them with information to support those choices.

Customer care and service is a priority, and our staff are trained to provide it.

THE ENVIRONMENT AND OUR COMMUNITY

The Body Shop is an expanding and successful company. We are also profitable, and we are concerned about the responsibility of those profits. It's a partnership of profits with principles. The company operates within the world, the environment, the community. That is where our responsibilities lie: we want to give something back to society.

THE BODY SHOP & THE THIRD WORLD

We source many of our products in the Third World, encouraging local communities in developing countries to grow ingredients. This then provides employment and trade.

We aim to have relationships with the Third World based on equality.

(Glynn Thomas, 1985)

35

Give this message to your partner over the phone. Note down the message
your partner gives you.

- Your partner's meeting with Michael Steadman in Philadelphia put
  back - now at 9 a.m. on Tuesday 14th, not Monday afternoon.
- Pick up your airline ticket from TWA desk when you get to Heathrow.
- Your outward flight is TW 755 at 09.55 on 13 March, arriving 12.50
- Return on BA 218 at 20.50 on 15 March, arriving back at 08.45.
- Take only carry-on hand baggage.
- Go straight to his office at 143 4th Street in the morning.
- Phone him to confirm all this on 0101 215 777 5482.

neon lights,
and barriers.

It is dominated by two team-based targets at either end of the room. Seven to 15 people are on each team and the goal is to "disrupt" as many of the people on the other team as possible and to wipe out the opponents' base target in six frantic minutes.

Of course, when players talk about the game they do not use gentle Photon lan-guage, they are out to shoot and kill their opponents.

"You have to massacre them and not let them kill you," Mr Matsumoto said.

To do this, they wear bat-tery packs around their waists, breastplate targets, and helmets in red and green team colours. Their guns are called phasers, after the ones used in Star Trek, but these models more closely resemble something Rambo might carry.

Before entering the game room they punch personal ID cards into a computer which keeps track of each player's and each team's score throughout the game.

Players score 10 points zapping an opposing and 200 points the o

37

You are Mr/Ms Warner of Acme Enterprises. You'll receive a call from a supplier, the Marketing Director of Zenith International, who spent an evening at your home on his/her previous visit. Study this information before answering the phone:

- On Friday 13th February you'll be busy all morning and are leaving for a long weekend at 4 p.m.
- You are not booked for lunch that day.
- The best restaurant in town is the Excelsior – but it is *very* expensive.
- You've heard that Zenith are soon going to introduce a new line of products, but you haven't received any literature about this – why not?

▶ When the 'observer' has given his or her feedback, return to page 165.

Find out what your partners think about these questions:

- If you were very well-off, would you give money to charity or keep it all for yourself and your family? Would you seek publicity or become a recluse?
- What would it be like to be retired?

── 40 ──────────

Judge Potter ordered Mr Bakker to be sent to the Butner Psychiatric Institution, 140 miles from Charlotte, where his condition would be assessed. Dr Jackson told the court yesterday that Mr Bakker was suffering from "acute depression, confusional reaction [and had] lost the ability to judge and evaluate reality."

Mr Bakker's troubles date from 1987, following revelations about his affair with a former church secretary, Jessica Hahn, which forced him to resign from the ministry. The scandal was compounded by reports that Ms Hahn received $265,000 hush money from PTL funds.

Dr Jackson, who has been treating the evangelist for the past nine months, said Mr Bakker's condition deteriorated on Wednesday after the collapse of Mr Steve Nelson, aged 39, a former PTL vice-president, who fainted on the witness stand.

Mr Nelson recovered but leaving the courthouse, Mr Bakker "suddenly felt the people outside took the form of frightening animals which he felt were intent on attacking him," Dr Jackson told the court. He was hallucinating, and had to be helped to his car.

Mr Bakker and Mr Nelson collapsed after another former PTL executive, Mr Richard Dortch, was taken to hospital. He has been sentenced to eight years in prison after admitting fraud and conspiracy related to ministry fund-raising, and was expected to testify against Mr Bakker.

── 41 ──────────

	Location	Length (km)	Opened
Suez Canal	Egypt	162	1869
– built by French engineer Ferdinand de Lesseps; without locks; transit time 11 hours between Mediterranean and Red Sea			
Kiel Canal	Germany	98	1895
– built to permit movement of German navy between Baltic and North Sea			
Hadrian's Wall	England	117	126
– protected Roman Britain from hostile Northern tribes in Scotland			
Lake Pontchartrain Causeway	Louisiana, USA	38	1956
– toll highway across lake north of New Orleans			
Verrazano Narrows Bridge	New York, USA	1.3	1964
– 18 metres longer than Golden Gate; 6 + 6 lanes; connects Brooklyn with Staten Island			
St Gotthard road tunnel	Switzerland	16	1980
– longest road tunnel; vehicles pay a toll to pass through			

42

You are the MANAGER of the Hotel California. Study this information before answering the phone:

- The Eagle Suite (capacity 150 persons) is available for conferences on the following dates in January:
4th–8th, 16th–17th, 20th–23rd – no smaller rooms are available.
Cost: £195 per day (this includes morning coffee and afternoon tea).
- Lunch arrangements: two possibilities:
  1 Lunch can be taken in the rooftop restaurant (cost £15–£20 per person + drinks) or sandwiches and snacks available in the coffee shop (cost £1.50–£5). Delegates would pay for their own meals in this case.
  2 Special conference meal in basement restaurant (£10 incl. wine) only available if *all* delegates take full lunch. Very good value!
- Special 25% discount on room rate for delegates if booked in advance.
- Ask for confirmation of booking by telex + 10% deposit in advance.

▶ When the 'observer' has given his or her feedback, turn to Activity 72.

THE CHALLENGE OF THE AIR

Flight was the adventure of the interwar years as developing technology briefly made aviation a competitive sport, in search of new speed and endurance records. None captured the popular imagination of the media so much as Charles Lindbergh's non-stop solo flight from New York to Paris in 1927. Competing for a prize of £25,000 which had claimed six lives in the previous year, 24-year-old Lindbergh took off in a Ryan monoplane he called "The Spirit of St Louis" from Roosevelt Field, Long Island on the morning of 20 May. Thirty-three and a half hours later he landed at Le Bourget, Paris.

Lindbergh's flight seemed to have an esthetic purity about it. Unlike his rivals, he flew alone. Although he had financial backing, his plane was built on a shoestring budget. It had no navigational system, and Lindbergh memorized his route. His exploits fed the hunger to discover new objects of attention, new sensations, new people. Christened "Lucky Lindy" and "the Flying Fool" by an already enthusiastic press before he took off, Lindbergh's story sold a record number of newspapers. After the flight, he appeared to confirm his heroic status by remaining aloof from movie offers and requests for testimonials. But in 1932 his baby was kidnapped, and Lindbergh again became front-page news for the weeks of the prolonged hunt for the child and then the trial of the alleged kidnapper Bruno Hauptmann. It offered the press and public another opportunity to gawk at a celebrity's private life; one imposter who claimed to know where the child was confessed that he had made his story up to "become famous". Later in the 1930s Lindbergh's open support for the Nazis led President Franklin Roosevelt to denounce him as a Fascist.

(from Dreams for Sale)

1 Work in pairs. Rewrite this passage using the exact words Max used.

Last Tuesday my friend Max told me that it was his birthday that day. He had had a card from his uncle in Australia the day before and one from his aunt the same day he spoke to me. He knew I couldn't go to his party the next day, so he invited me for a drink then or suggested I could meet him later that evening.

2 Now rewrite this passage as reported speech.

My friend Susan spoke to me on the phone last Wednesday and said: "I won't be able to see you next week. I had a call from my brother ten minutes ago. I've heard from him that my grandfather will be arriving here at the end of this week and this will be the first time I'll have seen him since he went to New Zealand in 1988. I hope you don't mind but I'd like to postpone our meeting from next week to the week after."

3 When you've finished, compare your versions with what your partners (in the other pair) have written and with the passages in Activity 9.

45

'The Menaced Assassin' by René Magritte, 1926, oil on canvas 150.4 × 195.2 cm. Collection The Museum of Modern Art, New York; Kay Sage Tanguy Fund.

Imagine that it is one year from now and you are at the airport. You are waiting to meet your old friend B, who you haven't seen since last summer (when *this* English course finished).

When your friend arrives, find out if he or she had a good flight and what he or she has been doing since you last met.

Marilyn Monroe (born 1 June 1926 – died 5 August 1962)

- Star sign: Gemini.
- Born Norma Jean Mortensen, raised by foster parents and in orphanages. Began modelling in 1945, signed up by 20th Century Fox in 1946. First starring role in *Niagara* (1952).
- Married 3 times: at 16 to aircraft worker Jim Dougherty 1942, for 9 months to baseball star Joe DiMaggio 1954, to intellectual writer Arthur Miller 1956.
- Affairs with Marlon Brando, Frank Sinatra, Charlie Chaplin Jr, John F. Kennedy, Robert Kennedy, Yves Montand, and many others.
- Most famous films: *Gentlemen Prefer Blondes* (1953), *How to Marry a Millionaire* (1953), *The Seven-Year Itch* (1955), *Some Like It Hot* (1959) – her films earned Fox over $100 million.
- Created and destroyed by the Hollywood star system.
- Committed suicide by an overdose of sleeping pills in 1962 at the age of 36 after being fired from her last movie.
- Reasons for her appeal even today: the ultimate embodiment of the desirable woman, a sex symbol who was vulnerable. She had real talent as well as sex appeal.
- Quotes:
  'Everyone is always tugging at you. They'd all like sort of a chunk of you.'
  'A sex symbol becomes a thing. I hate being a thing.'

Snake bite

1 DON'T cut the wound.
2 DON'T suck out the poison.
3 Reassure the patient that (in Britain) snake bites are painful but rarely fatal.
4 Encourage the patient to rest, lying down.
5 Wash the wound and apply a clean dry dressing.
6 Bandage firmly with a soft pad pressing on the wound.
7 Prevent the patient from moving the affected part – this reduces the spread of the poison.
8 You can give aspirin to reduce the pain.
9 Get the victim to hospital as soon as possible.

—— 50 ——

ROBINSON CRUSOE by Daniel Defoe (1719)

- Robinson Crusoe shipwrecked alone on a desert island.
- Got food, rum and guns from the wrecked ship, and dog and two cats.
- Made furniture, wrote a diary. Shot birds and wild goats for food. Planted seeds from old sack – grew corn and made bread.
- Made clothes from goat skins, and made butter and cheese from goat's milk. Built a boat and sailed round the island.
- Twelve years passed, found a footprint on the beach, but no people.
- Three years later, saw natives roasting meat on the beach with a captive. Crusoe shot some of the natives, scared the others away and rescued the captive. As it was Friday, Crusoe called the man 'Friday' – trained him as his servant and gave him English lessons.
- 35 years after Crusoe had first come to the island, a ship came to the island. Crusoe and Friday were taken back to England.
- Story based on real life story of Alexander Selkirk.

—— 51 ——

century, something went wrong."

In the book, A Vision of Britain (Doubleday £16.95), Prince Charles writes: "The fashionable architectural theories of the fifties and sixties, so slavishly followed by those who wanted to be considered 'with it', have spawned deformed monsters which have come to haunt our towns and cities, our villages and our countryside."

Unrepentantly answering his critics, he says: "Some people like to portray my views on architecture and the environment as thoroughly reactionary and opposed to progress and the requirements of the contemporary world.

"The further I delve into the shadowy world of architecture, planning and property development, the more I become aware of the powerful influence of various interest groups.

"Hence the frequently violent and vitriolic reactions to the points I have been making."

He lists 10 principles on which common ground can be found.

In su...........are:

52

The parliament building, shops, hotels, flats, leafy suburbs for the middle classes, schools, the university and the ministries are all located in separate zones. But looking more closely at the spectacular buildings you can see that they are falling to bits because they were built on the cheap. In a city where temperatures are normally over 30 degrees, the main indoor shopping centre is not even air-conditioned. And the poorer workers and their families are accommodated in large, squalid shanty towns on the edge of the city.

53

.... each ....nd each team's ....re throughout the game.

Players score 10 points for zapping an opposing player, and 200 points for hitting the other team's base target. They lose points for getting shot or for killing a teammate.

The helmets have red and green flashing lights so that players can see one another in the dark of the game room. The lights turn yellow when a player has been hit, and inside the helmet players hear buzzers when they are disrupted and beeps when they kill an opponent.

"It's like being on the inside of a video game," said Ms Akiko Itoh, who works at an insurance company during the week but becomes a Photon warrior named Cyber 2 at the weekends.

Photon was imported to Japan from America, but local managers said Tokyo's Photon base is one of the most successful in the chain.

"Japanese people love to be aggressive, but they are not supposed to be in their jobs or at home, so they come here," Ms Itoh said.

54

You feel VERY ANGRY because:

- You had to queue up at the bank for a long time only to discover that the money you were expecting hasn't arrived yet.
- When you came out of the bank you found your bike had a flat tyre and you had to wheel it all the way here.
- You spent a long time doing some homework but you left it at home – your teacher doesn't believe that you have really done it.
- You have just heard that your holiday plans have fallen through and now you'll have to arrange another holiday at the last minute.

Explain your problems to your partners and try to resist their efforts to calm you down.

55

When Gregor Samsa awoke one morning from uneasy dreams he found himself in his bed transformed into an enormous cockroach. He was lying on his hard armour-plated back and, if he raised his head slightly, he could see his arched brown belly, with its ridges and reinforced segments, on which his bed-cover was precariously balanced and just about to slide to the floor. His numerous legs, which were pitifully thin compared to the rest of him, quivered helplessly before his eyes.

'What has happened to me?' he thought. It was not a dream. His room, a normal, though smallish, human room lay quietly between its four familiar walls.

(from *Metamorphosis* by Franz Kafka)

56

How the soundtrack on movie film works

A stripe along the edge carries the soundtrack. The width of this sound stripe varies according to the sound signals produced during the recording.

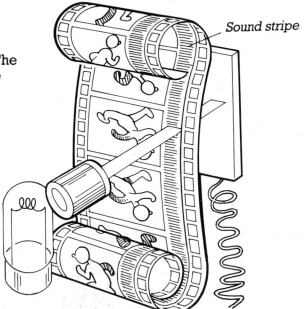

Sound stripe

1 Light shines through the sound stripe. Because of the varying width of the stripe, a varying amount of light passes through to a device called a photoelectric cell.

2 A photoelectric cell converts the light back into sound signals which are identical to the original sound signals.

3 The sound signals travel down a cable to the cinema's loudspeakers. These convert them into sound waves.

Did you know . . .?
- Before sound films took over from silent movies in the 1930s, large cinemas often employed a symphony orchestra to accompany each performance.
- A film is shown in the cinema at 24 frames per second. On TV the same film would be shown at 25 frames per second – a two-hour cinema film only lasts about one hour 55 minutes on TV.

57

Car accident
(If the emergency services are already at the scene, drive past slowly and
DON'T interfere.)
1 Control any serious bleeding and make sure victims can breathe.
2 Leave victims in the car unless there is danger from fire there.
3 Switch off the ignition and lights of any car involved. Make sure the brakes are on.
4 DON'T smoke or allow any bystanders to smoke.
5 Look to see if any victims have been thrown over a nearby wall or hedge.
6 Set warning triangles or send bystanders 200 metres behind and ahead of the scene to
  warn other drivers to slow down.
7 Get a bystander to call the ambulance (in the UK dial 999, in the USA 911),
  write down exactly where you are, the number of victims and apparent injuries.
8 Treat the victims as best you can without pulling them out.
9 Wait for the emergency services to arrive.

58

Find out more about these billionaires by asking your partner questions
about them:

the Morita family   Rupert Murdoch   Liliane Bettencourt   Queen Elizabeth II
the Brenninkmeyer family   Ingvar Kamprad   the Sainsbury family

Answer your partner's questions about these billionaires:

Yoshiaki Tsutsumi   (Japan)
Second richest man in world. Owns Seibu railroad, Seibu Lions baseball team, construction companies
and real estate. His half brother Seiji is also a billionaire: owns department stores and Inter-Continental
Hotels.

Sam Walton   (USA)
Richest American ($8.7 billion) – chain of Wal-Mart hypermarkets.

Roberto Marinho   (Brazil)
Owns newspapers and Rede Globo TV network (fourth largest in world after ABC, CBS and NBC in
the US).

Cox sisters   (USA)
Barbara Cox Anthony and Anne Cox Chambers: the richest women in the world – Cox
Communications owns many local radio and TV stations and newspapers.

Hans & Gad Rausing   (Sweden)
Their father founded Tetra-Pak (cartons for milk and soft drinks). Hans is chairman of the company,
Gad teaches archaeology part-time at Lund University, both live in UK.

Benetton family   (Italy)
Three brothers and one sister run the company and design the colourful clothes; network of small
shops all over the world and Nordica ski-boots.

Duke of Westminster   (UK)
Richest man in Britain; the family estate is worth $4 billion, including most of London's Mayfair and
Belgravia; only got two 'O' levels but has shrewd business brain.

59

Give this message to your partner over the phone. Note down the message
your partner gives you.

- Your partner's meeting with Jane Potter on Tuesday 14 June
  rescheduled - train strike.
- Meet her 12.45 in foyer of Grosvenor Hotel.
- Please book table for three for 1.30 (Hilda Meyer will be joining
  you).
- In case of problems getting out of London, book hotel room for
  yourself for Tuesday night - not too expensive!
- Recommended hotel: Cambridge Arms, 135 Alexander St - near Victoria
  Station (phone 071 222 9826).
- Bring your latest sales figures and forecasts on 3½ inch IBM-
  compatible floppy disks - not hard copies.
- Contact Ms Potter on 081 345 8921 or Ms Meyer on 01049 567 93220.

60

The chart shows the distribution of population of different ages in different
parts of the world. Discuss these questions with your partner:

- Why do you think these particular age groups have been chosen?
- Where would you 'choose to be born' if you wanted to live a long life?

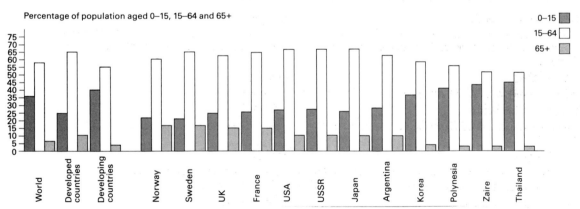

Percentage of population aged 0–15, 15–64 and 65+

Join another pair and find out what they have discovered. Share your ideas
and information with them.

How a movie projector works

1 Feed reel feeds film into the projector. The scene is recorded as a series of pictures taken rapidly one after the other.

2 Gate. Each frame, or picture, is pulled down one by one into the gate and held for a fraction of a second.

3 A shutter behind the gate opens as each frame is stationary in the gate. It closes while the film is moved on to a new frame.

4 Light shines on to the film when the shutter is open.

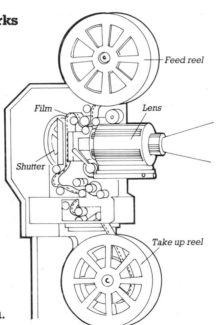

Feed reel

Film

Lens

Shutter

Take up reel

5 The lens enlarges the picture on the film and focuses it on to the cinema screen.

6 A take-up reel collects the film at the end.

Did you know . . .?
- A two-hour movie consists of 172,800 frames. Even a five-minute cartoon film consists of 7,200 separate drawings.
- Most films are shot on normal 35 mm film but projected in the cinema with the top and bottom of the frame cut off to give a wide-screen effect. On TV the whole frame is usually shown – if you look carefully you can sometimes spot the microphone at the top of the screen.

He felt a curious tingling in his hands and feet. He felt his nose becoming cold and wet, his ears becoming flappy.

Eric is a perfectly ordinary boy. Perfectly ordinary that is, until the night when, safely tucked up in bed, he slowly but surely turns into a dog!

What becomes of Eric – the adventures he has with his best friend Roy, and their joint efforts to puzzle out the *reason* for his transformation – makes a very funny and entirely believable book.

(*Woof!* by Allan Ahlberg)

Find out more about these billionaires by asking your partner questions about them:

Yoshiaki Tsutsumi   Sam Walton   Roberto Marinho
the Cox sisters   Hans & Gad Rausing   the Benetton family
the Duke of Westminster

Answer your partner's questions about these billionaires:

Morita family   (Japan)
Akio Morita founded Sony, but could have become master brewer in the family's *sake* plant. Their great rivals are the Matsushita family (National, Panasonic, Technics) who are also billionaires.

Rupert Murdoch   (USA/Australia)
Owns newspapers, entertainment companies and TV: *The Times, The Sun* and Sky TV and 20th Century Fox. Became a US citizen before buying TV stations there.

Liliane Bettencourt   (France)
Richest person in France – formerly president of L'Oréal, the world's largest cosmetics company.

Queen Elizabeth II   (UK)
Her land and castles really belong to the State, but she personally owns works of art, a stamp collection, properties abroad and racehorses worth over £2 billion.

Brenninkmeyer family   (Holland)
Richest family in Europe (apart from British Royal family); C&A clothes stores and retail chains in USA; very secretive.

Ingvar Kamprad   (Sweden)
Opened first IKEA furniture store (simple, well-designed furniture) in Almhult, Sweden; over 80 outlets in 20 countries. Lives in tax exile in Switzerland.

Sainsbury family   (UK)
First grocer's shop opened in 1869, now over 400 Sainsbury's supermarkets and Homebase do-it-yourself stores.

65

It's a city designed for the automobile with magnificent multi-lane highways but no pavements or pedestrian crossings because, in the future, everyone would have a car. Unfortunately, even today only one in eight of the citizens of Brasília has access to a car and the public transport system is chaotic. Most of the time the highways are empty but twice a day they are jammed with cars and pedestrians have to dodge the traffic to get across.

The one consolation for the very rich is that there are regular flights to Rio. It's scarcely surprising that on Friday afternoons all the flights out are fully booked.

66

Laze away the summer days down under ...

Come January, when the British Isles have plunged into yet another chilly old winter, Australia will be basking in blissful mid-summer temperatures hovering somewhere around the 25 degree mark. Celsius, that is.

To suggest summer Down Under is warm would be something of a classic Aussie understatement. Which is precisely why if anyone knows how to cook up a great holiday, we do.

We can't write a guarantee, but given the performance of the last couple of hundred years, bright sunny days, big blue skies, swaying palms and the soothing sound of clean sparkling waters tumbling on the finest golden beaches will all be waiting for you.

Wherever your travels take you through this great big, beautiful sun-soaked land, we'll accommodate your budget with secluded island hideaways, elegant international resorts, moderately priced hotels and motels, self-catering apartments, or homes on wheels.

You even have an invitation to be guest of the family in a fair dinkum outback country homestead.

NEW YORK! NEW YORK!

What a city! Thanks to television and the movies, visitors often feel they know the city before they've been there, but nothing beats the experience!

The five boroughs of New York City have a total population of some seven million, but it's the island of Manhattan that has shaped the city's reputation. From the razzle-dazzle of Broadway to the sober skyscrapers of the financial district, from the opulence of some of the world's finest hotels to the tranquility of Central Park, from the UN headquarters to Radio City Music Hall, New York has it all. The tallest buildings, the best department stores, the most superb museums and galleries, the widest range of restaurants (25,000 of them!), the most amazing choice of entertainment (400 theaters!), all combine to make the "Big Apple" like no other city on earth.

67

Find out what your partners think about these questions:

- What would it be like to be a multi-millionaire – what would be the problems and the pleasures?
- What would it be like to live in a cottage in the country?

68

Imagine that it is one year from now and you are arriving at the airport on a flight from London. Your old friend A, who you haven't seen since last summer will be waiting for you. When you spot your friend in the arrivals hall, find out what he or she has been doing since you last met (when *this* English course finished).

▶ To make this situation more realistic, you should move away from the others first of all.

69

He ___ ___ ___ on which common ground can be found.

In summary, these are:

- Place: "Don't rape the landscape."
- Hierarchy: "Where is the civic pride, and where is the entrance, to Chippenham's council offices?"
- Scale: "Buildings must relate first to human proportions and then respect the scale of buildings around them."
- Harmony: "The playing together of buildings."
- Enclosure: "An elementary idea with a thousand variants from the individual room to the interior of St Paul's."
- Materials: "Each town and village has a different hue, a different feel and fosters fierce loyalty ... We must retain this feeling."
- Decoration: "The training of the modern architect rarely encompasses the rules of ornament."
- Art: "Architects and artists should be betrothed at an early stage in any major public project."
- Signs and lights: "Ugly advertising, glaring street lights and banal logos must be outlawed."
- Community: "Pride in your community can only be generated if you have some say ... a community starts with local knowledge."

Study these instructions and secretly rehearse the trick together. Then join another pair and demonstrate the trick to them.

Prepare some strips of paper. Members of the audience say aloud a number of different words (e.g. vocabulary from this unit). You *appear* to write each one down on a separate strip of paper. Without looking at any of the strips of paper, destroy all but one of them and hand the remaining one to a member of the audience. Announce to everyone the word that's on the paper.

(You wrote the *first* word that was mentioned on *every* one of the strips, so it doesn't matter which ones were destroyed!)

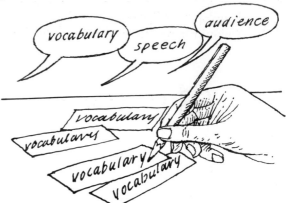

You feel VERY BORED because:
- You've got nothing to do – there are no films on that you want to see, no TV programmes on and you haven't got a good book to read.
- You have just come to the end of a twice-weekly evening course.
- You don't feel like doing anything energetic, like walking or sports.
- You're not in the mood for socialising with your friends.

Explain your problems to your partners and try to resist their efforts to interest you in things.

You are the 'OBSERVER'. Make notes on the call. After you have given the callers your feedback, return to page 165.

Find out what your partners think about these questions:
- If you suddenly became very wealthy, what would you do after you'd bought all the luxuries (home, car, yacht, villa abroad, etc.) you'd want?
- What would it be like to be a politician?

Imagine that it is one year from now and you are at the airport, where you have just said goodbye to a member of your family who is flying to America. Now you're in the arrivals hall buying an English newspaper.

Suddenly you spot your old friend A, who you haven't seen since last summer (when *this* English course finished). Say hello and find out what your friend has been doing since you last met.

▶ To make this situation more realistic, you should move away from the others first of all.

Paragraph 5 is from *Nineteen Eighty-Four* by George Orwell (1949).
This futuristic story tells of one individual's fight against a totalitarian State, where the Party controls everything in everybody's lives – even the way they think. A nightmarish vision of a totalitarian world. Many of the book's phrases ('Big Brother', 'the Thought Police', etc.) have passed into the English language.

Paragraph 6 is from *Conundrum* by Jan Morris (1974).
The story of how James Morris, a well-known writer and married man with children, became Jan Morris. This is an honest and moving account of the problems she faced during her life and how she eventually decided that the only way to overcome them was by having a sex-change operation. Full of surprising humour, wit and warmth.

The things you know to be true are shown with a tick ✓ and the things you are unsure about are shown with a question mark ? .

Adrian had to go to hospital for an X-ray ✓
Claire had a cold ✓
Frank had a job interview ?
Diane had a headache ?
Eric was suffering from sunburn ✓
Anne had a hangover ?

Betty's car wouldn't start ✓
Bill had hayfever ?
Dennis had a dentist's appointment ✓
Flora had flu ✓
Chris hurt her foot ?
Emma overslept ?

Acknowledgements

The author and publishers are grateful to the following authors, publishers and others who have given permission for the use of copyright material identified in the text. While every effort has been made it has not been possible to identify the sources of all the material used and in such cases the publishers would welcome information from the copyright owners.

Dover Publications, Inc. for the pictograms from *Handbook of Pictorial Symbols* by Rudolph Modley used in the chapter titles and on p. 116; Penguin Books Ltd for permission to reproduce the cover of *Castaway* by Lucy Irvine on p. 3, the covers of *Emma* by Jane Austen, *A Tale of Two Cities* by Charles Dickens, *Three Men in a Boat* by Jerome K. Jerome and *Nineteen Eighty-Four* by George Orwell on p. 151 and the cover and cover blurb of *Woof!* by Allan Ahlberg on p. 243; Hodder & Stoughton Ltd for permission to reproduce the cover of *The Islander* by Gerald Kingsland on p. 3; The Peters, Fraser and Dunlop Group Ltd for permission to reproduce 'The Castaways' by Adrian Mitchell on p. 5; *Punch* for permission to reproduce the cartoons on pp. 8, 15, 25, 29, 31, 91, 123, 172, 190, 196, 216 and 248; Earthworks, Hannibal Records Ltd, Realworld Records, Stern's Records, Virgin Records Ltd and World Circuit Records for their logos on p. 11; Orion Pictures Corporation for the *Robocop* poster © 1987 on p. 19; Goldcrest Films and Television Ltd for the *Local Hero* videobox liner on p. 19; Camera Press Ltd for the photograph on p. 21; Christopher Reed for the articles on pp. 21, 55 and 58; Town and Country Taverns Ltd for The Clifton menu on p. 35; *The Daily Telegraph* for the article from *The Young Telegraph* © The Daily Telegraph plc on pp. 37–8; Kevin Jones of Kevin Jones Associates for the illustrations on pp. 37–8; *The Guardian* for the articles on pp. 42, 183 (bottom), 186, 194–5, 223, 225, 233, 237, 245 and the photographs on p. 184; Barnaby's Picture Library for the three photographs on p. 49; Basil Blackwell for the extract from *Coping with Japan* by Randall and Watanabe on p. 60; Chatto and Windus and The Julian Bach Literary Agency Inc. for permission to reprint the extract from *The Complete Book of Running* by James Fixx © 1977 by James Fixx on p. 60; Grafton Books (A Division of the Collins Publishing Group) for the cover blurb from *Empire of the Sun* by J. G. Ballard on p. 60; Longman Group UK for the extract from the introduction to *Call for the Dead* by John Le Carré (Longman Simplified English) on p. 60; Saatchi and Saatchi Advertising for permission to use the extract from the advertisement for Intercity train travel on p. 60 and for the advertisement on p. 203; Sony for the headphone instructions on p. 60; Working Software Inc. for the QuickLetter advertisement on p. 62; Longman Group UK Ltd and Chronicle Communications Ltd for permission to use the extracts from *Chronicle of the 20th Century* © Chronicle Communications, London, © Jacques Legrand SA, Paris, © for the Chronicle System, Harenberg Kommunication, Dortmund on pp. 66 and 224; Harrap Publishing Group Ltd and Equinox (Oxford) for the extract and cover blurb from *Dreams for Sale* (originally published from *Dreams for Sale* Harrap, London, *Passing Parade* Oxford University Press) on pp. 67 and 234; Format Partners Photo Library for the photograph on p. 75; *The Listener* for the article on pp. 75–6; Anna Tomforde and *The Guardian* for the article on pp. 80–1; United Biscuits and Nicklin Advertising Ltd for the advertisement on p. 83; Associated Press Ltd for the photograph of Cory Aquino on p. 92 and for the photograph on p. 207; Syndication International Ltd for the photograph of Benazir Bhutto on p. 92; Jerry Bauer for the photograph of Simone de Beauvoir on p. 92; Alexander Walker of Conundrum Ltd for the article on pp. 93–5; Rex Features Ltd for the photograph on p. 96; Twentieth Century Fox Film Corporation for the photograph of Marylin Monroe on p. 97; Munro and Forster (PR Agency) for the photograph on p. 99; Tucci and Frank Spooner Pictures for the photograph on p. 101; Paul Almasy and Camera Press Ltd for the photograph of Guayaquil on p. 104; The Telegraph Colour Library for the photograph of roulette on p. 104; Desmond Morris for the extract from *Manwatching* on p. 111; Mercedes Benz AG Germany, for permission to reproduce their three pointed star trade mark on p. 115 and Campaign for Nuclear Disarmament for their symbol on p. 115; Her Majesty's Stationery Office for the signs from the British Highway Code on p. 116; Coca-Cola ('Coca-Cola' and 'Coke' are registered trademarks which identify the same product of the Coca-Cola Company), IBM and Sony for permission to use their logos on p. 116; Cambridge University Press for the extract from *The Cambridge Encyclopedia of Language* by David Crystal on pp. 118–19; W. W. Norton & Company, Inc. for the extract on pp. 127–8 reprinted from *The Vanishing Hitchhiker, American Urban Legends and Their Meaning* by Jan Harold Brunvand, by permission of W. W. Norton & Company, Inc., copyright © 1981 by Jan Harold Brunvand; Cordon Art for 'Relativity' by M. C. Escher © M. C. Escher Heirs/Cordon Art, Baarn, Holland) on p. 129; *The Sunday Correspondent* for the articles on pp. 113 and 206–7; Transcendental Meditation for the leaflet on pp. 132–3; Collins Publishers and Aitken Stone Ltd for the extract from *For Love and Money* by Jonathan Raban on p. 136; Martin Secker & Warburg Ltd and Macmillan Publishing Company for permission to reprint the extract from *Small World* by David Lodge (copyright © 1985 David Lodge) on pp. 144–5; Mills and Boon Ltd for the cover of *Stormy Vigil* by Elizabeth Graham on p. 146; The Julian Bach Literary Agency, Inc. (copyright © 1975 by Jan Morris) and A. P. Watt Ltd on behalf of Jan Morris, for the extract from *Conundrum* by Jan Morris on p. 150; Curtis Brown Ltd on behalf of the Estate of Daphne du Maurier (copyright 1938 by Daphne du Maurier Browning) and Doubleday, a division of Bantam, Doubleday, Dell Publishing Group Inc. for the extract from *Rebecca* on p. 150; The estate of the late Sonia Brownell Orwell, Martin Secker & Warburg Ltd, and Harcourt Brace Jovanovich, Inc. for the extract from *Nineteen Eighty-Four* by George Orwell (copyright Harcourt Brace Jovanovich, Inc. and renewed 1977 by Sonia Brownell Orwell) reprinted by permission of the publishers on p. 150; Pan Books for the cover of *Rebecca* by Daphne du Maurier on p. 151; Epson UK Ltd for the advertisement on pp. 161–2; Chris Schwarz for the photograph on p. 165; Greenpeace UK for the articles and the photograph on p. 171; Anglia Television and Dr Richard Laws for the article on pp. 176–7; Paul Popper Ltd for the photograph on p. 177, the photographs of a highjacking and a robbery on p. 189 and the photograph on p. 224; *The Sun* for the top article on p. 183; The Press

Association for the photograph on p. 183; Ed Vulliamy and *The Guardian* for the bottom article on p. 183; Andrew Moncur and *The Guardian* for the article on p. 185; Hampshire Constabulary for the letter on p. 187; Oxfam for the photograph of floods in Bangladesh on p. 189; The Hogarth Press for the extract from *Cider with Rosie* by Laurie Lee (1959) on p. 196; Tom Smithies and *The Guardian* for the article on p. 199; Shyama Perara and *The Guardian* for the article on p. 202; Anuradha Vittachi and *New Internationalist* for the article on pp. 210–11; James M. Rodengen for the advertisement on pp. 215–16; Cynthia Owens and *The Guardian* for the articles on pp. 218, 233 and 238; The Body Shop International plc for the leaflets on pp. 219, 226 and 230; Hamish Hamilton and Houghton Mifflin Company for the extract from *Kingdom by the Sea* by Paul Theroux on p. 221; Adidas, Esso, Fiat, Ford and VAG (UK) Ltd for their logos on p. 222; Kellogg Company for kind permission to reproduce the Kellogg's logo on p. 222; the Kodak logo on p. 222 is reprinted courtesy of Eastman Kodak Company; Collins Publishers and Aitken Stone Ltd for the extract from *Coasting* by Jonathan Raban on p. 228; Glynn Thomas for 'Shingle Street' on p. 231; The Museum of Modern Art for 'The Threatened Assassin' by René Magritte on p. 235; Martin Secker & Warburg for the extract from *Metamorphosis* by Franz Kafka (translated by Willie and Edwin Muir) on p. 239; Usborne Publishing Ltd for permission to reproduce the diagrams from *Invention and Discovery* on pp. 239 and 242; the Australian Tourist Commission for the middle advertisement on p. 244; American Express Holidays for the bottom advertisement on p. 244.

Drawings by Tony Hall, Leslie Marshall, Chris Pavely, Clyde Pearson, Trevor Ridley and Shaun Williams. Artwork by Peter Ducker, Hardlines and Wenham Arts.
Book design by Peter Ducker MSTD.

Index